CW01655410

HAPPY BIRTHD ,

BE LUCKY !

Bob —

BOB OSBORNE

CONSTRUCTIONS

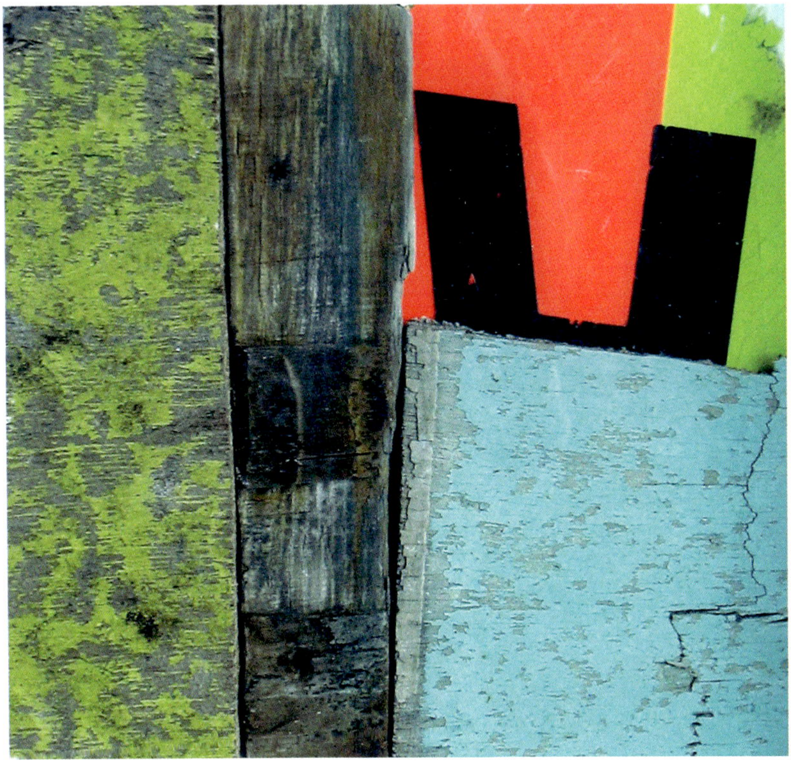

Peter Davies

'The artist does not observe the world, he lives it.'
– *Naum Gabo*

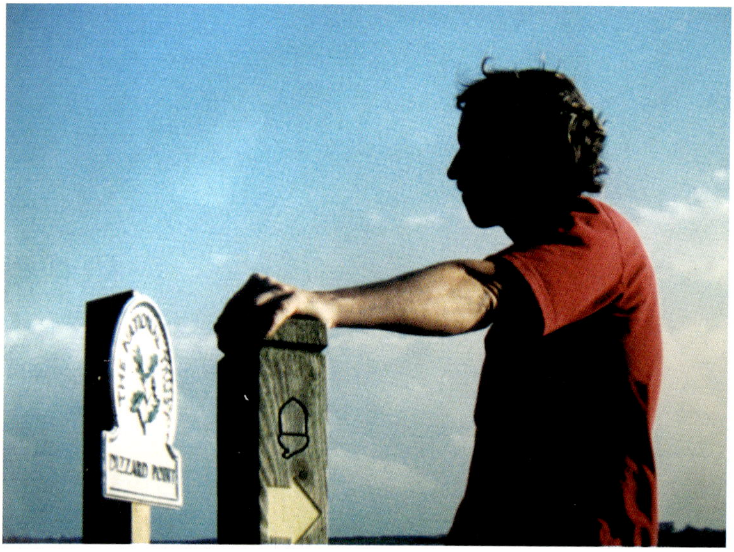

All rights reserved. No part of this publication may be reproduced, converted or archived into any other medium without relevant permission first being obtained from the publisher. Nor should the book be circulated or resold in any binding other than its original cover.

Bob Osborne - Constructions

Text © Peter Davies

First Edition published 2012

Front cover: Mad in England Plaque, 2012 - Carrie Reichardt
Frontispiece: The Geometry of Driftwood, 2000 - Bob Osborne
Rear Cover: Addison Place, 1956 - Roger Mayne

Designed by Bob Osborne

Printed & Published by:
The St Ives Printing & Publishing Company,
High Street, St Ives, Cornwall TR26 1RS UK.

www.stivesnews.co.uk

ISBN: 978-0-948385-58-2

CONTENTS

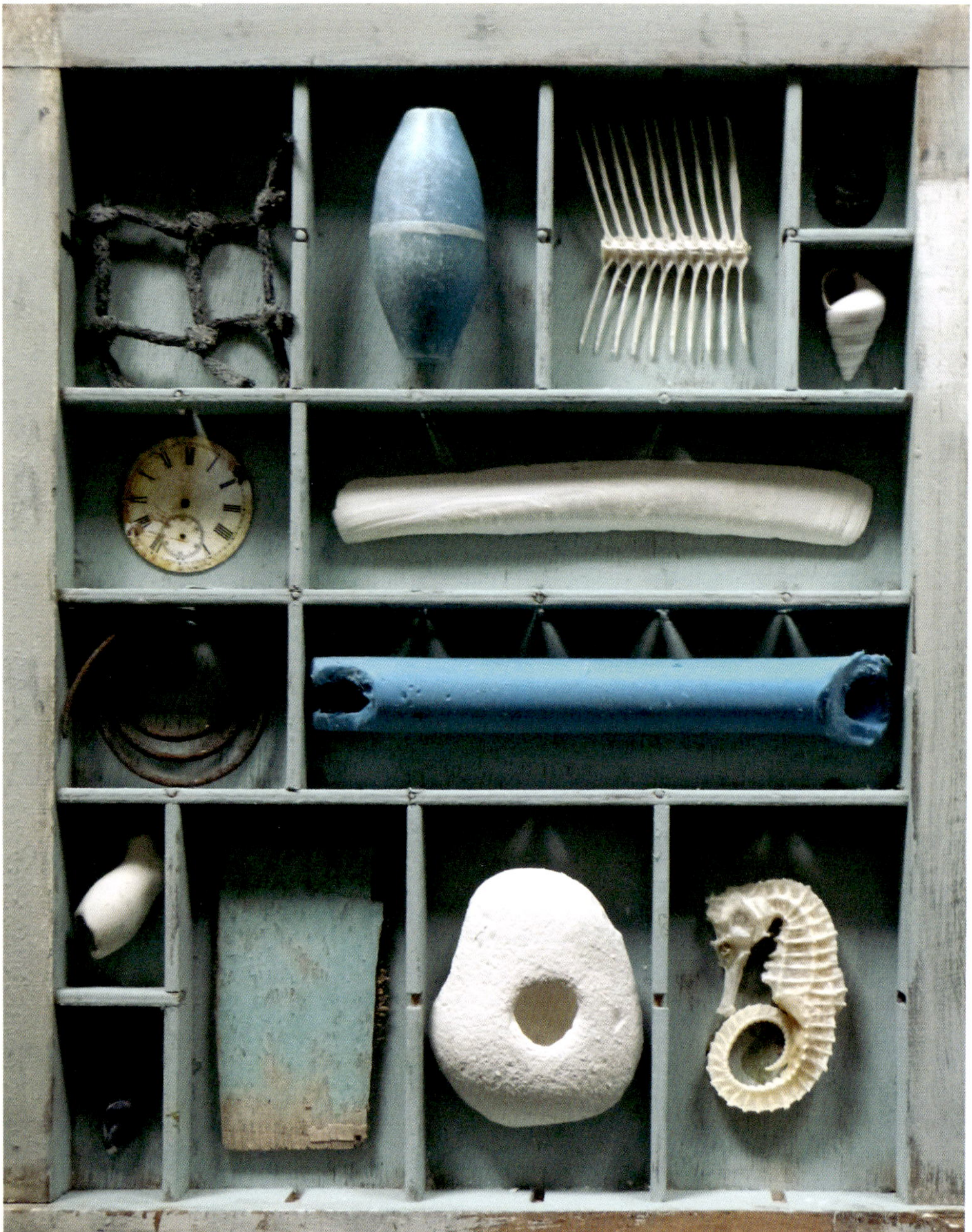

Out of the Blue, 1999

FOREWORD

by Sylvette David aka Lydia Corbett

I have always loved driftwood and looking at found objects in nature. Natural creation of such beauty seen in soft bits of wood: having floated on the sea for months or years, and suddenly found on a beach they become eternal and lovable. The pebbles and the seashells shining on wet sand are irresistible and are art works in themselves.

In my youth Picasso inspired me so much, seeing him creating things from found objects, and having such fun constructing works of art. Making a pyramid out of Gitanes cigarette packets, to see how much he smoked! He would be amused at his installation. Also he made a sculpture of me, using objects from a potter's kiln. He called it *The Lady with the Key*. That all happened in 1954 in Vallauris in the South of France.

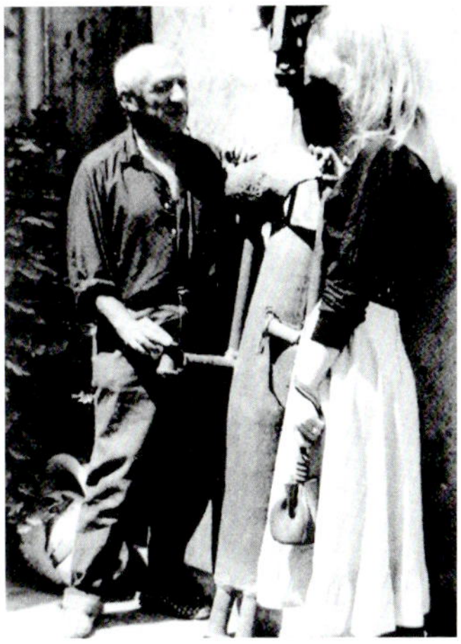

Picasso and Sylvette with "The Lady with the Key," 1954 *photograph: Tobias Jellinek*

So Bob Osborne has the artistic eye for making beautiful art out of found objects, which are his own ideas and which people love–like a poem for the eye and the imagination–containing memories and reveries of past and present, ever changing like the sea.

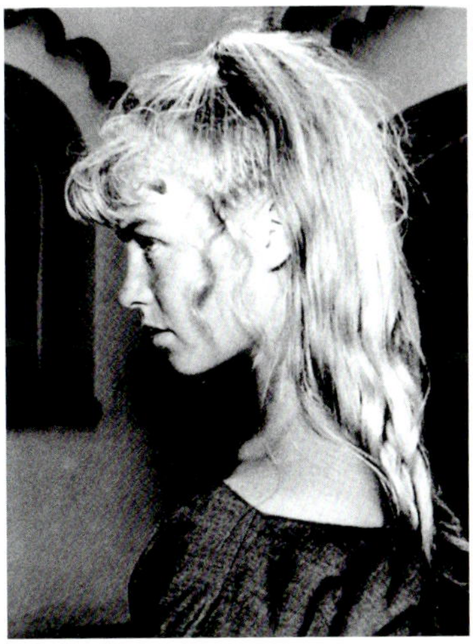

Sylvette David, 1954 *photograph: Andre Villers*

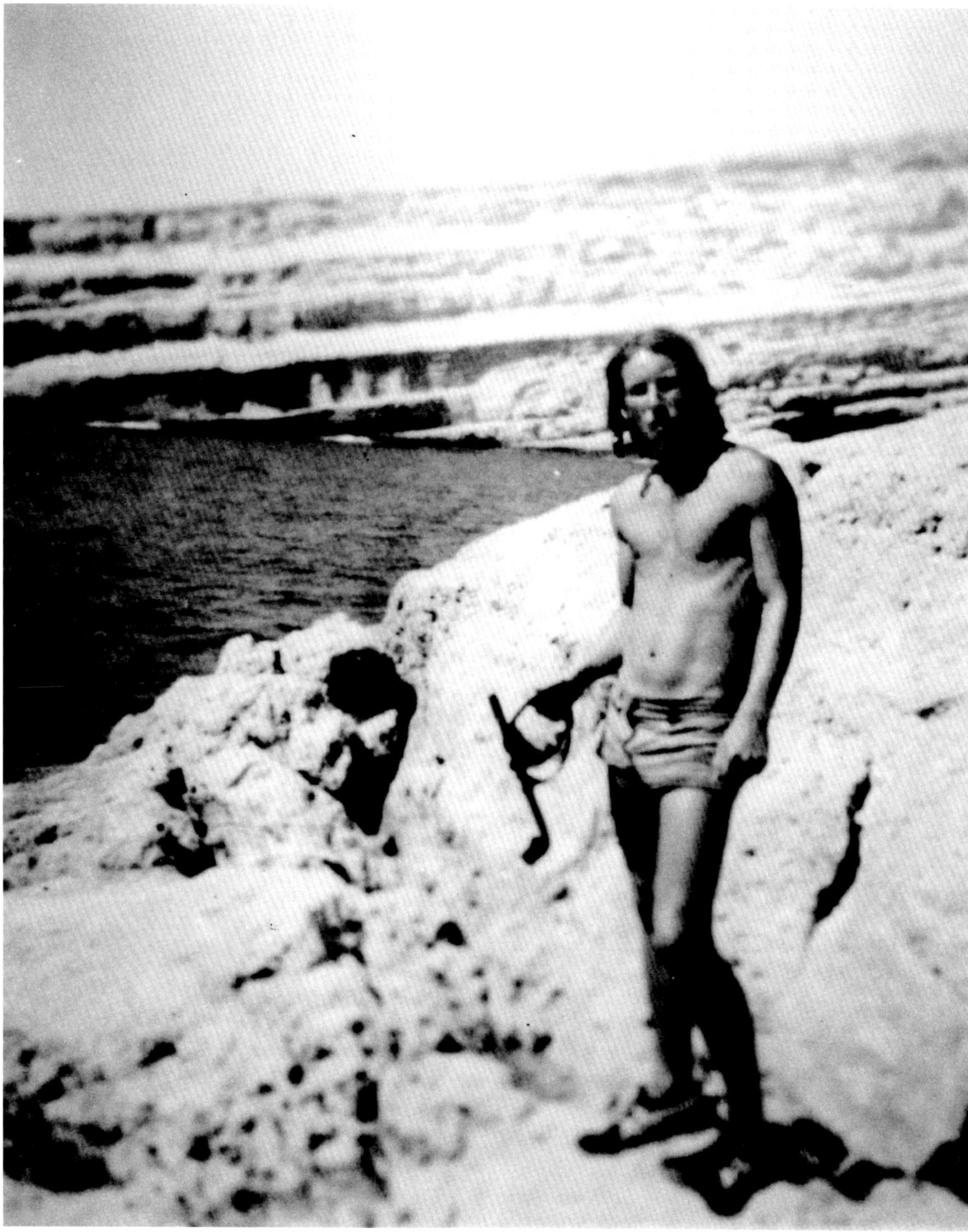

Bob Osborne, Living in a cave in Crete, 1977.

'Living well is the best revenge'
– George Herbert, Metaphysical Poet (1593-1633)

INTRODUCTION
by Peter Davies

My earliest recollectons of Bob Osborne go back to the autumn of 1972 when we were both first year students at the University of East Anglia. A sandy haired beach boy in a donkey jacket who arrived in Norfolk after exploits in the contrasting arenas of building sites and European travels, Osborne seemed to have a point to prove. From the outset he was always an independent, even rebellious spirit, and his déclassé stance was real for he hailed from gypsy street traders and the rough end of West London Bohemia.

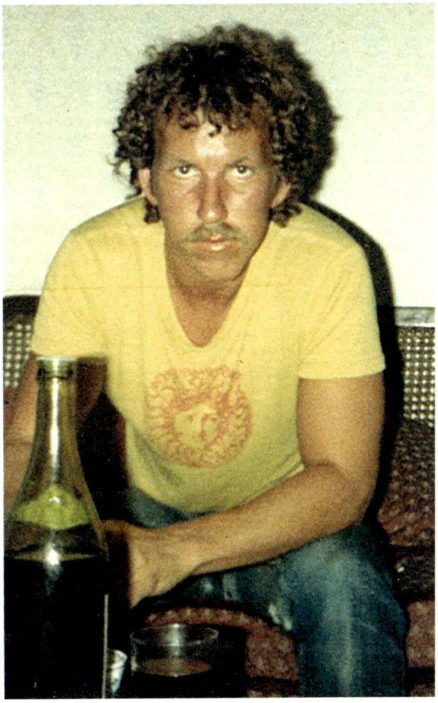

We went our separate ways as students but, 30 years later, made re-acquaintance in St Ives, where his dream of a Dionysian, creative and hedonistic accord by the sea found fulfilment. Although he came to art late - though not as belatedly as Alfred Wallis - there is something personal, endemic and natural in his chosen *modus operandi.* After all, as a child he went out on a horse and cart and witnessed his father, a scrap metal dealer, turn discarded junk into a source of livelihood. The random excitement of finding objects stayed with him providing a formative and motivational factor in his scouring of London skips and Cornish harbours and beaches. From these humble materials he fashions collages and wall-bound relief constructions.

Beachcombing and the poetic retrieval of rough and weathered *objets trouvés* - driftwood, metal, boat parts and netting - bridged the gap between art and life. Osborne's art-making is a natural extension of his lifestyle and links raw and instinctive processes with an intellectually informed sensibility. Since 1998 his boxed or free-hanging compositions have developed from nostalgic or literary juxtapositions into purely formal arrangements, whose shape, colour and texture embodies poignant association with obsolescence, redundancy and a salutary, if sad beauty.

A former literature and creative writing student who - not bad for an aspiring poet - knew Robert Graves in Deia, Mallorca, he developed his art along inevitable plastic and architectonic lines once he began working in St Ives.

Time as well as place exerts a hold on Osborne's work. His reliefs function as self-imposed diaries of a given day, each excursion 'chronicled' in terms of a captured spontaneity and subject to only minor adjustments in the studio. Osborne knowingly strikes a compromise between the concrete and lyrical qualities of St Ives modernism. But his beachside and maritime constructions introduce an unruly note to the ordered purity of St Ives constructivism. Whilst assisting in the studios of his close friends Sandra Blow and Denis Bowen, Osborne learnt directly from inspirational sources.

Osborne never uses scale gratuitously, enjoying the challenge of restricted and ramshackle working spaces. The improvisational nature of the Cornish imagination is reflected in the art of this schooled primitive whose work also extends to printmaking. The simple but eye-catching litho print Waves is an emblem of the flux of sea and sand enshrined in the static clarity of memory. Memory and the distance of time are held in check by a sensual delight in the direct and physical manipulation of materials.

'Every act of creation first involves an act of destruction'
– Pablo Picaso

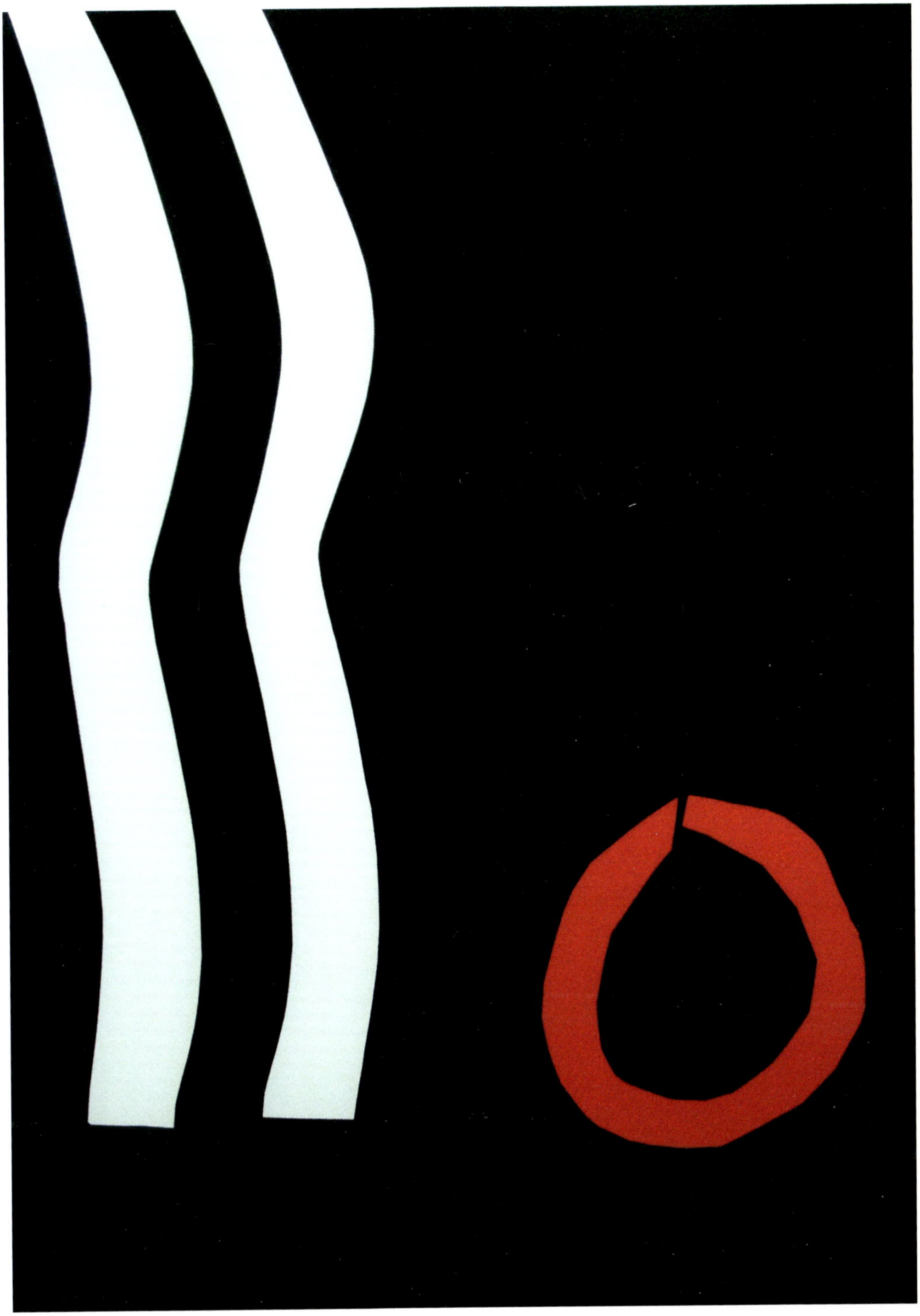

Waves, 2001 litho print

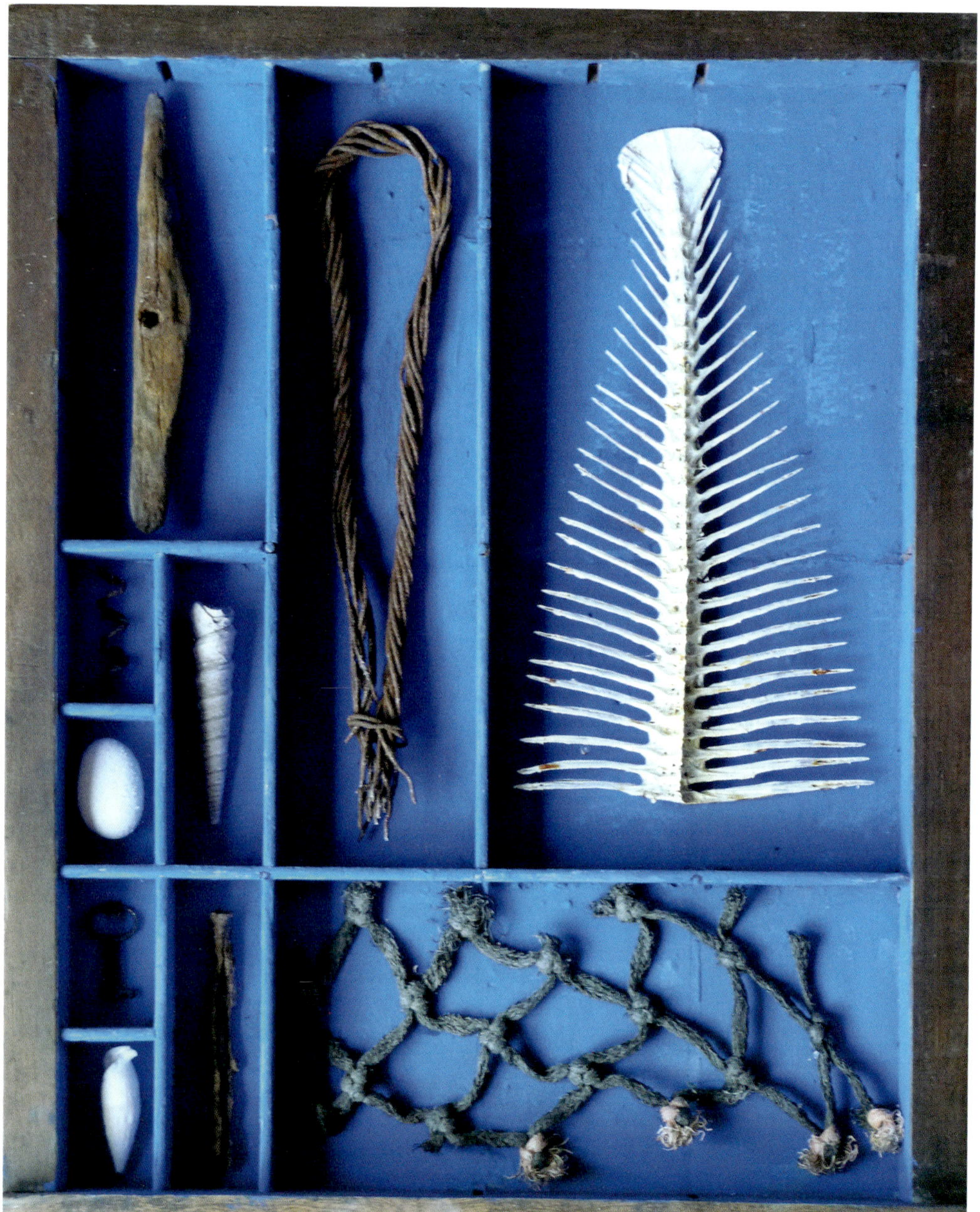

Cornwall, 1998

REBEL NOT TAKEN

by Bob Osborne

For those with an historical bent, my own ancestry can be traced back to a long line of downtrodden peasants, hawkers, bare knuckle boxers, convicts, rag-and-bone men and all-round riff-raff - the heroic sort that has always scratched a dodgy living on the outside edge of society.

Like my forbear Alexander Osborne, one of the nonconformist rebels who fought against the King's men in the 1685 Monmouth Rebellion. A West Country farm labourer, Alexander Osborne joined the ill equipped 'pitchfork' army rounded up by the wayward Duke of Monmouth, who hatched a plot to capture Bristol with a rabble of untrained yokels and then march on London to claim the throne. Not a good idea!

They came second in the Battle of Sedgemoor and it was a good job Alexander Osborne escaped after the final whistle, because those unfortunate wretches captured were dragged up before the infamous 'hanging' Judge Jeffreys at the "Bloody Assizes". Their brutal punishment was either to be sold as slaves to the colonies or sent to the gallows, after which their corpses were quartered, boiled in salt, dipped it pitch and then exhibited as a fearful lesson to all who contemplated defiance to the King.

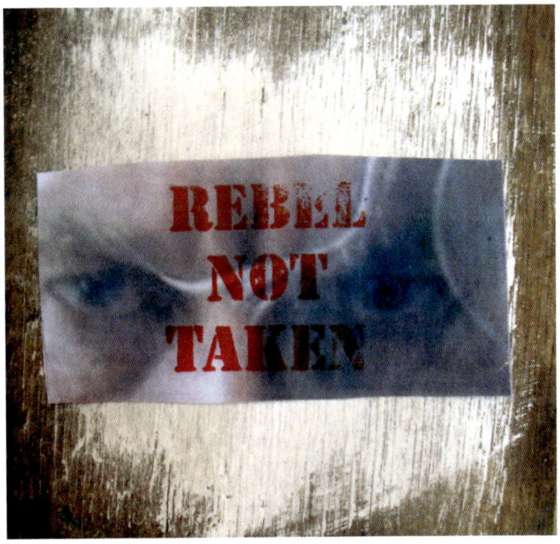

This explains how my lucky ancestor Alexander Osborne is listed in the annals of history as 'rebel and not taken'.

As for those miscreants who were 'taken', two names might ring a bell: Dr Peter Blood – found guilty of aiding the wounded Monmouth rebels and transported to the West Indies, where he started his second career as a pirate and became the model for Captain Blood of *Pirates of the Caribbean*. And the young Daniel Defoe, who, whilst hiding in a churchyard to avoid capture, noticed the name *Robinson Crusoe* carved on a gravestone. Luckily for the future of the English novel Daniel Defoe was in receipt of The General Pardon in 1686.

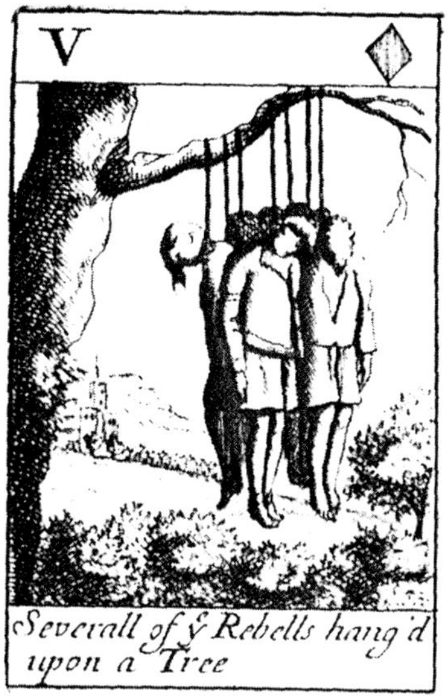

And there's another 'Art' link. After the defeat at Sedgemoor, the charismatic Duke of Monmouth (King Charles II's bastard son) was captured hiding in a ditch disguised in the clothes of a shepherd. He was duly charged with treason and beheaded seven days later on Tower Hill. It took eight blows of the axe from Jack Ketch (a butcher and part time headsman) to sever his bonce, finishing off the job with a butcher's knife.

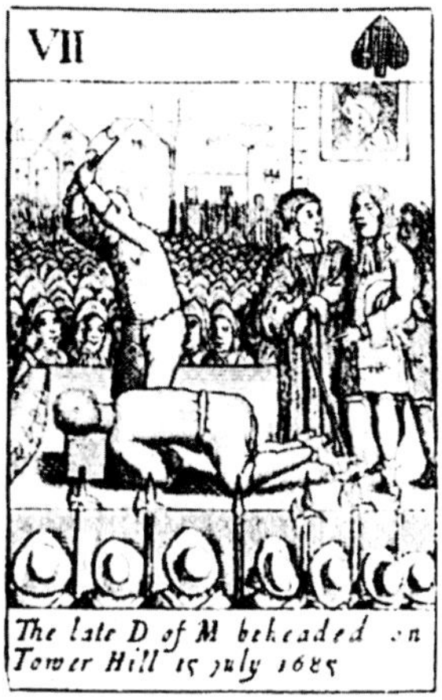

After this well attended public exhibition, it was realised a terrible mistake had taken place. The son of a former king, albeit illegitimate, had been executed without his portrait being painted. So a Yeoman Warder was sent to retrieve his head after the body was exhumed and the Surgeon General was commissioned to sew it back on. The portrait was knocked out in double quick time and has hung in the Royal Portrait Gallery to this day.

'Actions receive their tincture from the times,
And as they change are virtues made of crimes.'

Daniel Defoe: *A Hymn to the Pillory*

These are Alexander Osborne's direct descendents:

Alexander Osborne b 1687-farm labourer
Alexander Osborne b 1710-farm labourer
Henry Osborne b 1751-farm labourer
Isaac Osborne b 1796-farm labourer
Edward Osborne b 1821-farm labourer
Edward Osborne b 1851-fish hawker
Edward Osborne b 1887-scrap metal dealer
Robert Osborne b 1925-totter
Robert Osborne b 1953-artist

Descendents of Alexander Osborne were variously listed in censuses as 'worker in the field', 'scavenging haulier', 'horse dealer', 'pauper' and 'yarn spinner in sail cloth factory'. Children's occupations included 'plough boy' and 'Gentleman's errand boy'. Many were given 'assisted passages' to Australia in Victorian times.

My Great Grandfather migrated from the West Country to Notting Hill in the 19th century (called Notting Dale then). An unplanned shanty town developed in the Dale known as the 'Piggeries and Potteries'. This area was to develop a reputation for being rough with Pottery Lane being nicknamed 'Cut-throat Lane' by the locals. Charles Dickens called the Potteries 'a plague spot scarcely equalled for its insalubrity by any other in London.'

In 1893 the *Daily News* published an article denouncing the conditions in the Dale with the author stating that he had never seen 'anything more degraded and abandoned than life in these wretched places.' The Kensington Vestry put these conditions down to the evil habits of the people who were 'largely made up of loafers, cab-runners, beggars, tramps, thieves and prostitutes.'

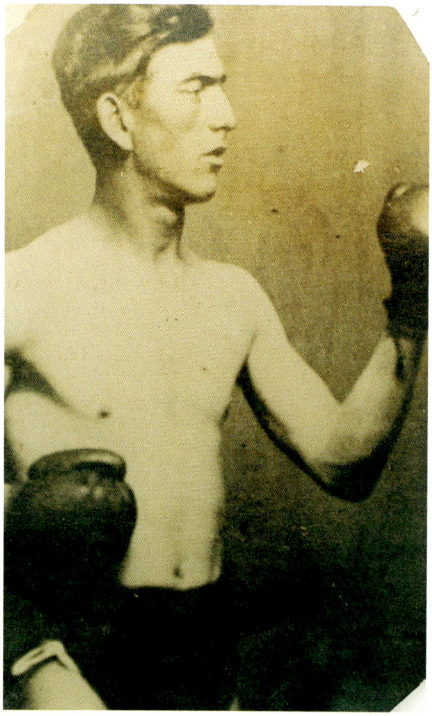

Ted Osborne (grandfather) c.1912, at the Rugby Boxing Club in Walmer Road. The mission was founded by old boys of Harrow and Rugby Public Schools to provide social activities and discipline for the slum dwellers of Notting Dale. 'Digger' Stanley, a local gypsy who had started boxing in fairground booths and became Bantamweight champion of England in 1909 also fought there and was a neighbour of the Osbornes. Another lively local was Alf Mancini who fought for the British Welterweight title in 1928. The Mancini family had an ice cream parlour in Bramley Road and one of Alf's brothers modelled for the sculptor Augustus John.

Albert Osborne (great uncle) wearing a flower hawking suit with slits in the trousers to display stems c.1930's, with his wife and sister Alice (left), who smoked a pipe.

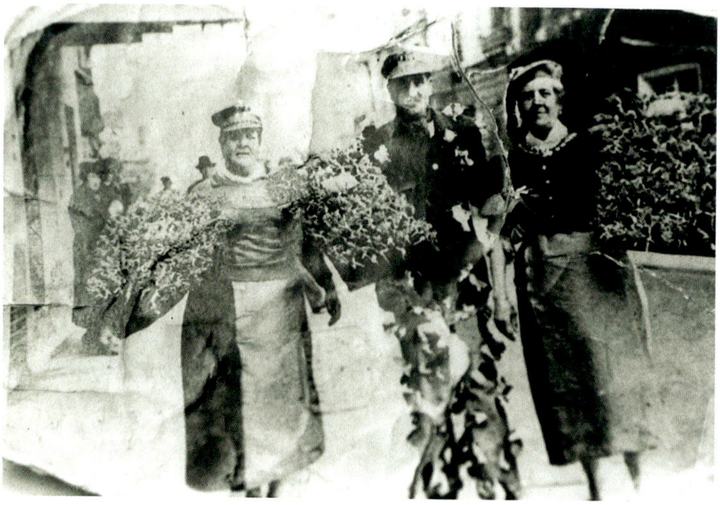

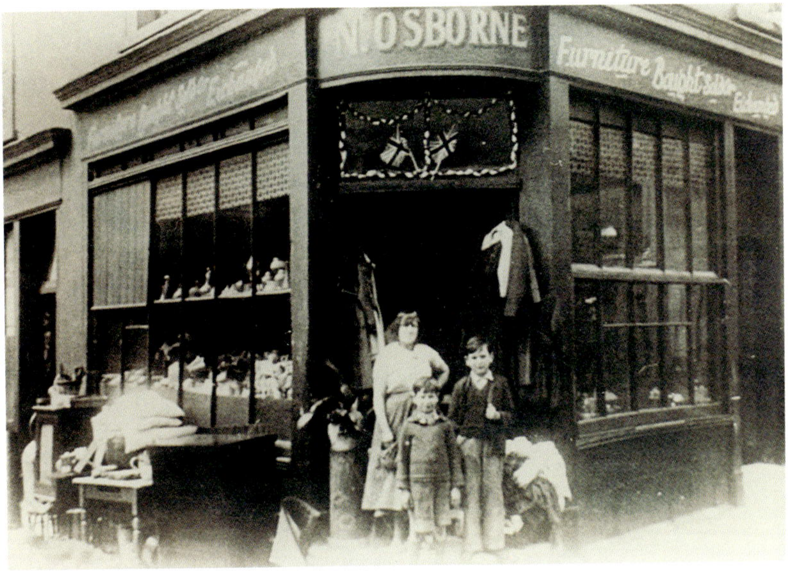

Nellie Osborne (grandmother), who was a Romany gypsy, photographed outside her shop in Portland Road on Coronation Day 1937, with Bobby and Billy, two of her twelve children. She received a letter of congratulation from the King of Spain for having a large family and taking in orphans from the Spanish Civil War.

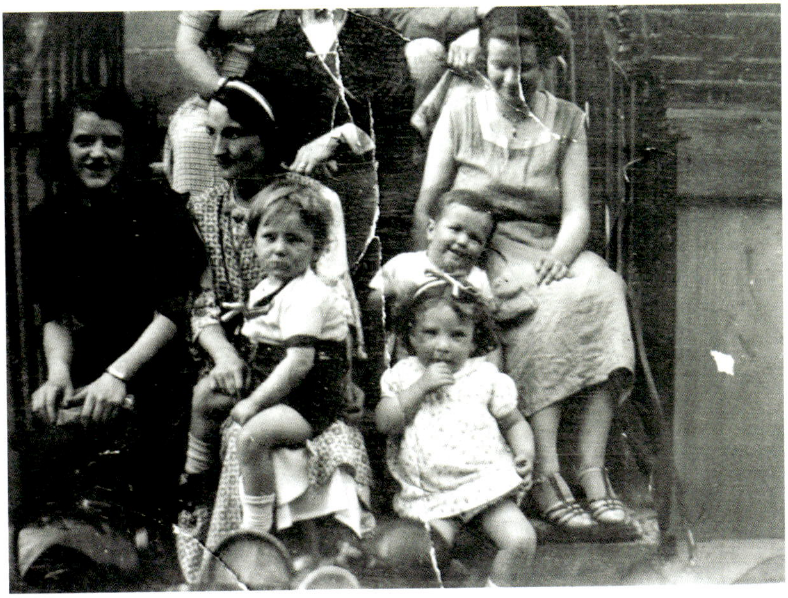

Patricia Osborne (mother – front right), with neighbours on the steps at 14 Dartmoor Street (now Hillgate Place), Kensington c.1936.

Growing up in the turbulent post-war decades of the 1950's and 1960's provided rich material for an artist. The Osbornes, mostly rag-and-bone men and ne'er-do-wells, crossed paths with serial murderer John Christie of 10 Rillington Place, frequented slum landlord Peter Rachman's illicit gambling dens in North Kensington, were drinking mates with local gangster Joe Cannon (who had links with the Krays) and socialised with assorted 'actresses'.

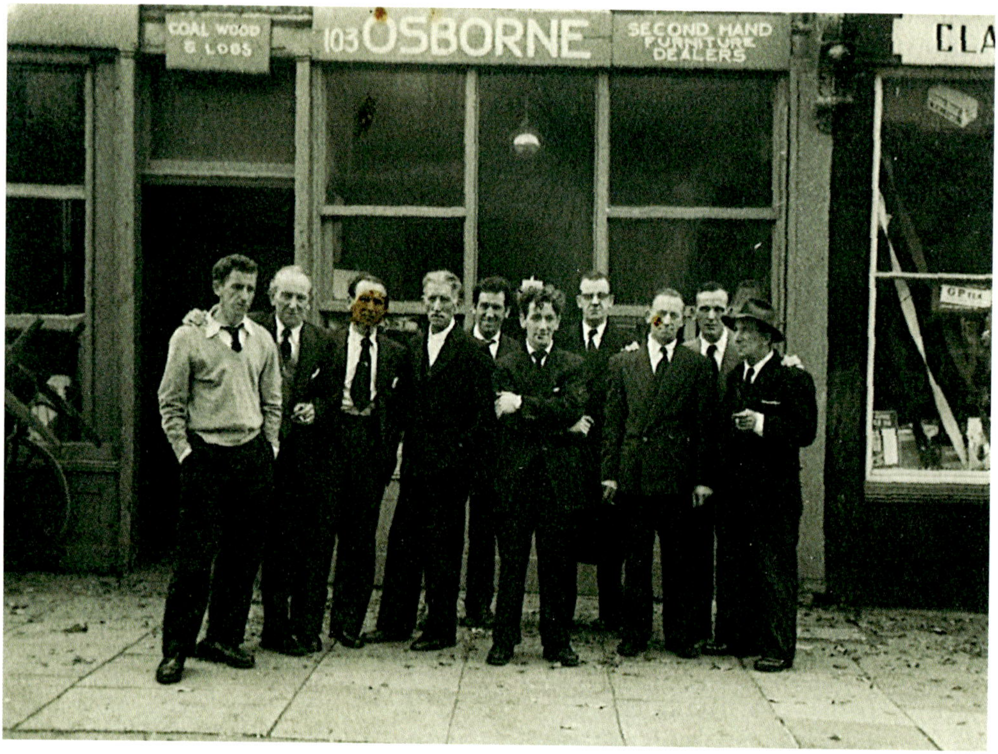

Osborne junk shop in Clarendon Road, Notting Hill Gate, 1957. Ted (4th from left) with 9 of his surviving sons. They had stables for horses and carts in Latimer Road and stalls in Portobello Market.

> 'All along the gutter rickety stalls and barrows were piled high with rags, torn jerseys, mismatched shoes, chipped china, bent tin trays, 3-legged furniture and malfunctioning appliances from the early days of electricity.'
>
> Monica Dickens, novelist and great-granddaughter of Charles Dickens, writing about Portobello Road.

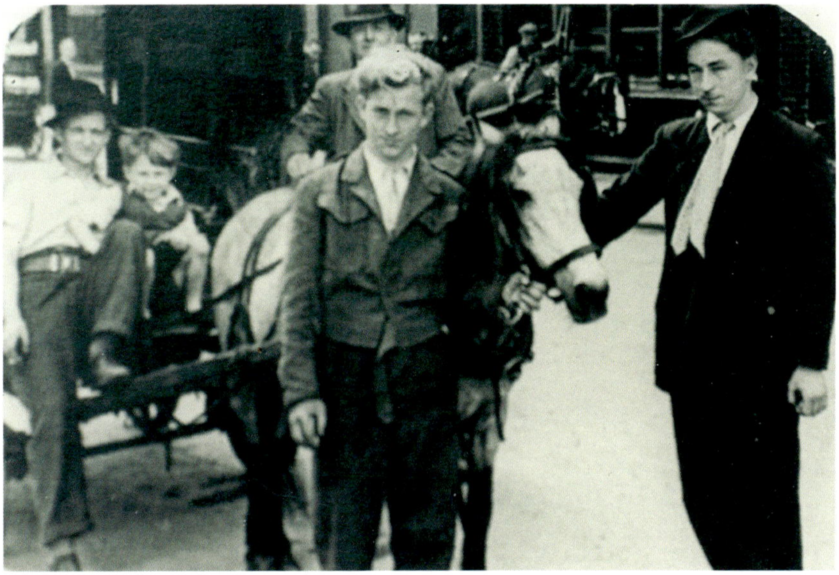

Osborne rag-and-bone men totting with 'Nelson' the one-eyed horse, c. 1960's.

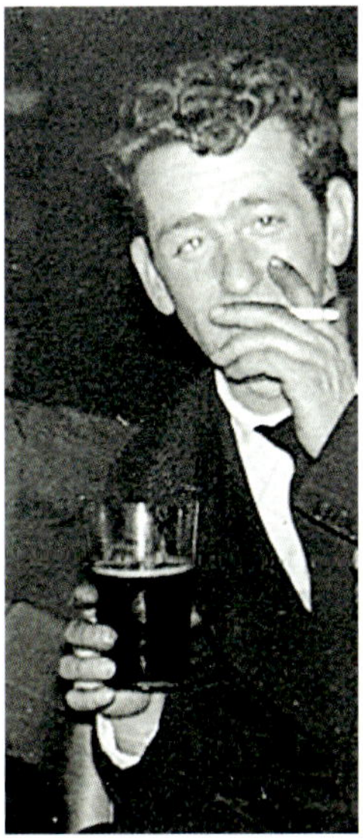

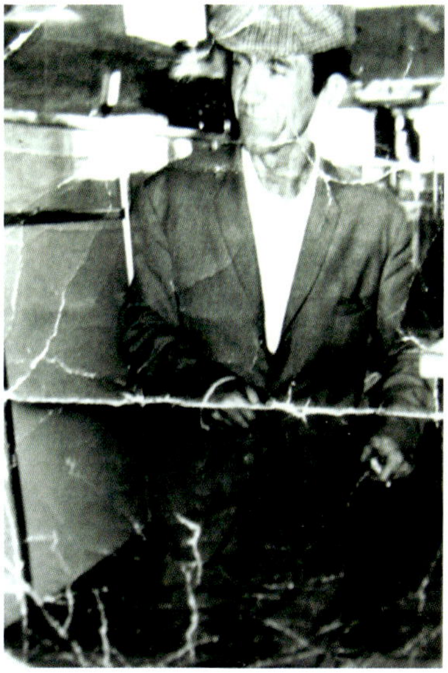

Left: Tommy 'Popeye' Osborne (uncle) who could smoke and drink with both hands.

Right: Georgie Osborne (uncle) 'walking on his knees'. He had a pet monkey called 'Wanker' and a parrot that he taught to swear. He also worked as a waiter on cruise ships to Australia.

Leslie 'Spike' Osborne (uncle) served 21 years in Brixton. He was a friend of Buster Edwards and was 'questioned' after the Great Train Robbery, c.1960's. Rumoured to have burgled the Lord Mayor of London's house in the 1940's and suspected of making rings and jewellery from the gold chain.

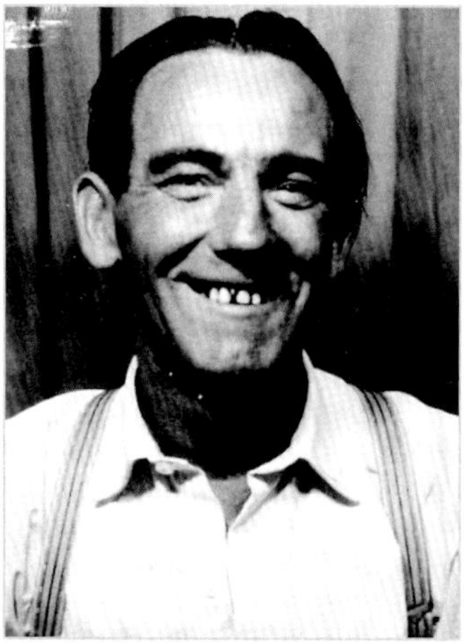

Those decades were also a time of radical social change with the pubs and streets morphing into a cultural melting pot and photographers and writers lighting up the pockmarked bombsites and dark corners of Notting Hill. The film director Ken Russell, who lived on Portobello Road during the mid 1950's, was one of many artists who had a keen eye for the surreal and eccentric.

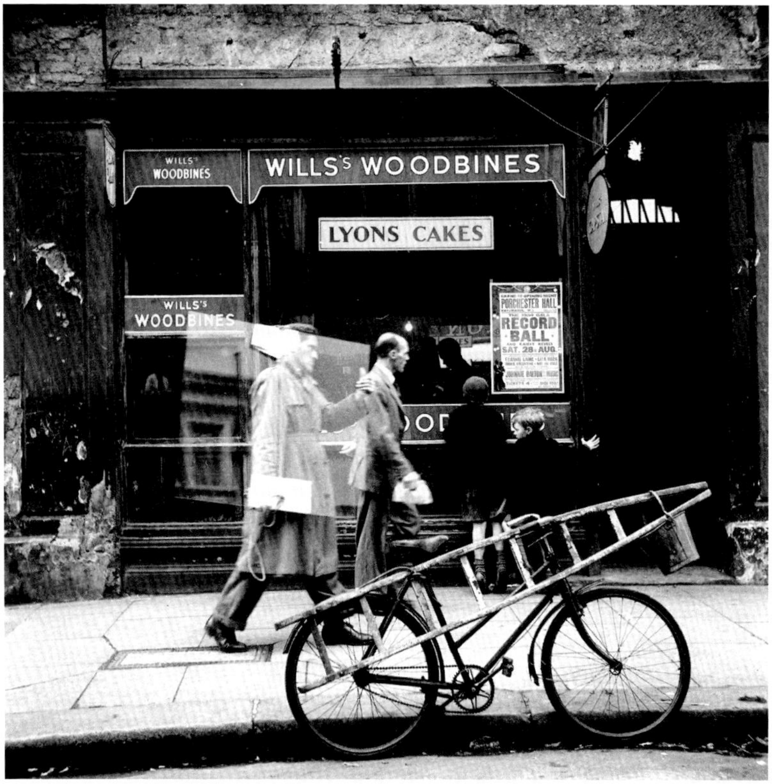

Portobello 1954, Ken Russell *photograph courtesy of Topfoto*

During the 1950's, Fascist Oswald Mosley had his election campaign headquarters in Princedale Road. The race riots were breaking out in Notting Dale and fly on the wall photographer Roger Mayne was documenting local Teddy Boys and children (including Osbornes) running wild in decaying Southam Street and Portland Road (1956-61). Roger Mayne's pictures of the fledging youth culture in Notting Hill appeared on numerous Penguin covers during the sixties, most famously Colin MacInnes' novel *Absolute Beginners* and George Orwell's *Keep the Aspidistra Flying*. He also photographed many of the painters in the Cornish art colony of St Ives, who, coincidentally, I was to work with and befriend 50 years later. In the 1960's Princedale Road became the location for the scenes in *Blow Up* and the hippy magazine *Oz* had its office there.

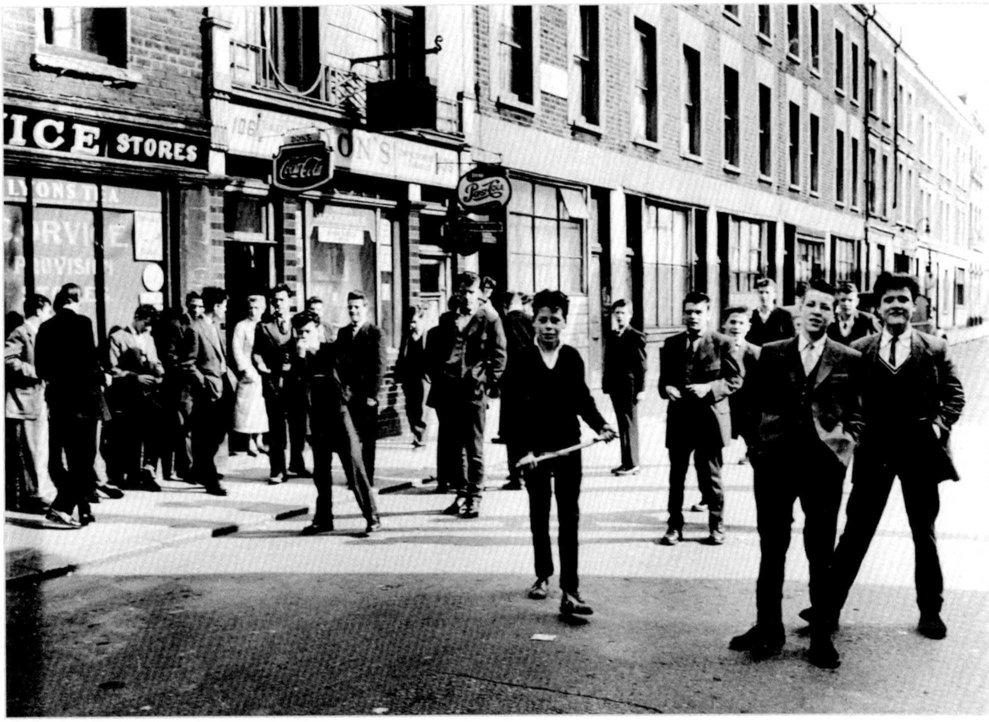

Princedale Road 1956, Roger Mayne.

Photograph courtesy of Mary Evans Picture Library

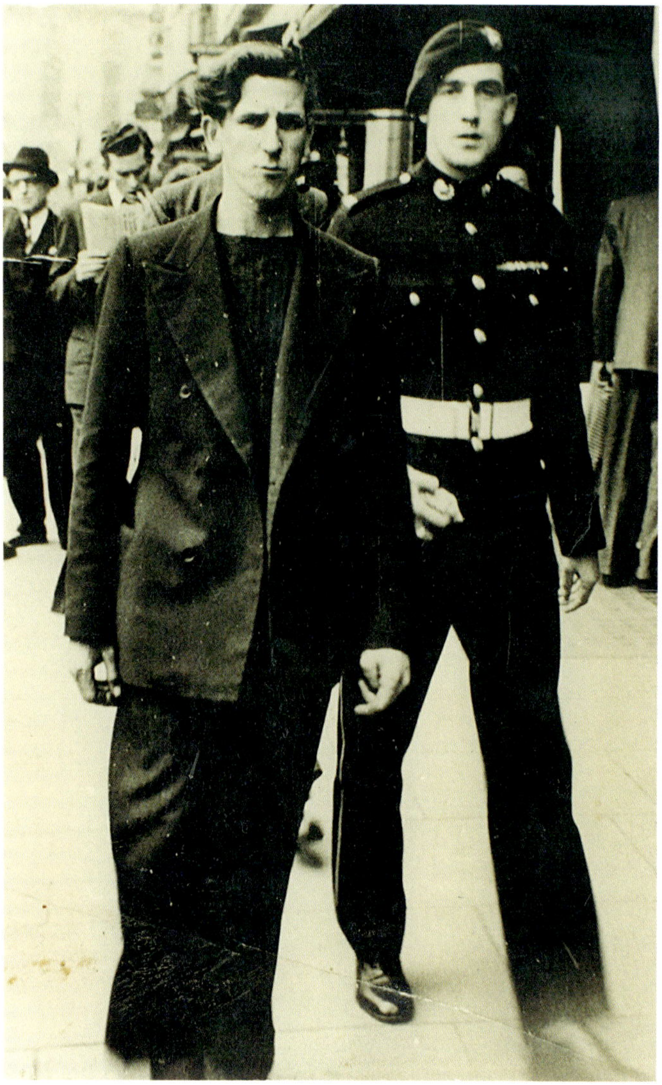

Bobby Osborne (father) being arrested by the Military Police for absconding from National Service and escorted to 'The Glass House,' a colloquial term for the Military Corrective Centre in Colchester c.1950's.

In the 1960's actors and musicians mixed freely with 'faces' from the 'underworld' and class barriers and conventions were being deconstructed. During these interesting times, the Osbornes continued their picaresque journey through history with a genetically mixed cocktail of insouciant contempt for authority and feckless hedonism. An existential way of confronting the world that proved to be a recurring and dominant leitmotif in my work.

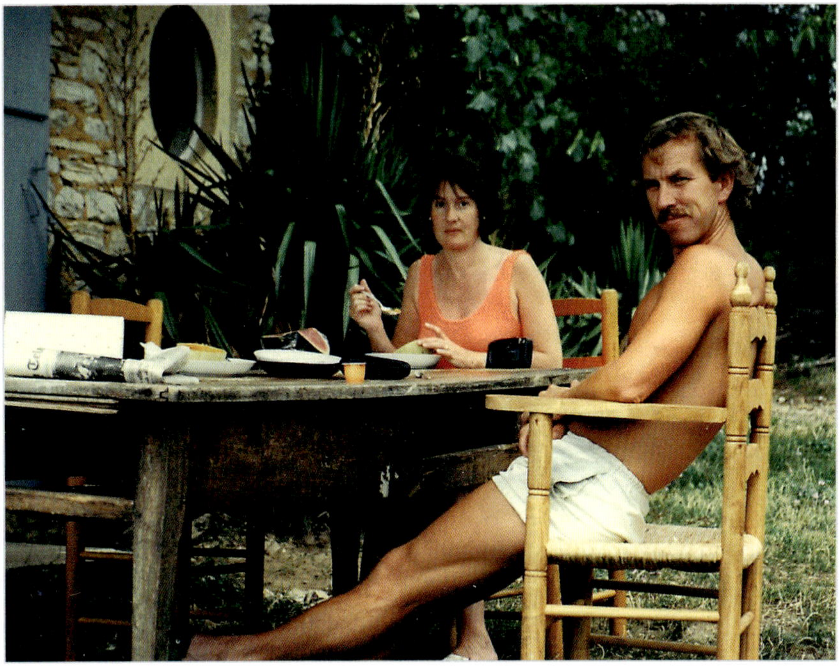

Bob Osborne and Lynda Davies at Canteloube in the Lot valley, 1989, home at the time of the novelist Mario Reading, who was later to write the bestselling Antichrist Trilogy.

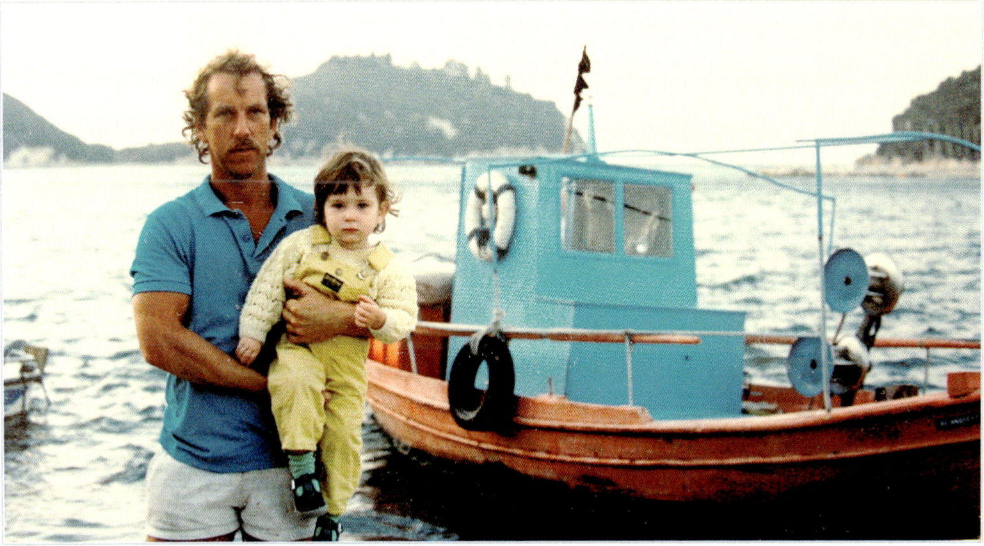

Bob and Sophie Osborne, Paxos, Greece, 1988.

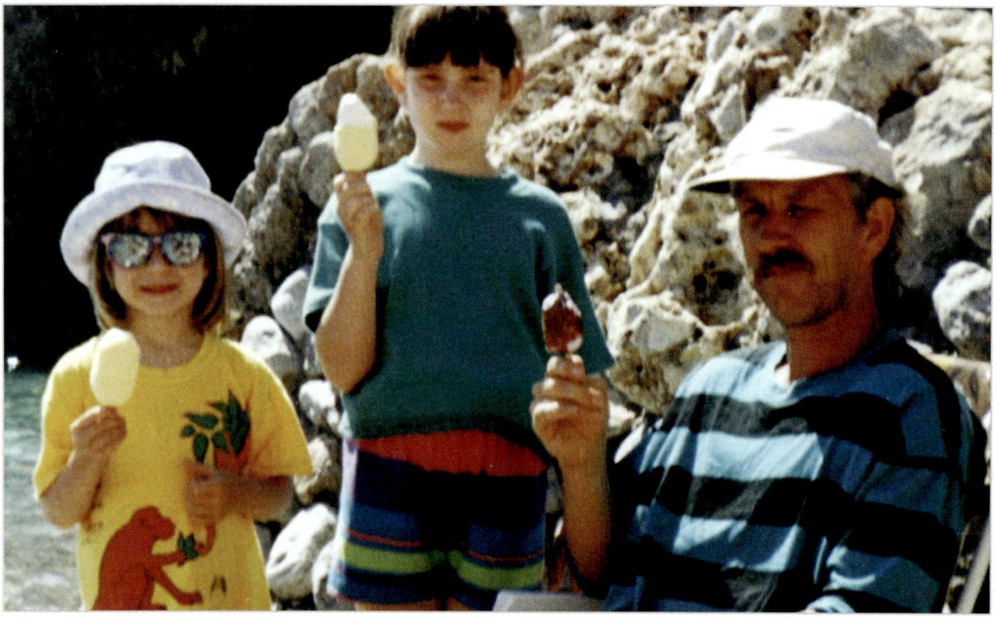

Bob Osborne with daughters Sophie (right) and Rosie (left) on Porthgwidden Beach, St Ives, Cornwall,1998.

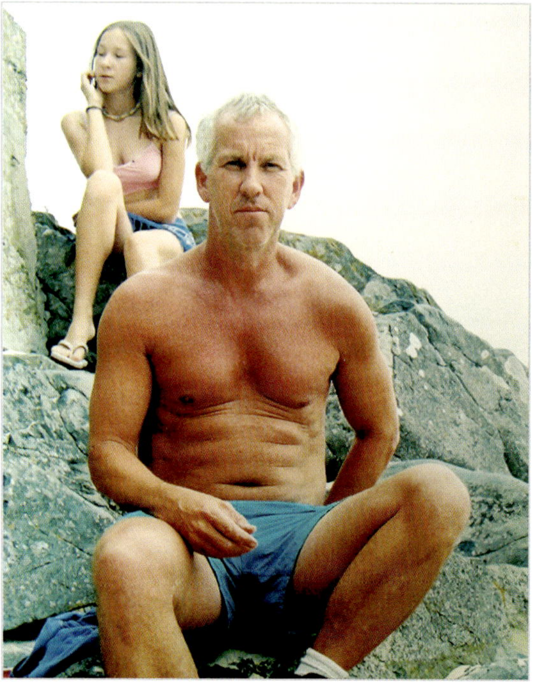

Bob and Rosie Osborne, St Ives, Cornwall, 2000.

DRIFTWOOD CONSTRUCTIONS

The driftwood constructions that form an important part of Osborne's output since the 1990's trade in the discarded poetry of marine life. The weathered texture and fortuitous colour of these objects-frequently broken up boat fragments, oars, sackcloth, machine parts or piping-lend an automatic distinction to works that are subjected to a synthetic régime of post cubist composing and re-arranging. Here automatic or more conscious impulses interact to create an uncanny synthesis between chance and order.

Broken, and subject to natural decay, the objects find artistic salvation and boxed permanence as they are constructed in an entirely new, this time non-utilitarian context. The salvaging of order from chaos is, however, of a random kind finding ultimate and final rationalisation within the tight parameters of wall-bound boxes or framed pictorial objects. In *Cornwall 1996* and *Cornwall 1998,* made just after he started living in a property overlooking Porthmeor Beach in St Ives, Osborne slots shells, bones, pebbles, metal fragments and beach detritus into ready-made grids adapted from printer's block boxes. These pictographic compartments are unified using the vivid ultramarine blue paint patented by the French artist Yves Klein and known as International Yves Klein Blue. As part of his open-ended notion of aesthetic democratisation Klein saw IYKB as a chromatic commodity for general artistic use. Not only binding Osborne's diverse found objects into a whole the blue contrasts with the pebble greys, fishbone whites and rope greens of the composition's members. As in the Hayle painter John Miller's use of deep blue skies to express the timeless quality of Cornish high summers, Osborne's deployment of IYKB evokes the carefree tranquillity of the seaside. The intrinsic linear patterns of fish vertebrae instils a natural visual interest with the biographical accoutrement of it's derivation from an actual fish consumed by the artist and his friends.

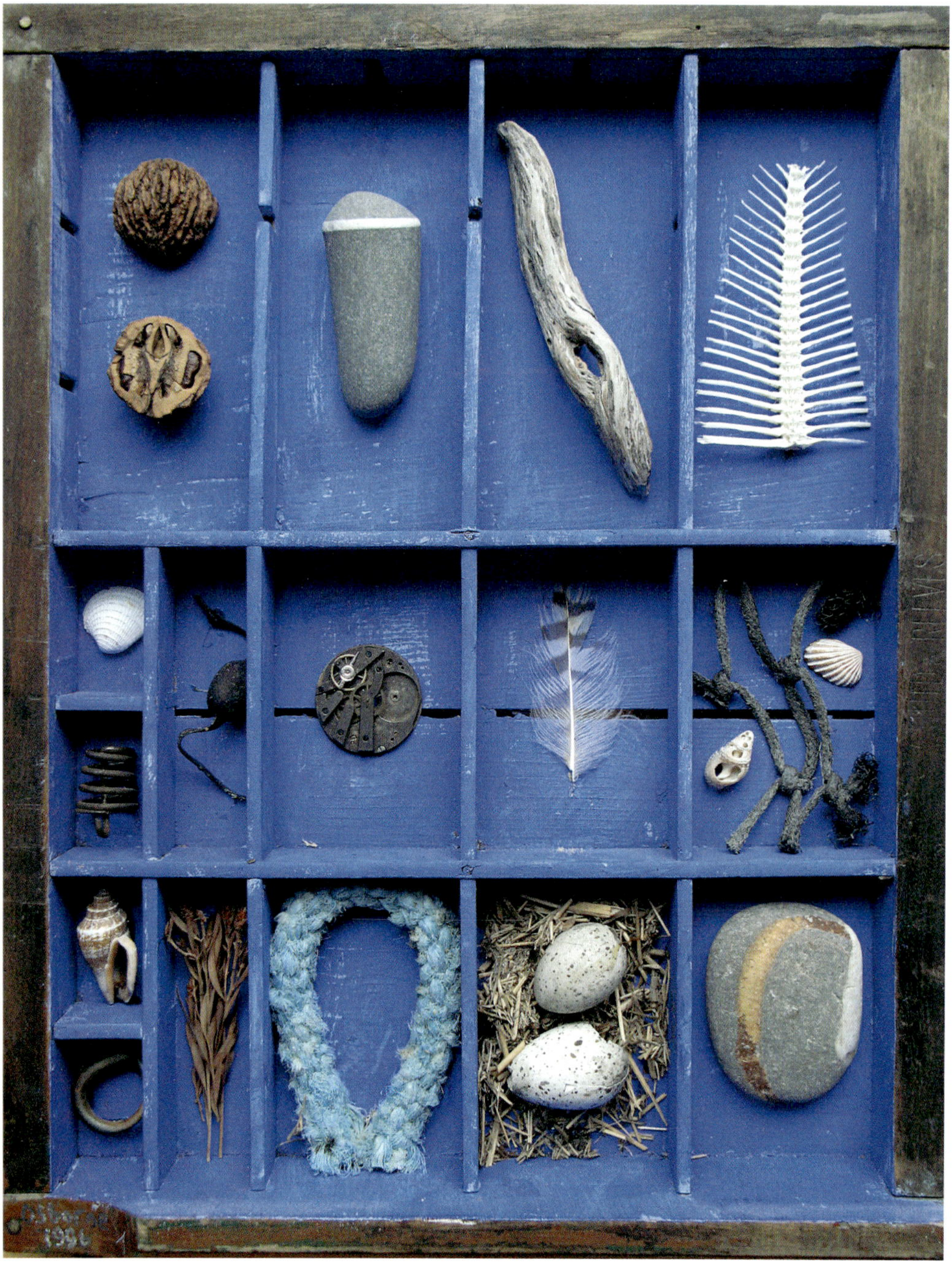

Cornwall, 1996

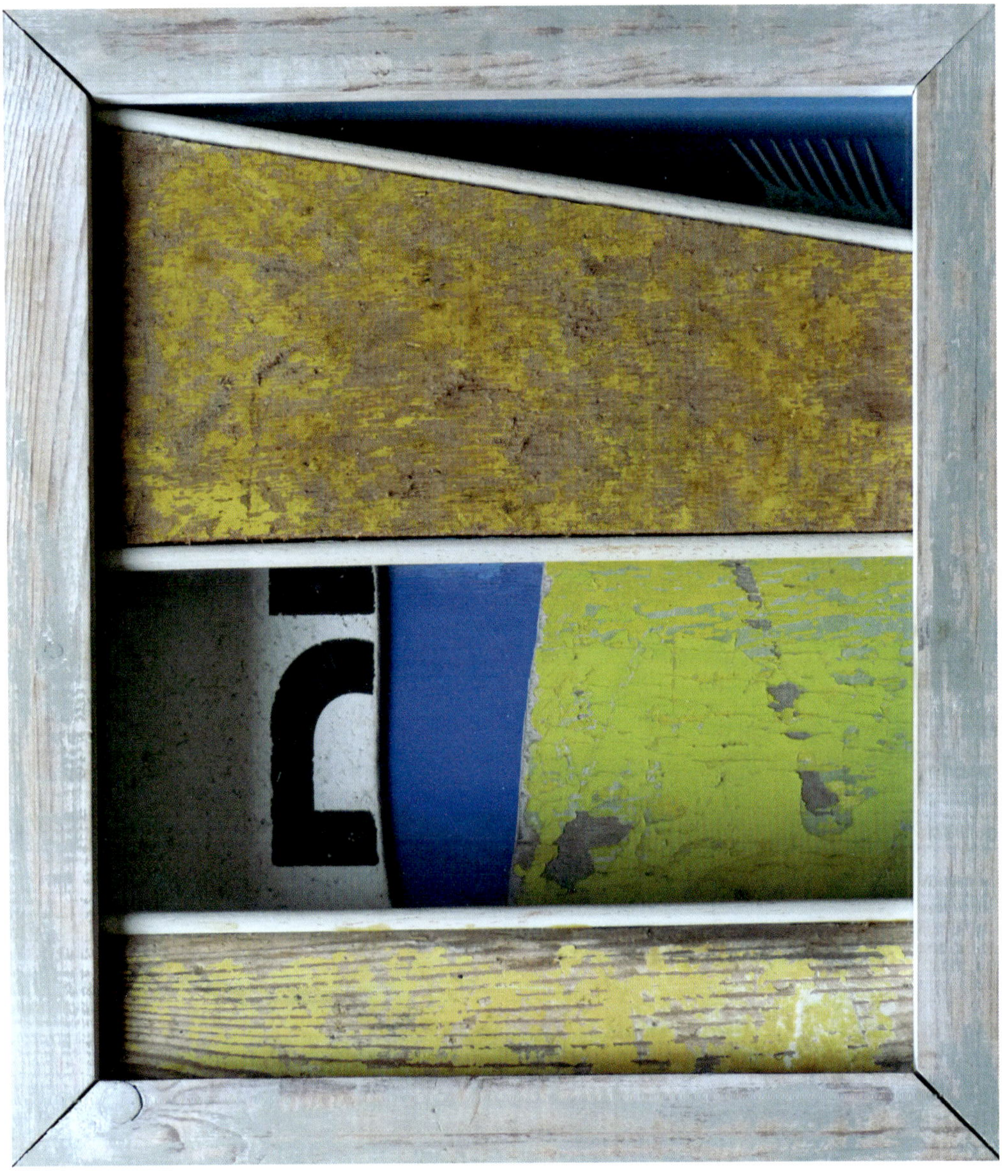

Yellow Driftwood, 1998

Newlyn, by contrast, relies on the intrinsic textures and colours of burnt or distressed wood fragments, blue tubing and red canvas offcut. Slotted together as a tightly-composed ensemble, this semi-sculptural relief reads more like an *informalist* abstract painting with random and multifarious paint textures.

Some constructions, while pinned to the wall, forgo the pictorial 'packaging' of framing and stand-or rather hang-as raw, naked, found objects. In these instances the works are the product of a sculptor manqué, their coloured morphologies the Duchampian outcome, not of the traditional methods of carving or modelling, but rather of direct construction using maritime members or pastoral parts. They are attached like trophies to the wall. Picasso, Schwitters and their British (St Ives) successors Peter Lanyon and Margaret Mellis are the precursors of this romantic, nature-inspired constructivism- at once art historically specific yet both primitive and timeless. In *After The Fire*, made up from elements salvaged from a summertime bonfire on Porthmeor beach, near to his St. Ives studio, Osborne's *modus operandi* becomes more opportunist and autobiographical.

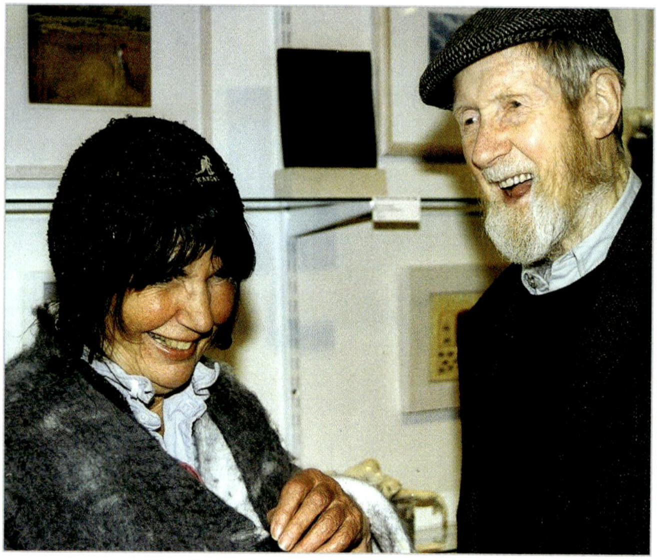

Sandra Blow RA and Bob Crossley at Osborne's exhibition of constructions held at the Cornerstone Gallery in St Ives in 2002. The painter Bob Crossley was a neighbour of Osborne, who was, at that time, living and working in Zelah studio (previously used by Patrick Heron) overlooking Porthgwidden Beach

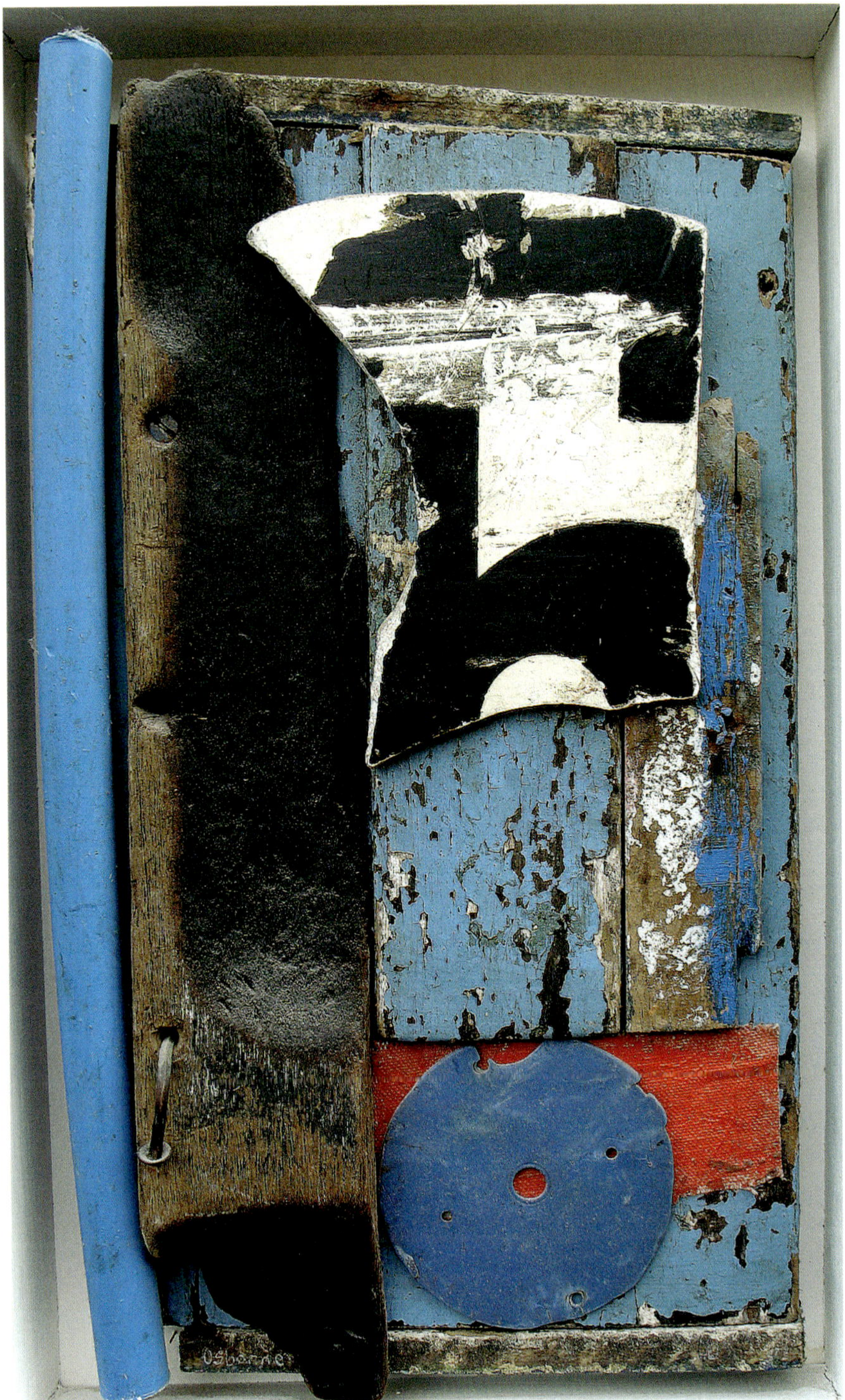

Newlyn, 2001

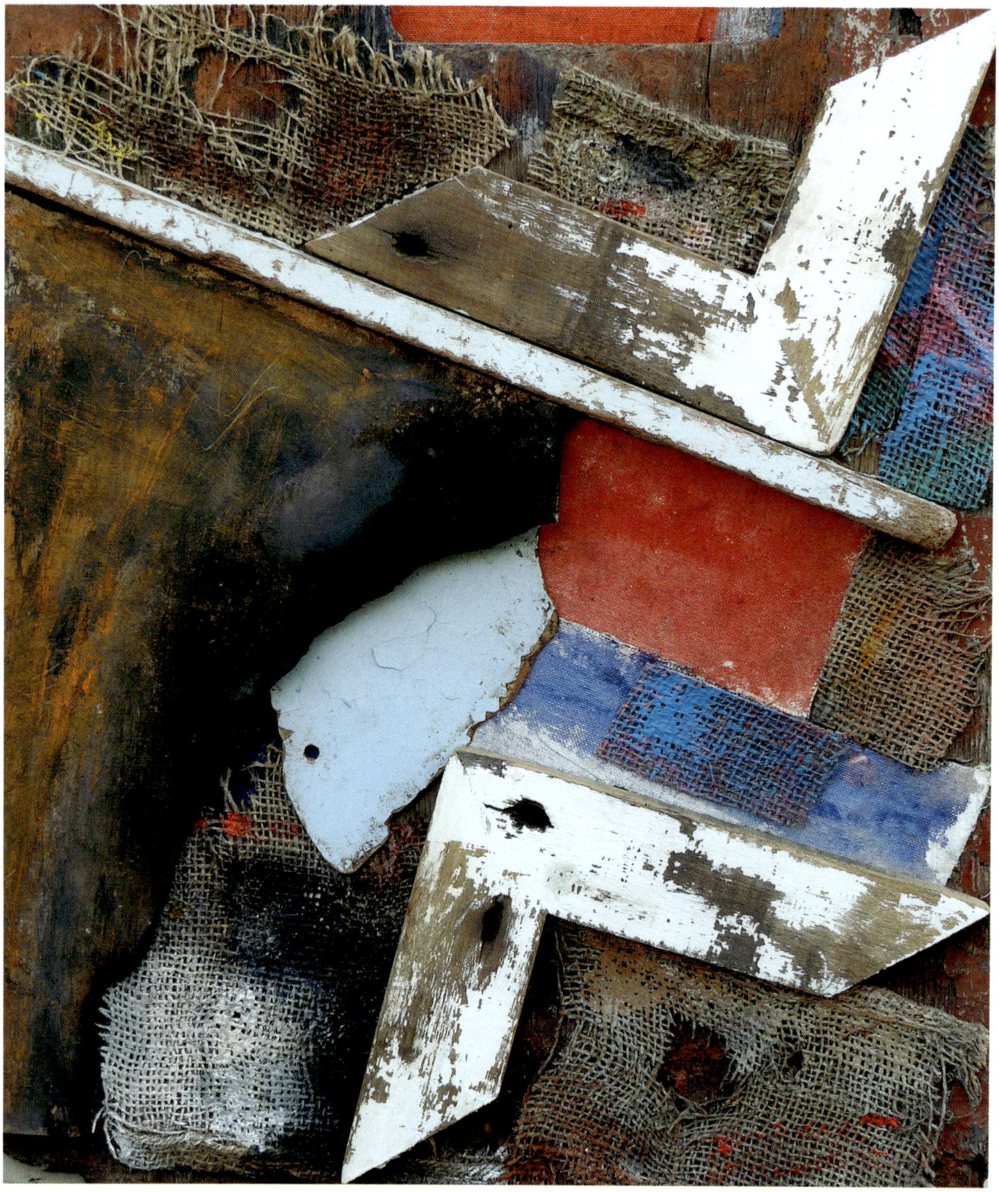

After the Fire, 2001

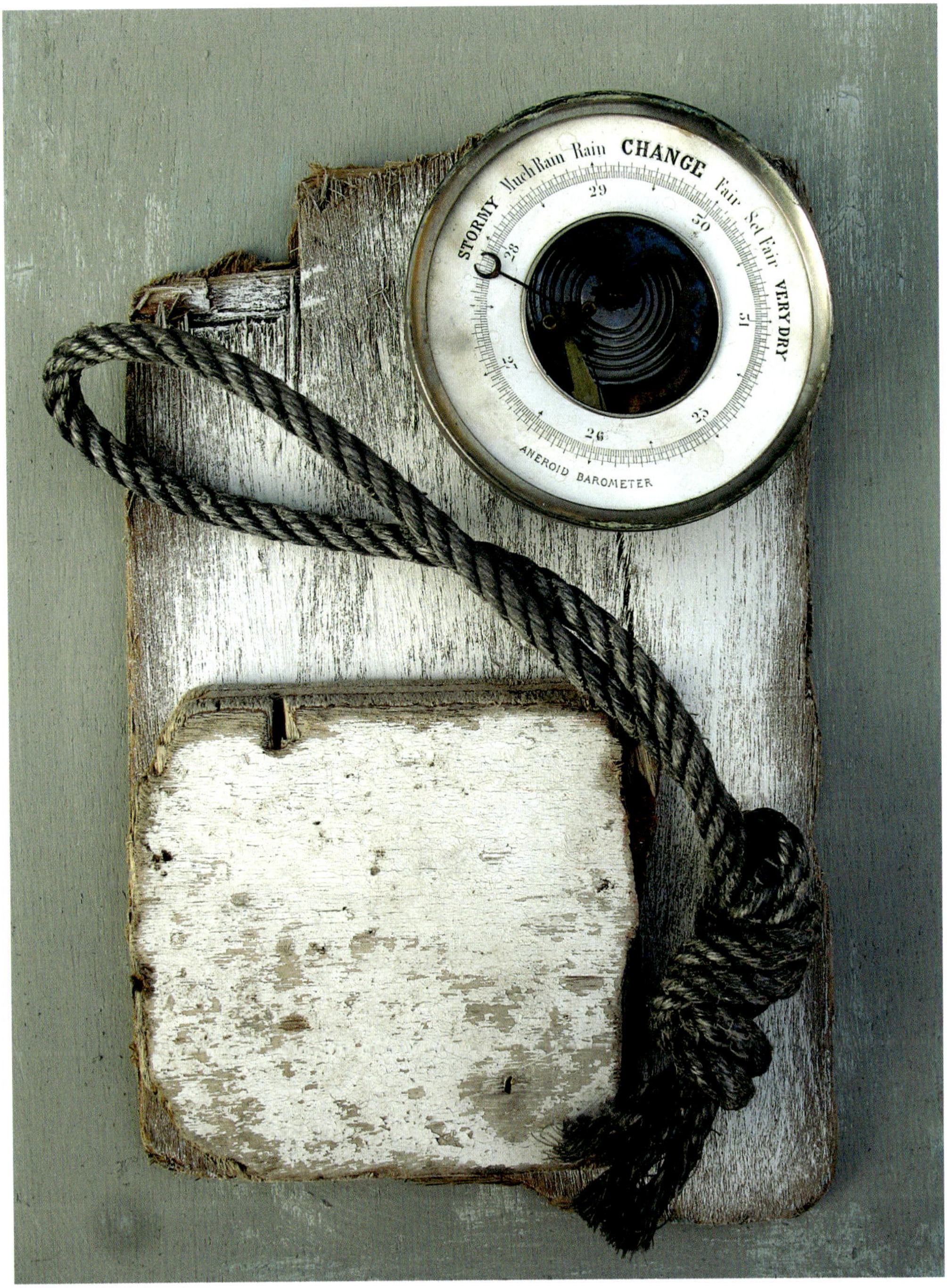

Marazion, 2000

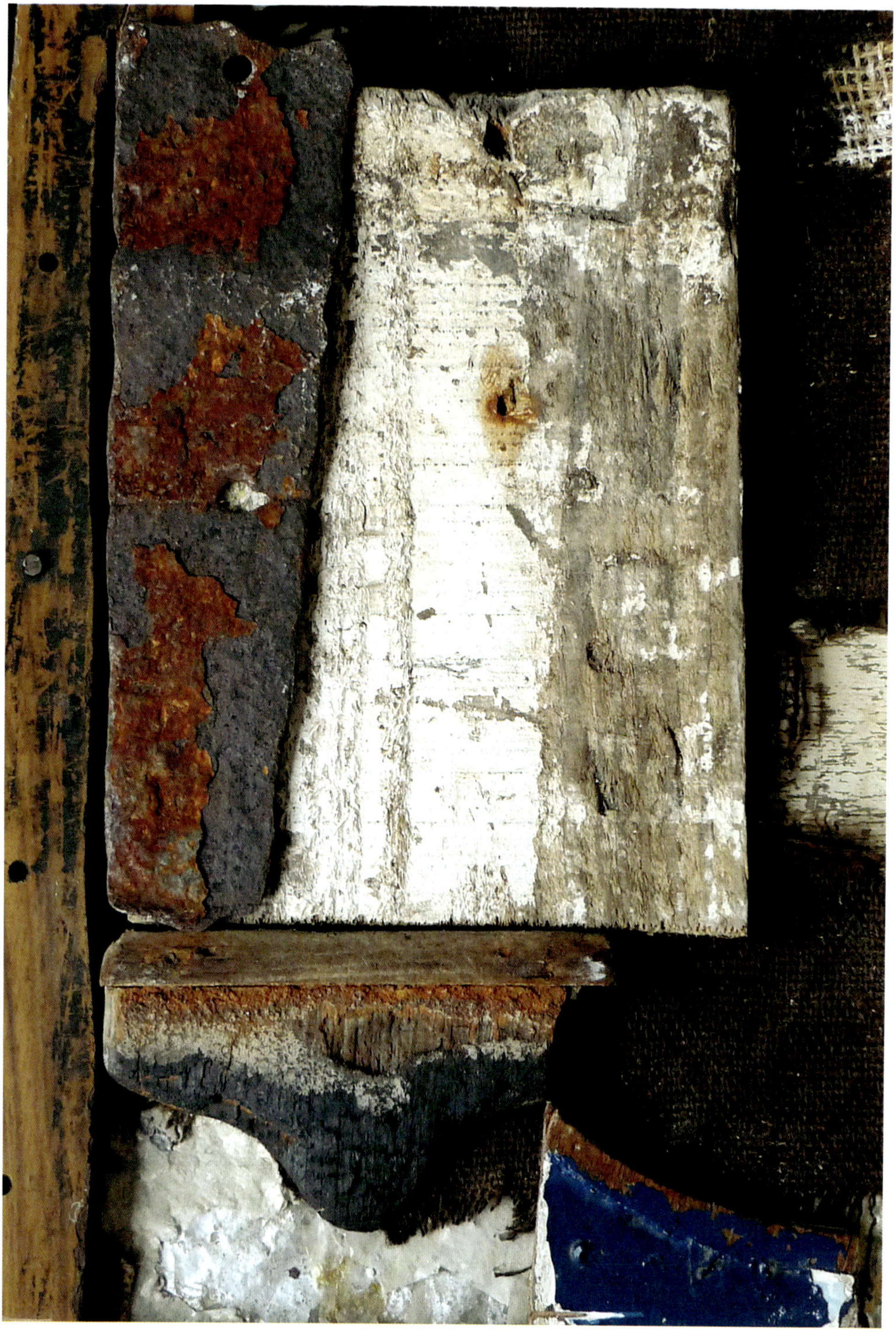

Crossing Boundaries, 2001

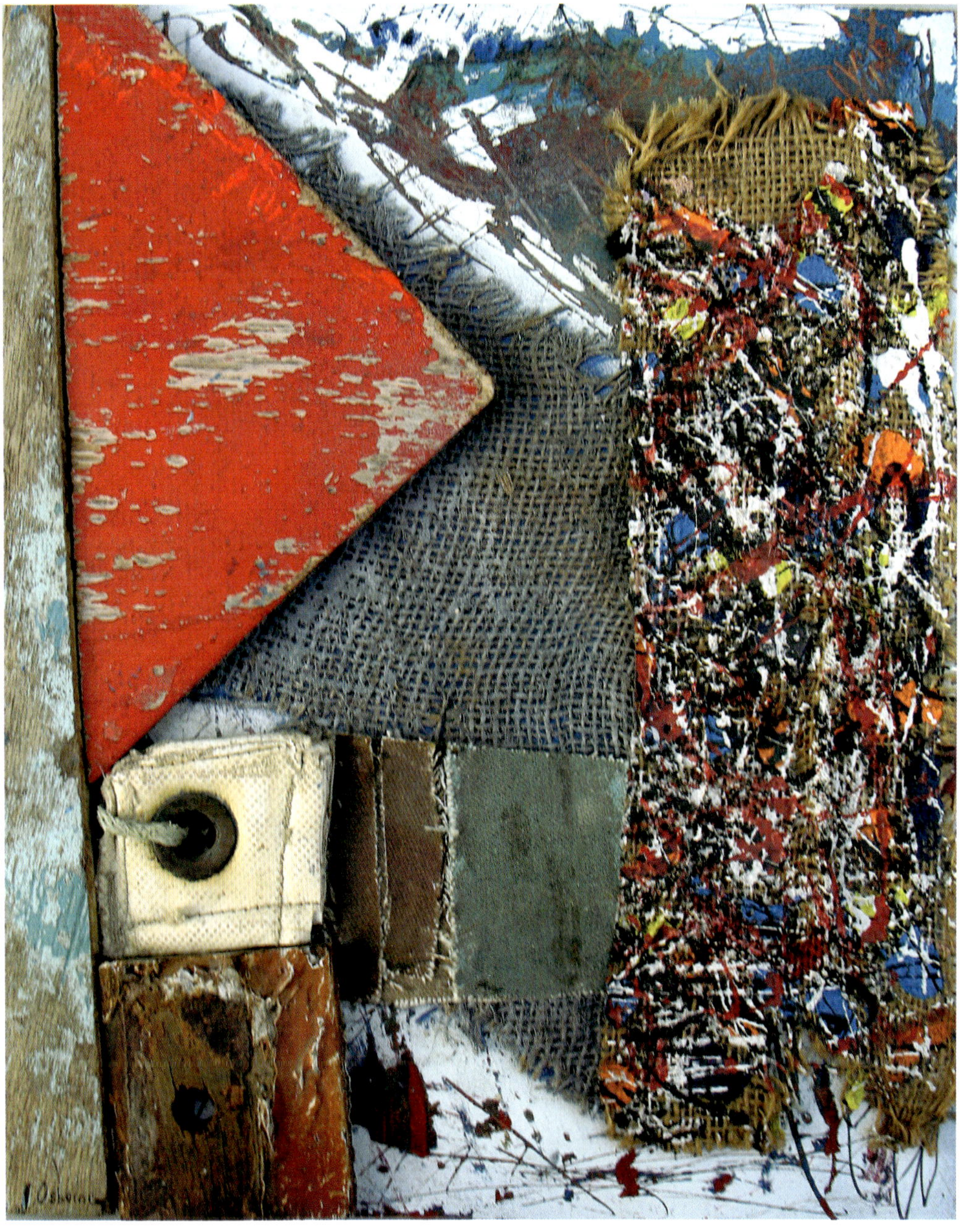

Combing the Towans, 2002

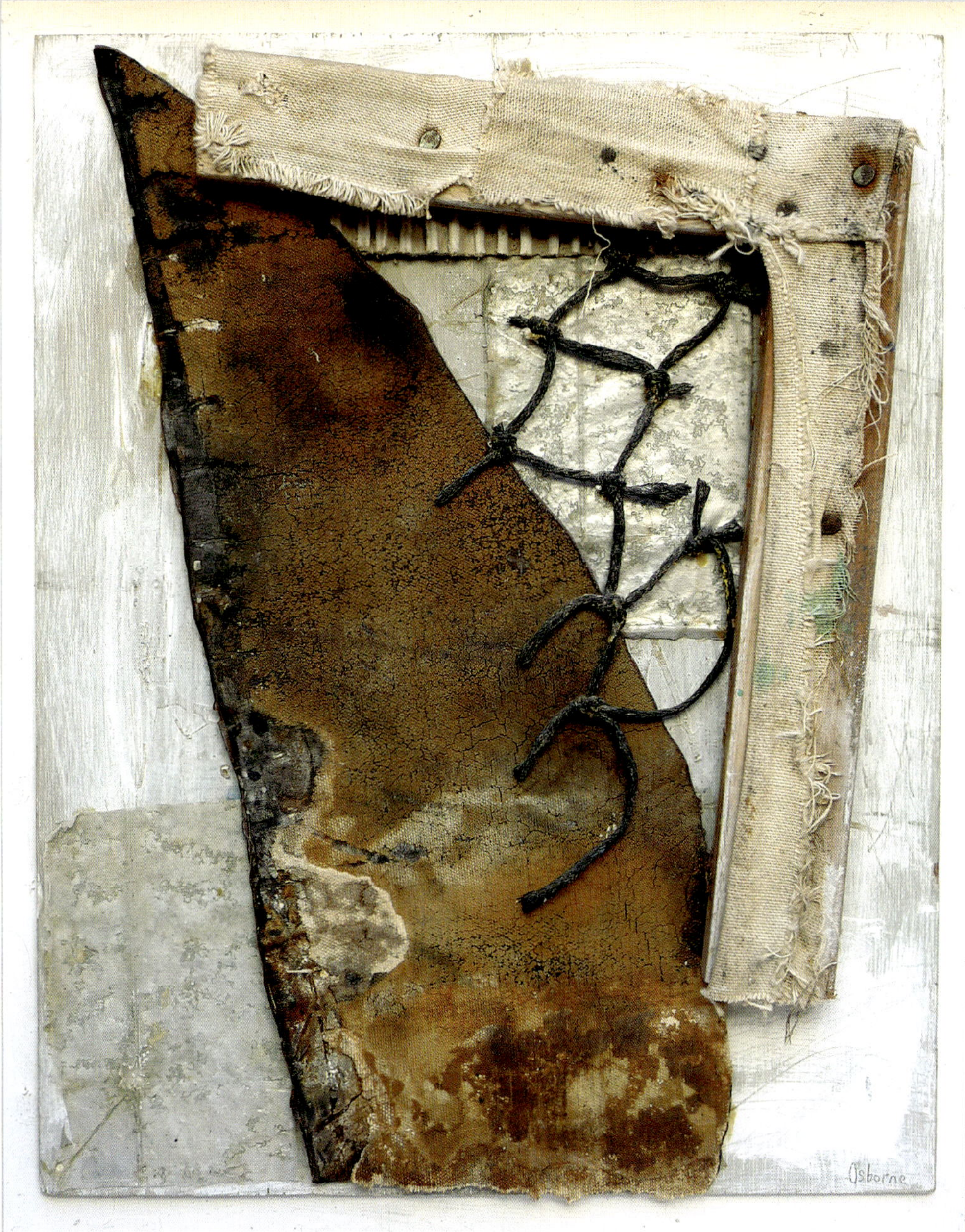

Porthmeor Beach, 2002

In 1999, Osborne and I visited Southwold on the Suffolk coast to spend the day with the celebrated former St Ives painter and collagist Margaret Mellis. Mellis' breadth of experience, as a 'child' of the wartime Carbis Bay constructivist enclave, informed her relaxed and literally down to earth working practice. This entailed composing ad-lib from a pile of dried out and domesticated driftwood and boat parts kept in a spare room. Mellis' late husband, the paper collagist Francis Davison, also extolled the virtues of direct handling of found materials.

The rawness of Mellis' latter day wall-bound constructivism-though at variance with the neater collaged, paper configurations of her wartime Carbis Bay beginnings that had originally drawn on the site specific influences of Hepworth, Nicholson and Gabo-recalled Schwitters, Lanyon's late constructions and the recent work of Janet Natham, a Hampstead constructor and partner of the painter Patrick Caulfield.

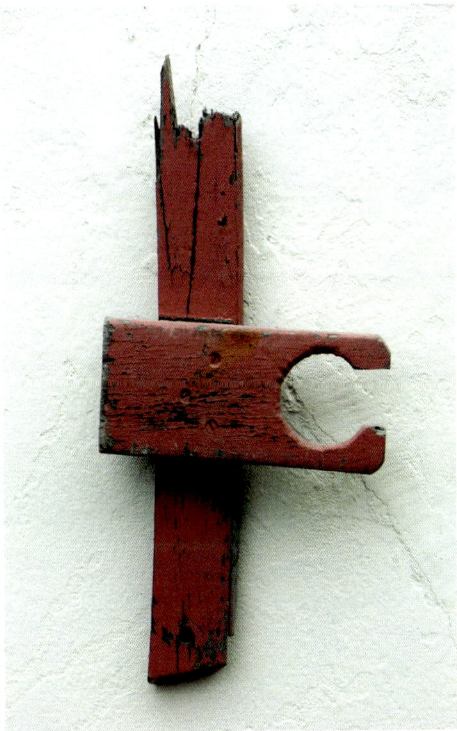

Found Boat Part (Marazion)

Although London based, Osborne was already collecting and working with the salt-licked debris of broken boat parts in his Porthmeor Beach studio, and must have seemed a kindred spirit to the older Suffolk artist. Mellis hung some of Osborne's constructions on her kitchen wall later that afternoon, along with her own works for comparative effect. This open-ended democratisation, where art became a shared process and experimental adventure conjured up the communal spirit and carefree atmosphere of the immediate post-war years in St. Ives.

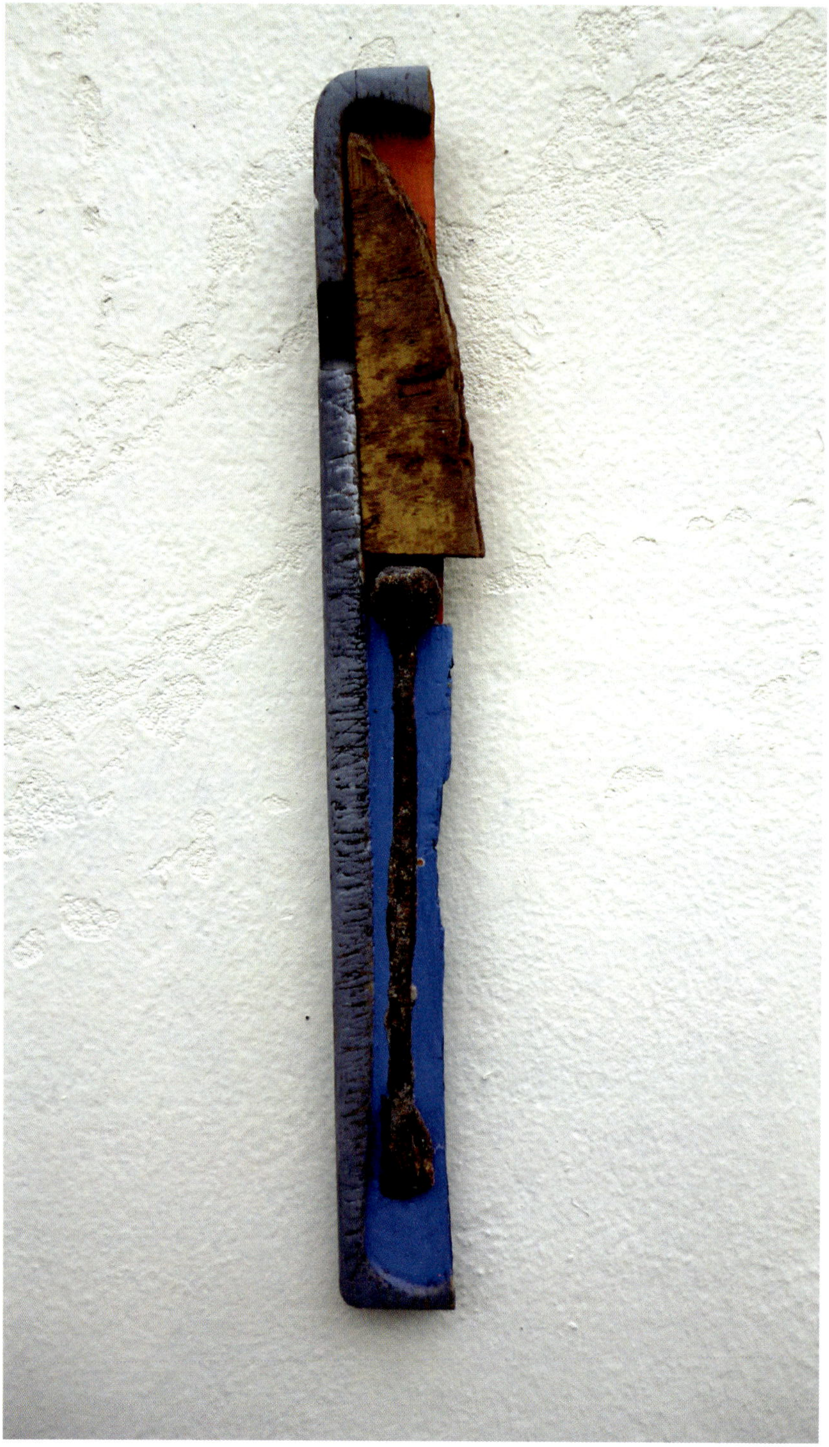

Sea Instrument 1, 2000

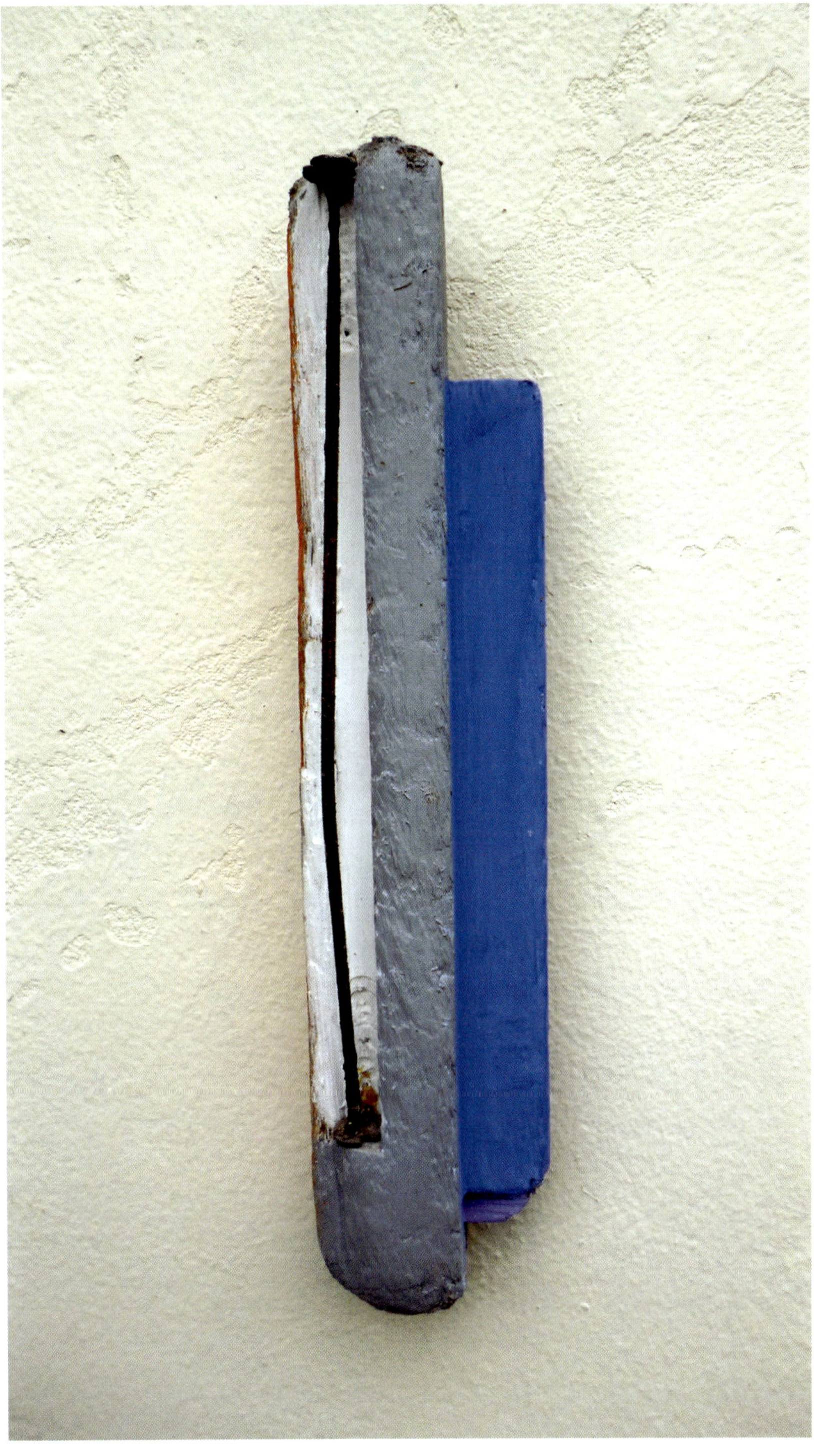

Sea Instrument 2, 2000

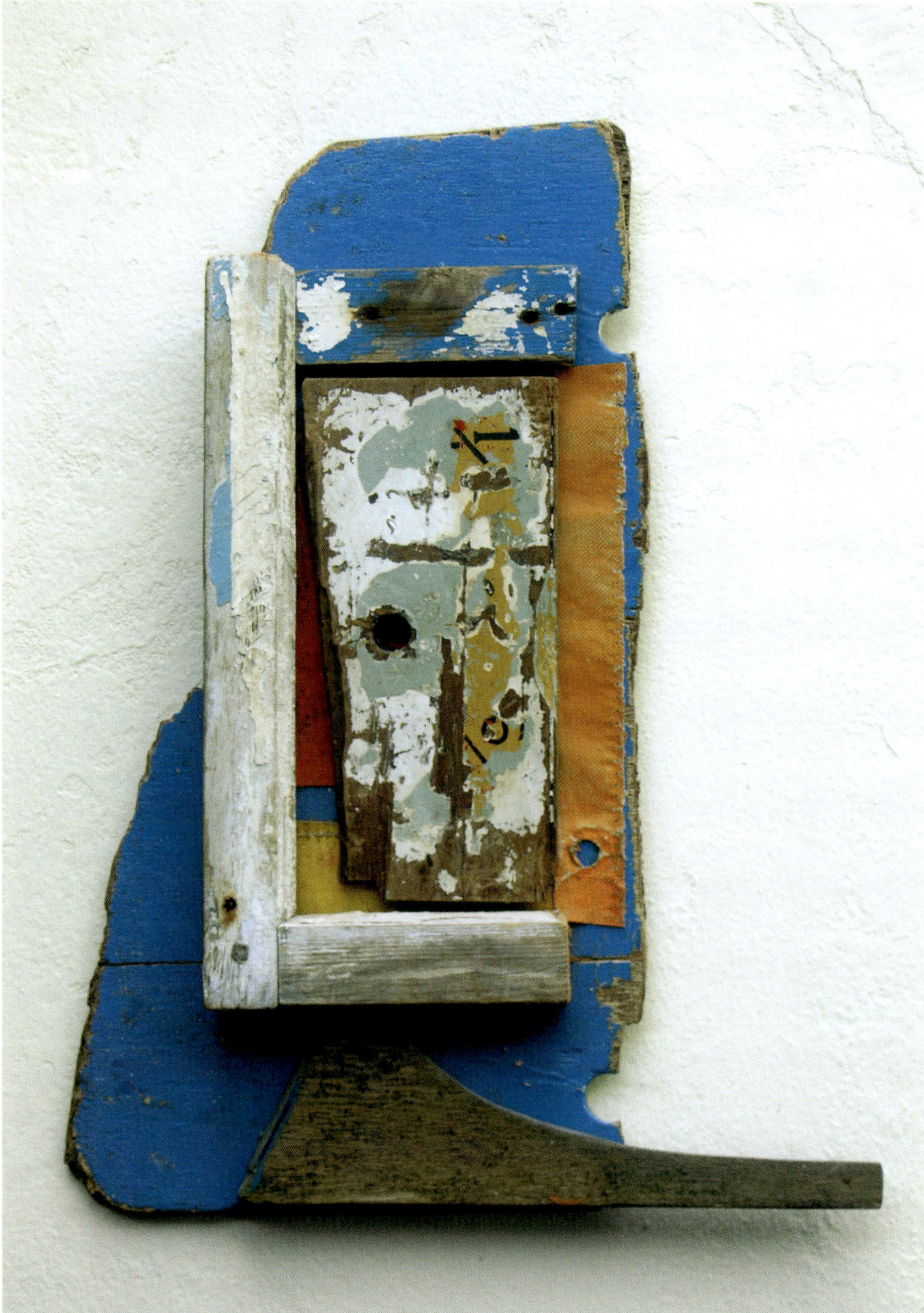

To the Lighthouse, 2001

During the first few years of the 21st century Osborne regularly visited the small Cornish fishing village of Mousehole where he was able to collect boat fragments from the harbour and keep them in the cellar at The Fish Store, a house originally used for packing pilchards and inhabited by Augustus John and his family. Mousehole had also been a base for the painters Adrian Ryan and Mary Jewels. After one particularly heavy winter sea storm Osborne salvaged wood from the wreckage trapped in the tiny harbour and constructed a series of works which were exhibited in 2005 in a group show at the Royal West of England Academy in Bristol.

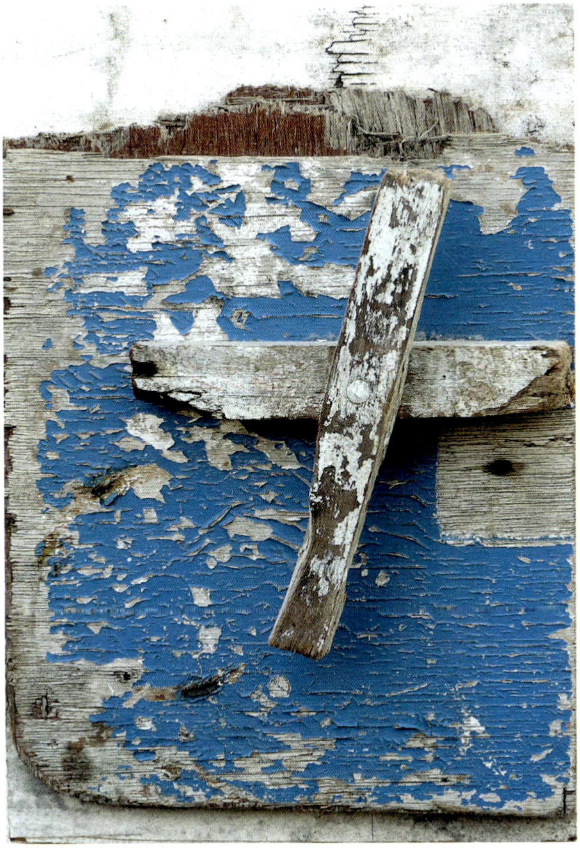

Found boat part (St Ives)

These constructions were pinned directly to the wall without any framed context or constraint, their banged-together rawness the exact compositional equivalent of their fortuitous shapes and colours. ***Mousehole 1, 2 and 3*** are generally vertical in orientation and use partially recognisable boat parts such as oars. Their bright colours-reds, yellows and rich blues-enliven the surrounding space and introduce a sense of the wild outdoors into the tame, reposeful and settled environment of the domestic or gallery arena.

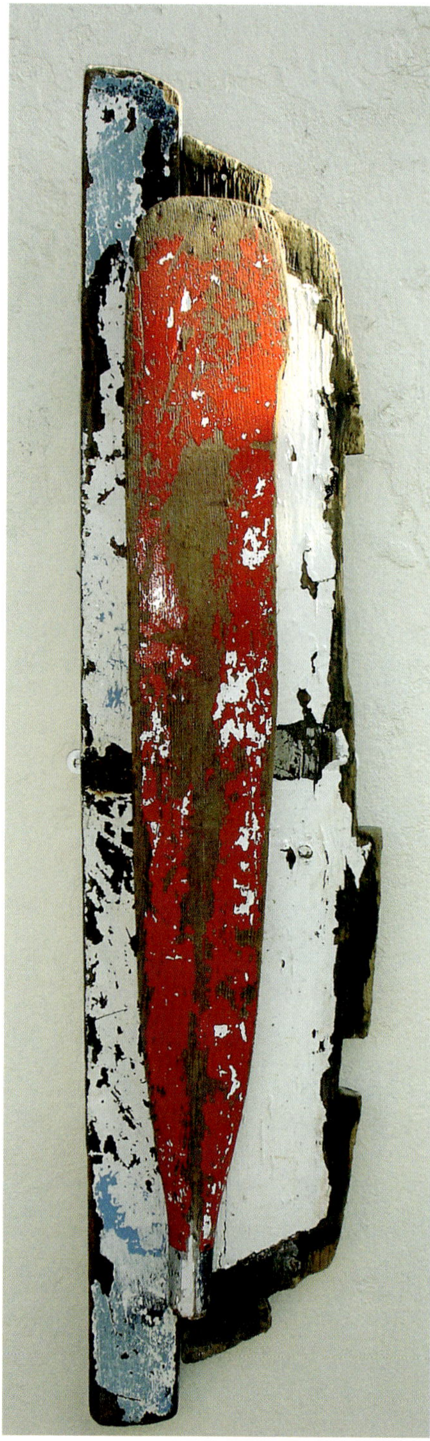

Mousehole 1, 2005

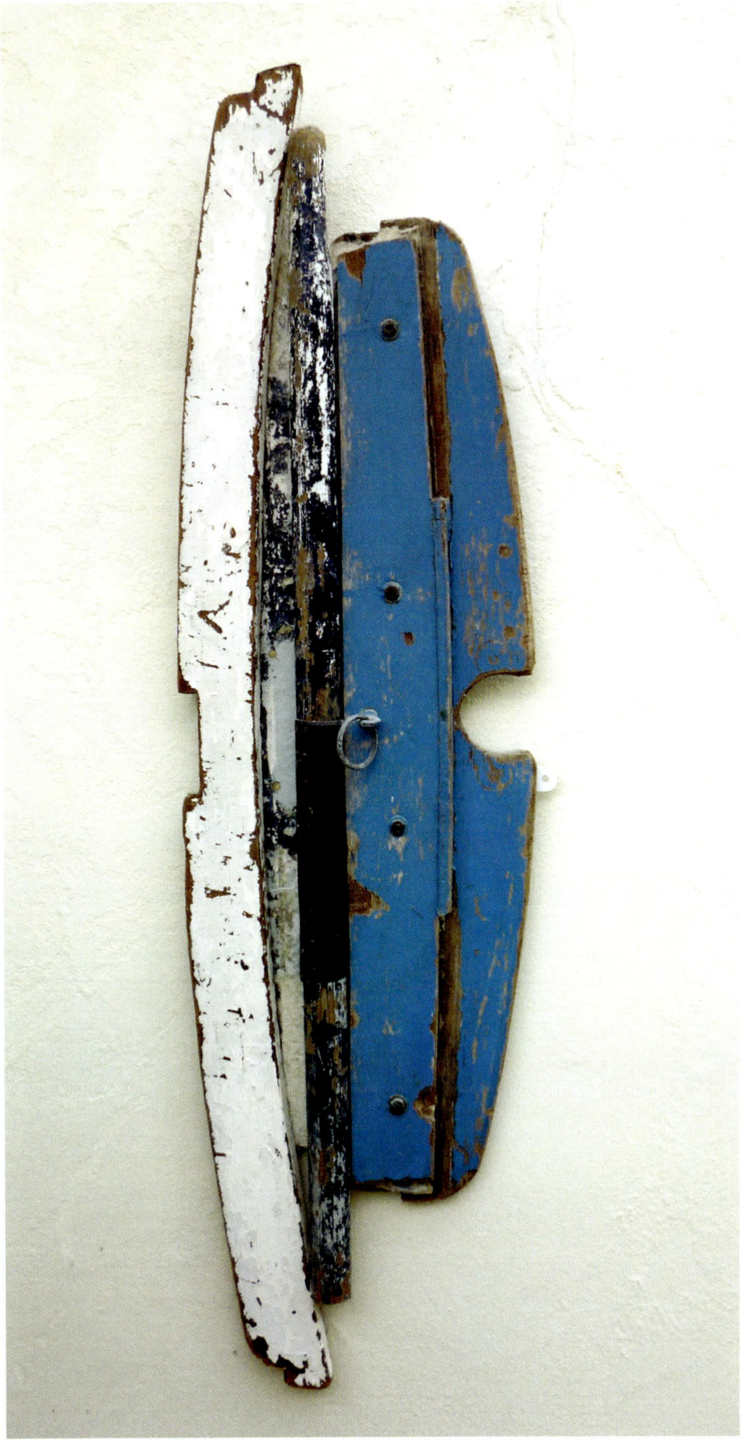

Mousehole 2, 2005

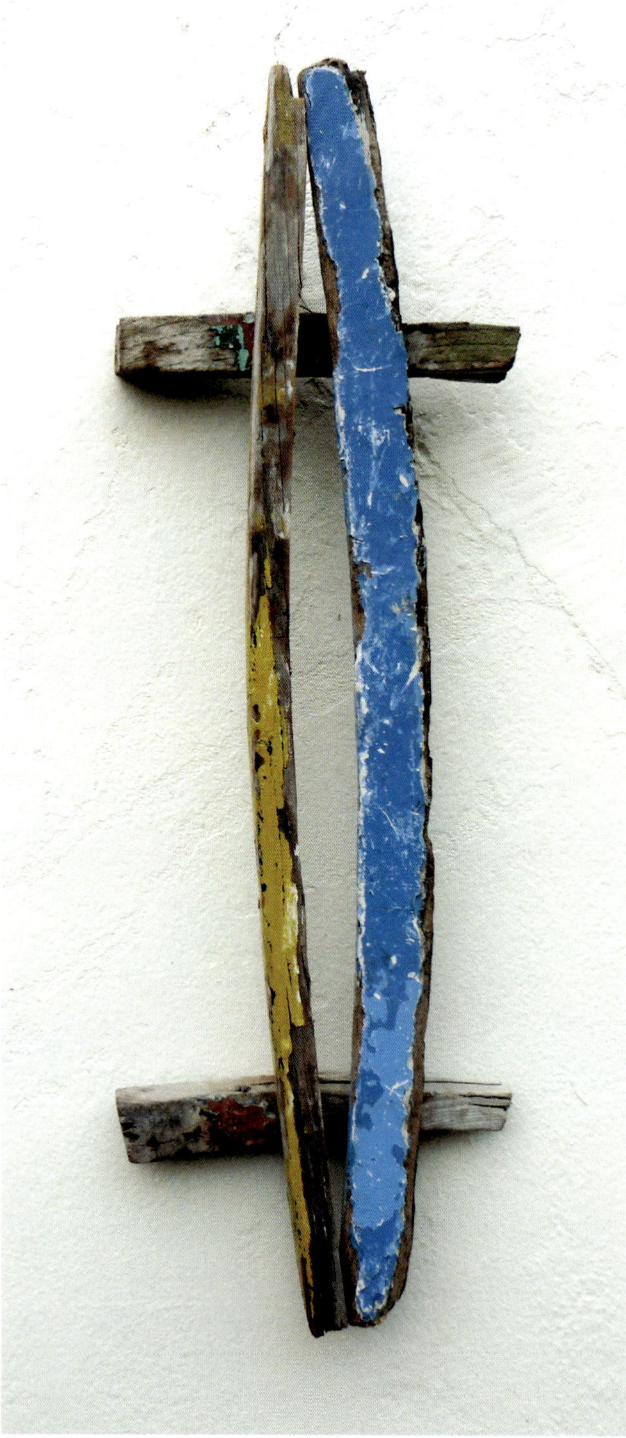

Mousehole 3, 2005

The association with The Fish Store seems apt given Osborne's gypsy roots and Augustus John's notorious fascination for, and repartee with bohemia. A self-styled John 'follower', Sven Berlin, had pursued the same fascination with outsiders. In 1953 Berlin left his St Ives base and removed to the New Forest where he associated with the local gypsy communities. The colourful, northern painter Alan Lowndes spent a valedictory summer living and working at the Fish Store in 1977. Osborne later befriended Lowndes' widow, Valerie, who had lived in St Ives In the 1960's, and made several visits with her to see Terry Frost in nearby Newlyn.

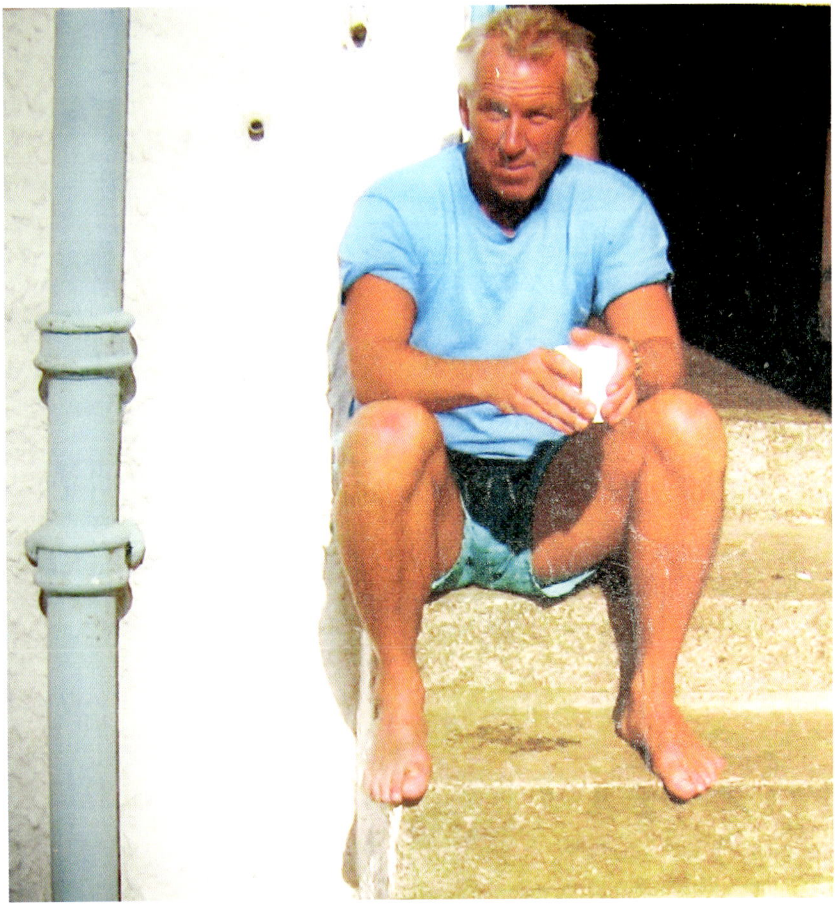

Bob Osborne in Mousehole.

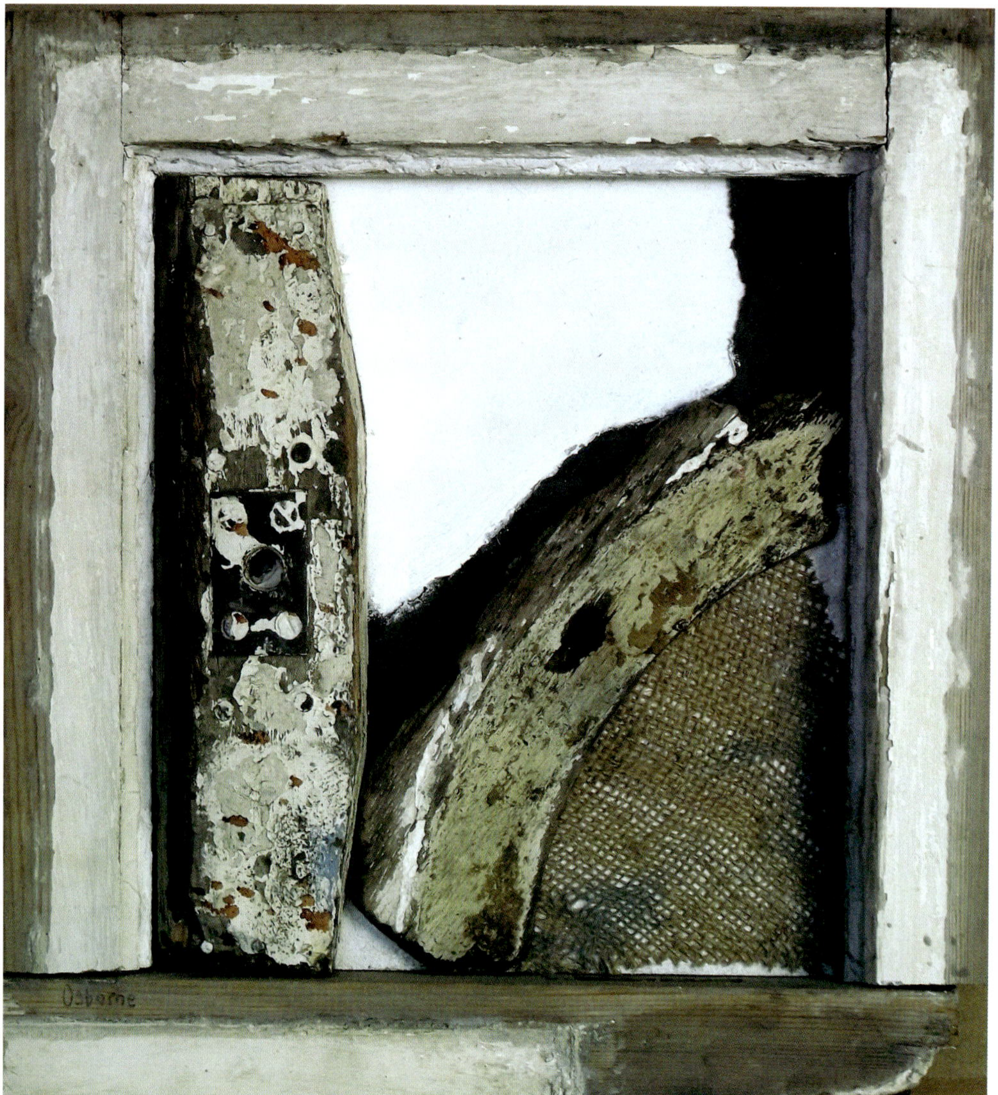

Mousehole Window, 2003

As a schoolboy in August 1970 Osborne hitchiked to the Isle of Wight pop festival at Afton Farm near Freshwater Bay. 37 years later he would exhibit at nearby Dimbola Lodge Museum in Freshwater. The former Victorian home of pioneering photographer Julia Margaret Cameron, Dimbola today celebrates the epochal festival as a key event in Wight's cultural history with a bronze statue of legendary guitarist Jimi Hendrix, whose virtuoso performance in that summer proved his penultimate 'gig'.

Given Osborne's use of old postcards and photographs as collage material, it is apt he should have exhibited at Dimbola during the summer of 2007 in the 'Sharing A View' group as the chosen 'guest' artist of Denis Bowen. Preceding working visits to West Wight yielded the driftwood compositions ***Chale and Brightstone***, two tightly assembled, irregular off-square constructions where painted and intrinsic colours of boat parts establish a specific chromatic and textural character.

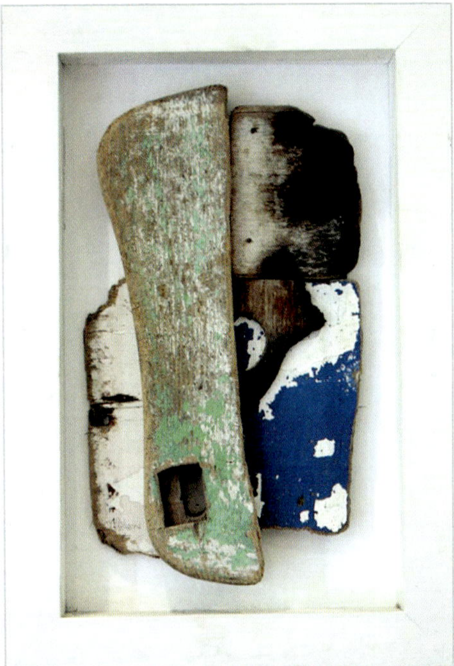

Chale, 2007

Equally aptly, Dimbola Lodge Museum in making its acquisitions of each member's work for its permanent collection chose, not a driftwood construction, but a collaged stencil work depicting Mick Jagger, which was commissioned to be reproduced as a poster to herald the June 2007 pop festival outside Newport on the island. Five years later the Dimbola connection saw Osborne and I attend photographer Carinthia West's exhibition of her portraits of rock musicians at the Julia Margaret Cameron Museum where Jagger's brother Chris performed with his band.

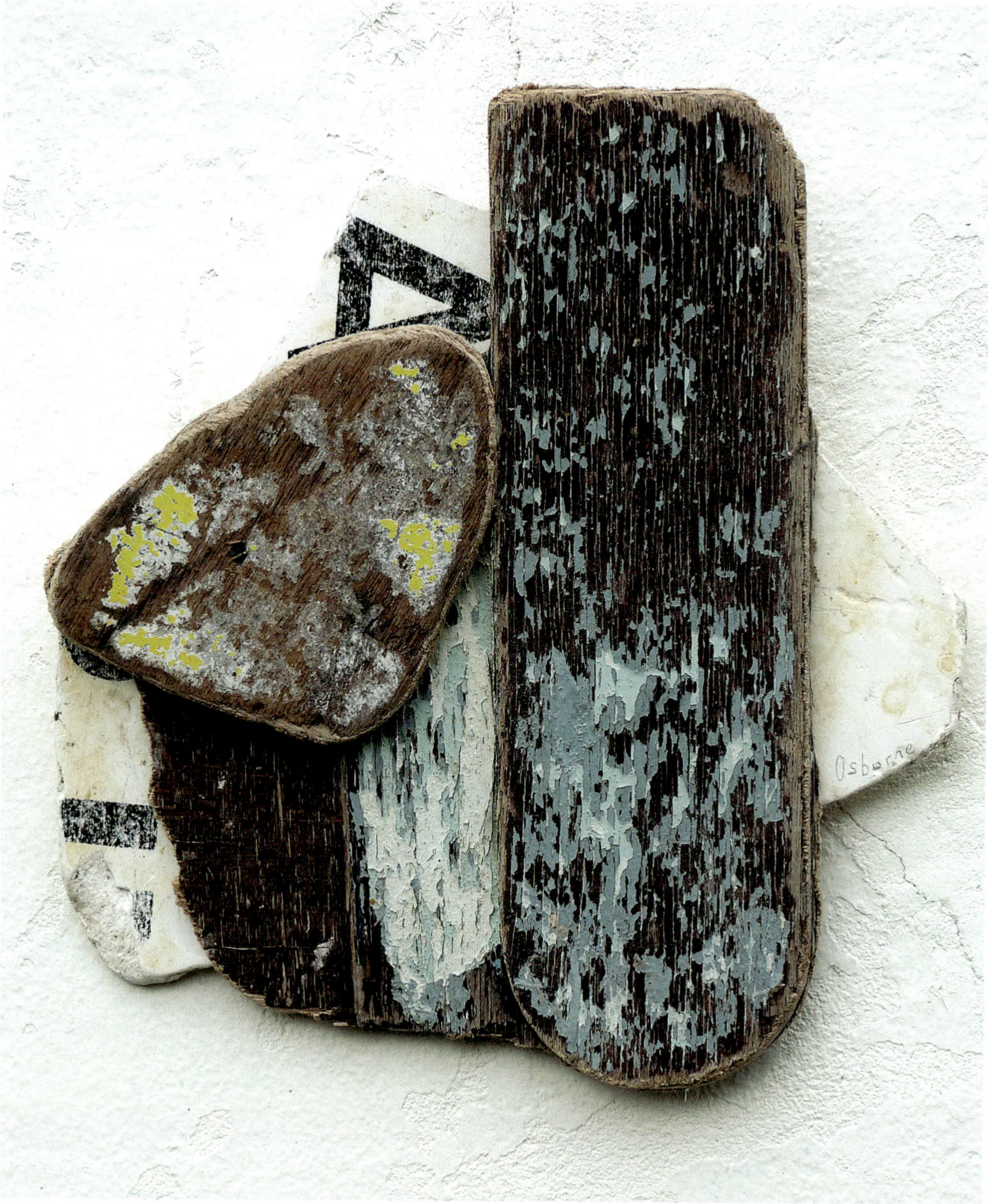

Brightstone, 2007

SACKCLOTH COLLAGES

The common material of sackcloth has found its way into modern art in general, and the *arte povera* movement in particular. It's tactile and expressive possibilities were exploited by its leading proponent, the post war Italian artist Alberto Burri. Its coarse weave possesses a rough tactility making it a poor cousin to the finer surfaces of artist's canvas. It's soaked, stained or ripped surfaces provide an ideal ground plan in Osborne's collages and constructions for the superimposition of driftwood, corrugated card or other 'found' detritus.

The axiomatically titled box construction ***Finding Common Ground*** is composed from three vertical 'bands' of driftwood, card and sacking. Its typical brown and cream colour scheme is an unmodified record of its common state. Similarly ***Sennen Cove*** is put together from the given shape and colour of sacking and driftwood found on Sennen's wide beach on New Year's day 2001. The washed out Cornish colours are a product of nature's bleaching or corrosive actions on broken boats.

Osborne describes his "pathway to Burri" as coming through his collaborations with Sandra Blow, once a Burri disciple and then a St Ives based artist, in whose studio at Porthmeor Beach he assisted. Osborne was clearly influenced by the elder artist's working practices and in 2000 bought a large Blow composition *Sacking and Acrylic*. This work hangs alongside Osborne's own sack cloth reliefs which generally, however, do not include Blow's painted passages. Exceptions are ***Pandora's Box*** and ***Reinventing the Past,*** where a frenzy of red, white, blue and ochre paints dribble crisscross in an *informalist* mêlée. The almost Pollockian action of these violent paint trails creates a surface counterpoint against a vivid torn orange and earth coloured collaged background. These painted passages notwithstanding, Osborne's work prefers a Duchampian directness and a Burrian gravitas to the doctored decorativeness of a more laboured or craftmanly approach.

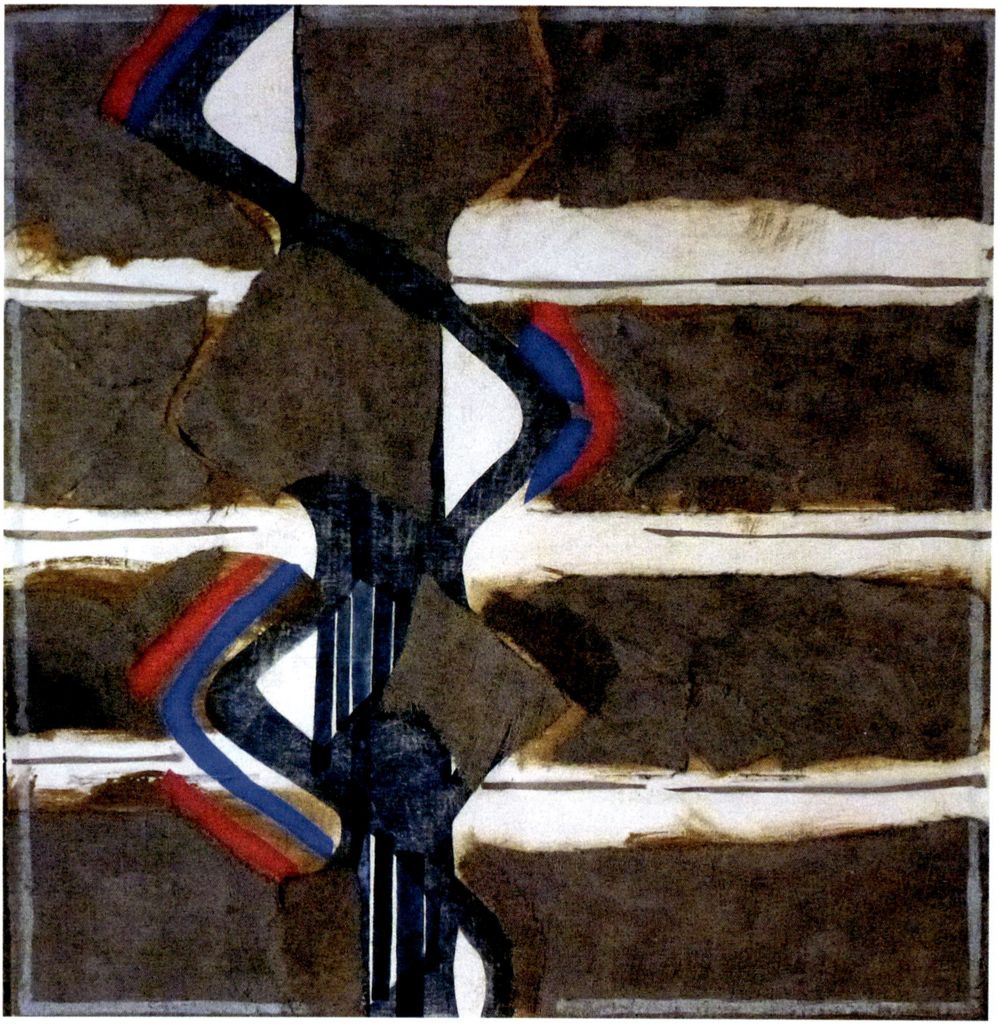

Sandra Blow's Sacking and Acrylic, 1967/68

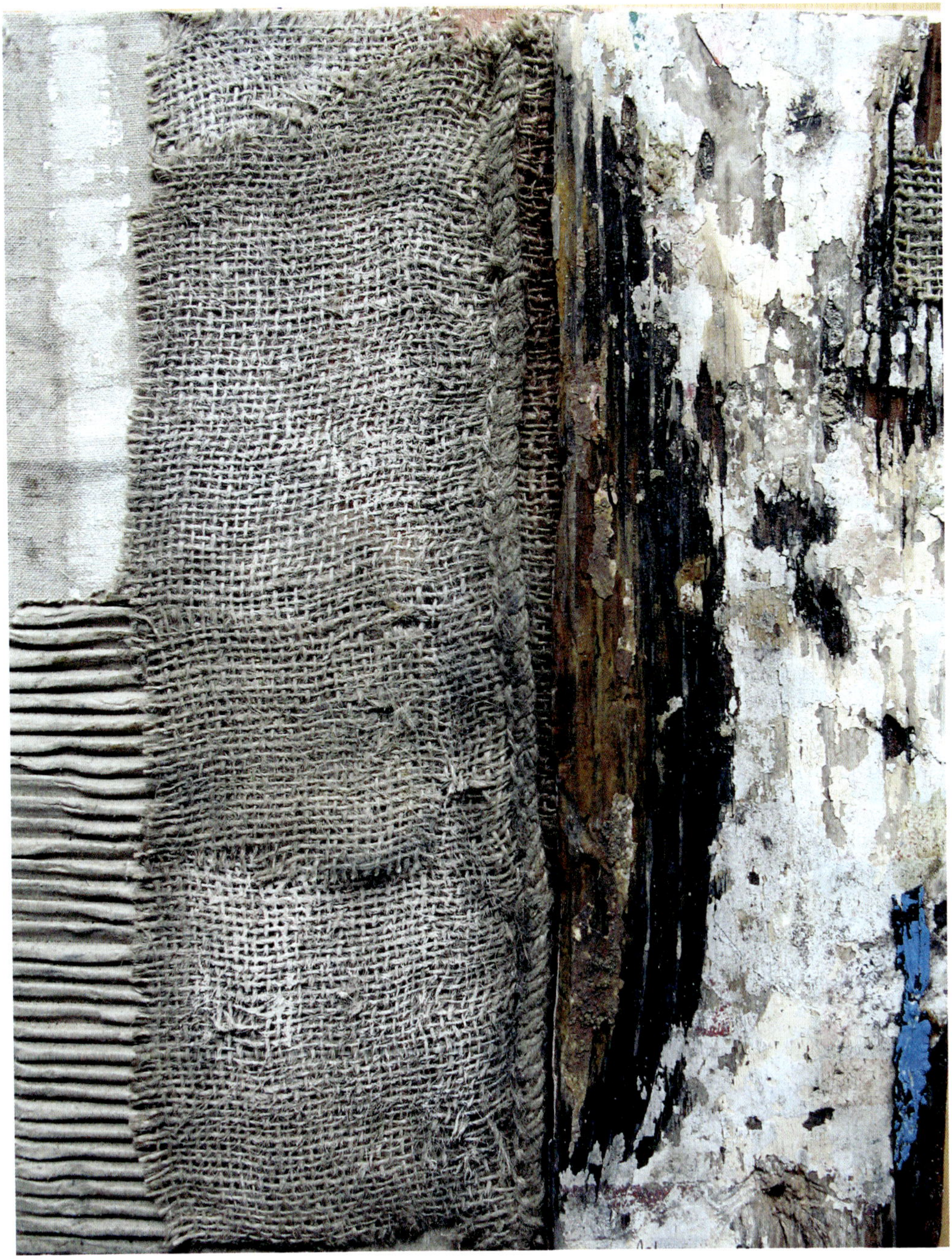

Finding Common Ground, 2002

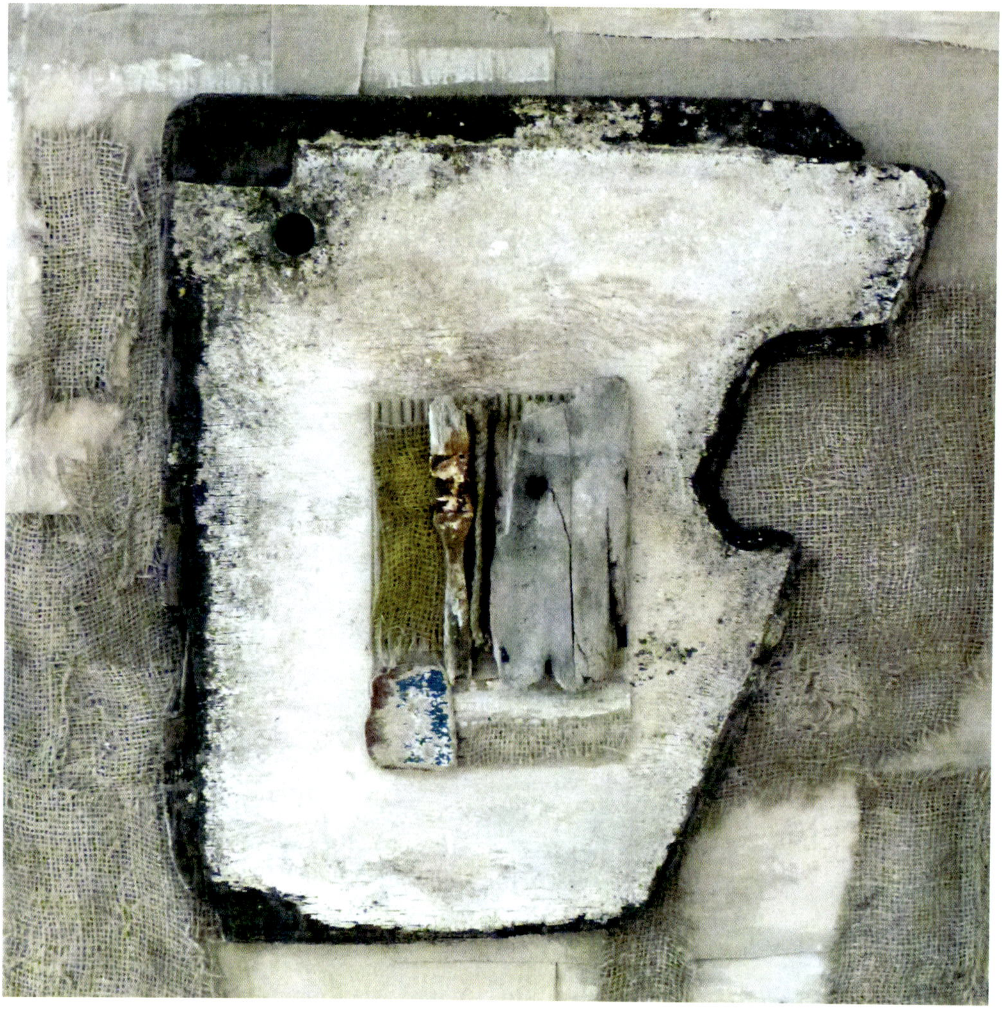

Sennen Cove, 2001

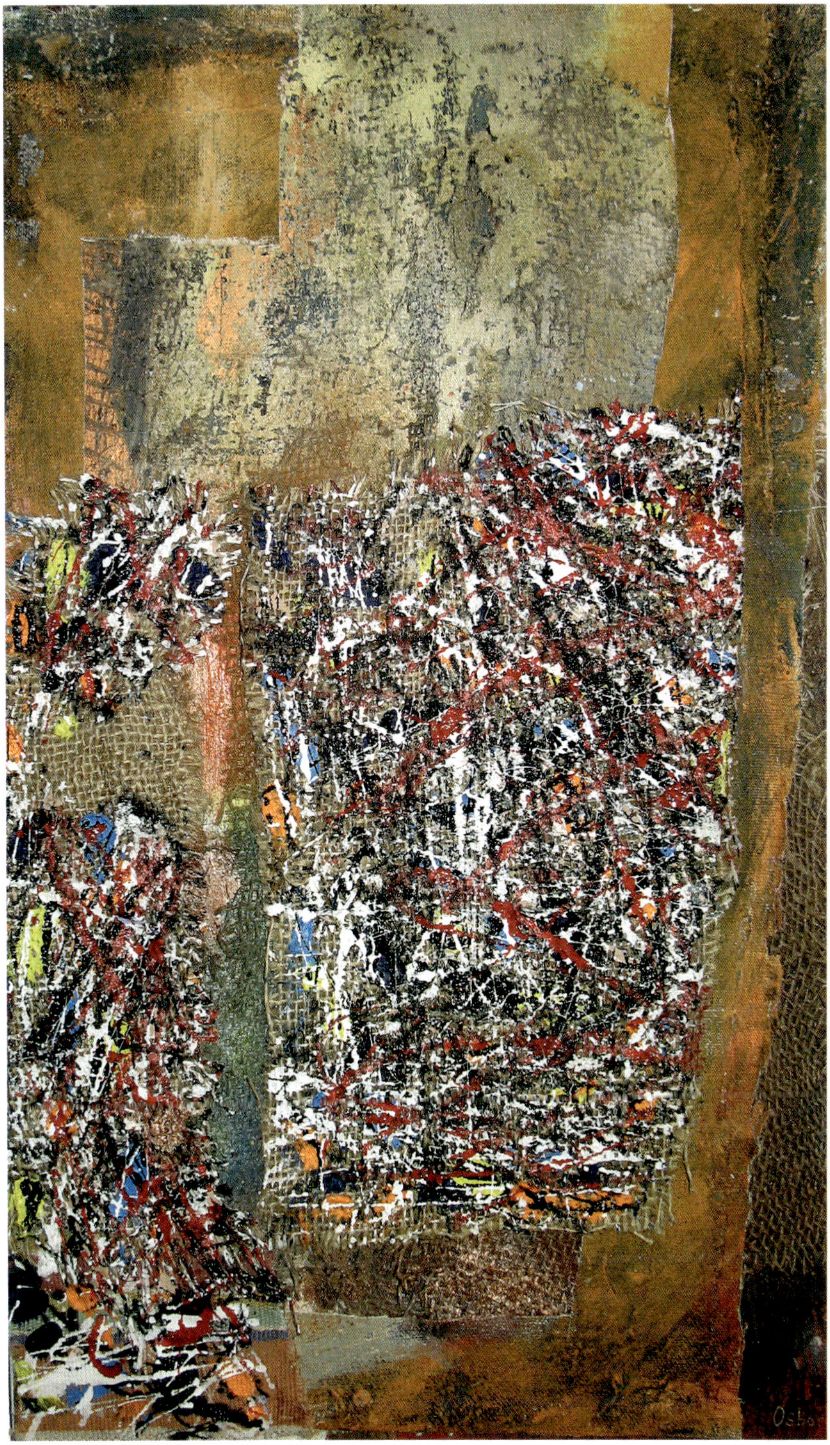

Reinventing the Past, 2001

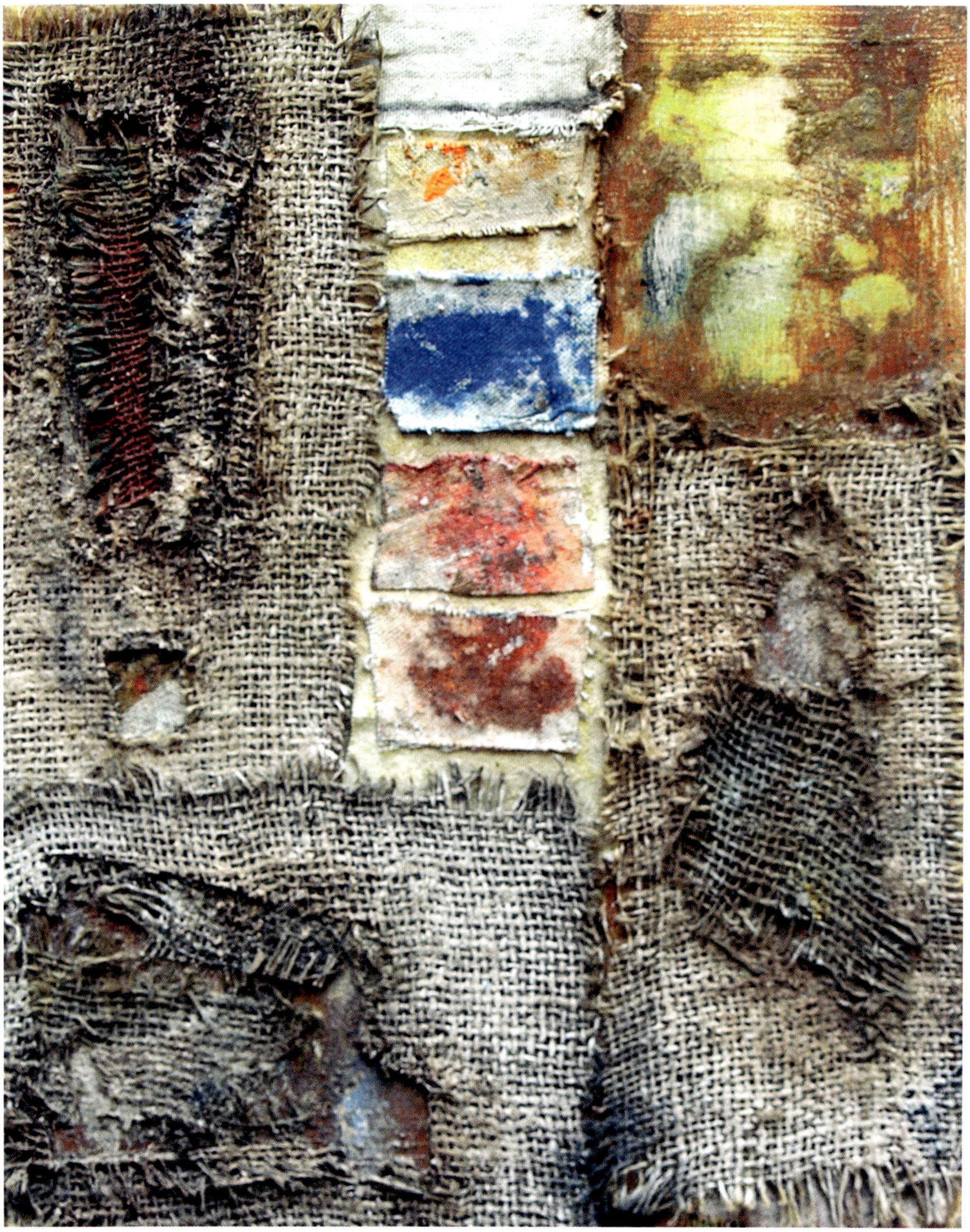

Pandora's Box, 2002

Bob Osborne's crucial connection - both personal and professional - with the well-known painter and collagist Sandra Blow RA proved mutually advantageous and added a sophisticated and 'arty' spin to the messy business of constructing imagery from the humble detritus of discarded materials and 'found' objects. Blow's influence was to help Osborne develop his natural collaging facility towards large scale *pictorialism*. This *pictorialism* linked in with the spontaneous, improvisatory and gestural currents of avant-garde mid-century abstract painting.

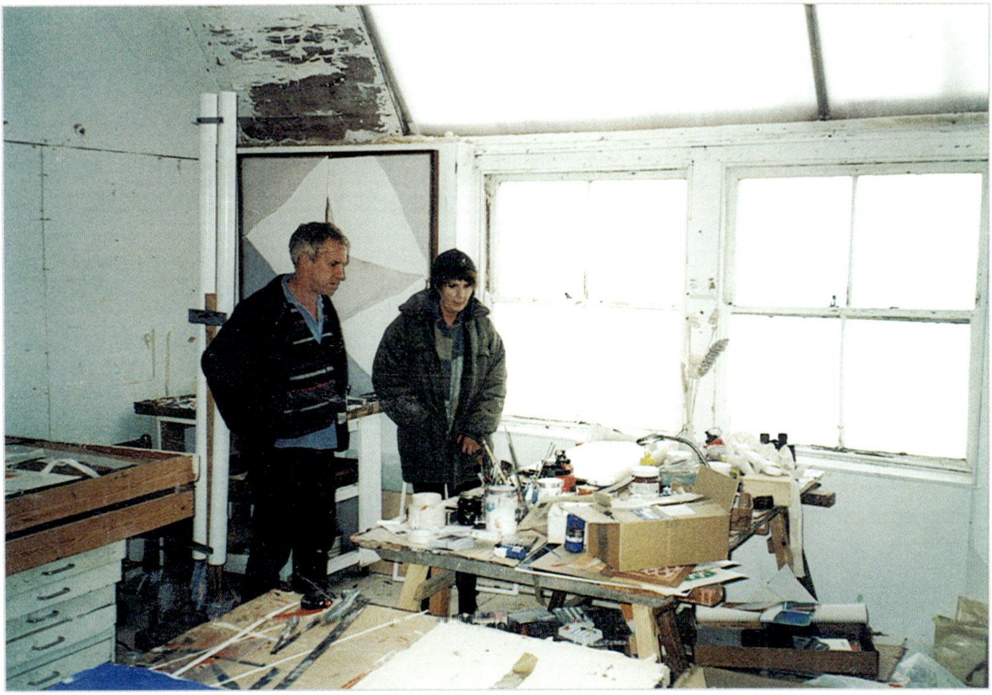

Sandra Blow and Bob Osborne in No. 9 Porthmeor Studios, St Ives, 2000

The enhanced textural and chromatic feeling for paint as an independent expressive substance informed and inspired much post war abstract art. The dichotomy between flat, illusionistic elements, on the one hand, and concrete, collaged imagery that extended into the third dimension on the other, linked painting and low relief sculpture in the 'combines' of Robert Rauschenberg and the collaged paintings of Jasper Johns, late Lanyon, Joe Tilson, Michael Kenny and others. Art historically aware, Osborne tapped into this strand with an innate conviction.

Sandra Blow, by contrast, followed her early association-again both personal and professional-with the Italian *arte povera* master Alberto Burri, by drawing on the flat, decorative, specifically pictorial legacy of Matisse's late cut-outs. In this context Osborne was obliged, through assisting in Blow's St Ives studio in the physical execution of work, to make tactile as well as visually explicit surfaces courtesy of sack clothing, torn paper strips, corrugated cardboard and other textually sensual collage materials. These processes invested his work with decorative largesse and gave physical impact and imaginative daring to Osborne's subsequent plastic and psychic automatism.

The crucial experience of assisting in Blow's St Ives studio paid direct dividends in terms of Osborne's fast developing methods. To have a bookish admiration for the *arte povera* or random collage ethos was one thing, but to learn directly about the risk-taking ambition of Blow's studio practice gave an immediate authenticity to Osborne's evolving work. In particular, the open-ended process of incorporating chance effects, accidents and mistakes inspired a physically engaging and real, rather than cerebral or precious, attitude to the creative process. The intuitive search for what Blow termed "resolution" or "startling rightness" suggested to Osborne that final perfection was a product of raw, imperfect means. Osborne always admired the demonstrative physical presence of Blow's early masterpiece *Space and Matter (1959)*, a work whose *pentimenti* of unerased matter formed a template for the younger artist's own approach.

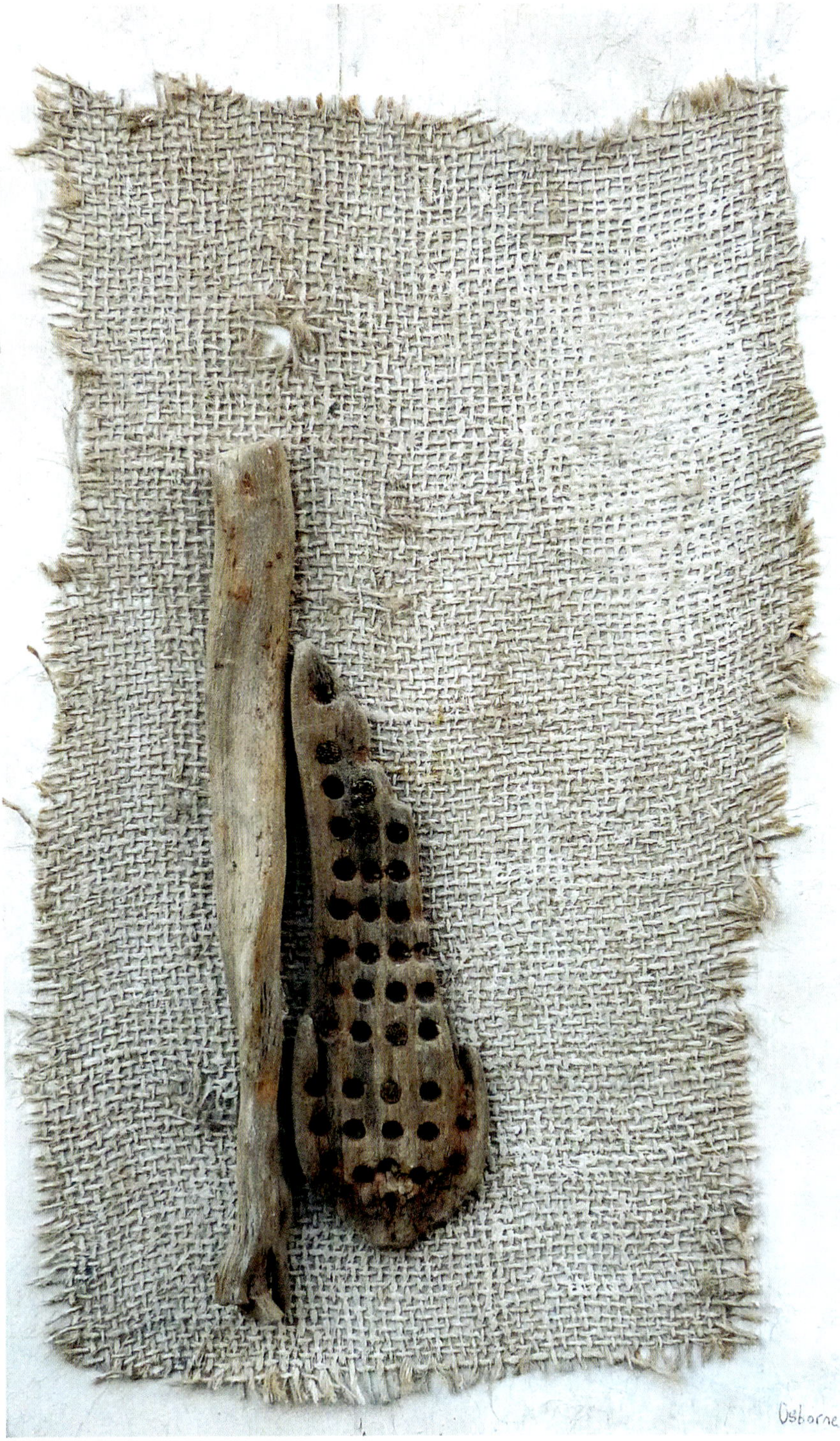

Winter, 2002

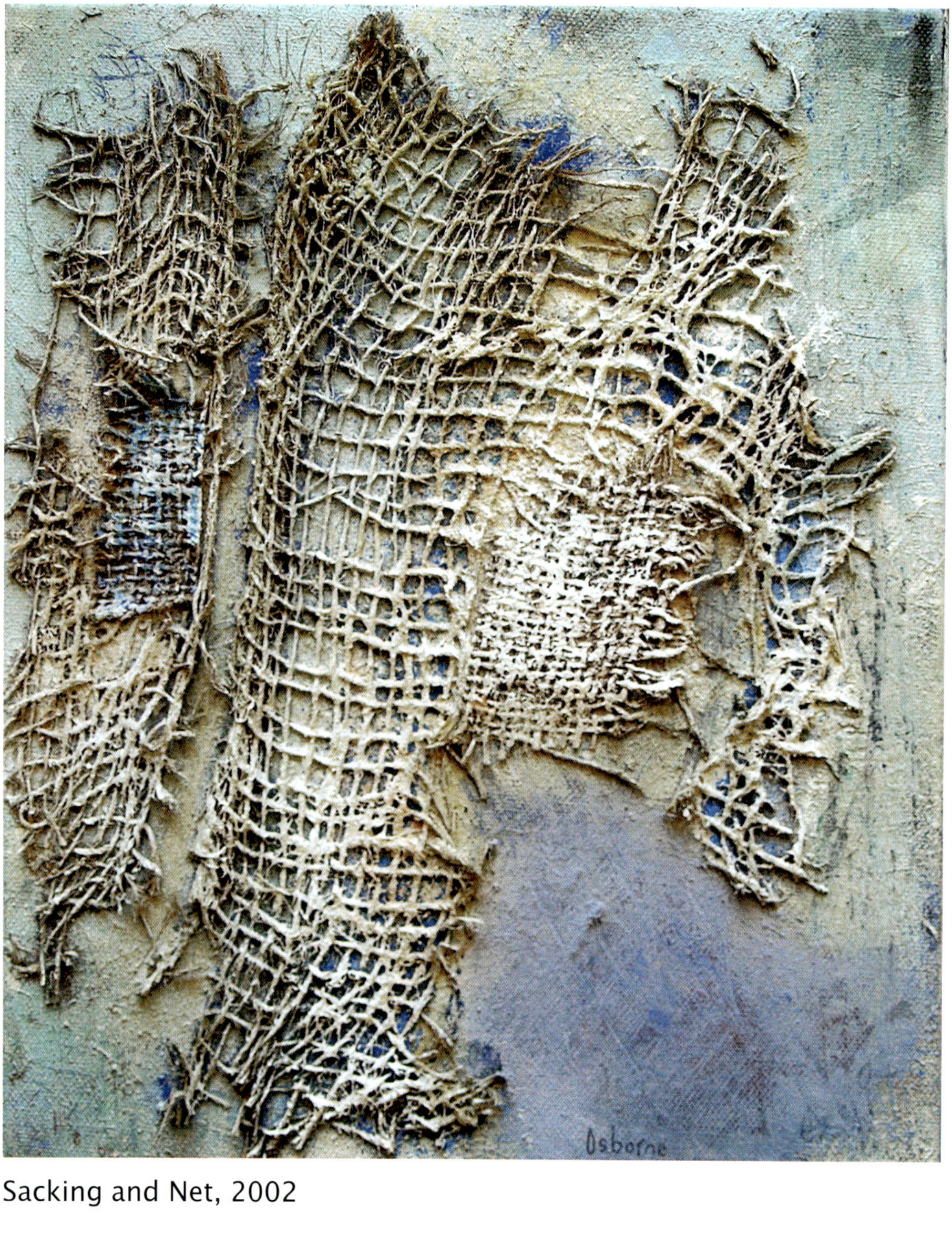

Sacking and Net, 2002

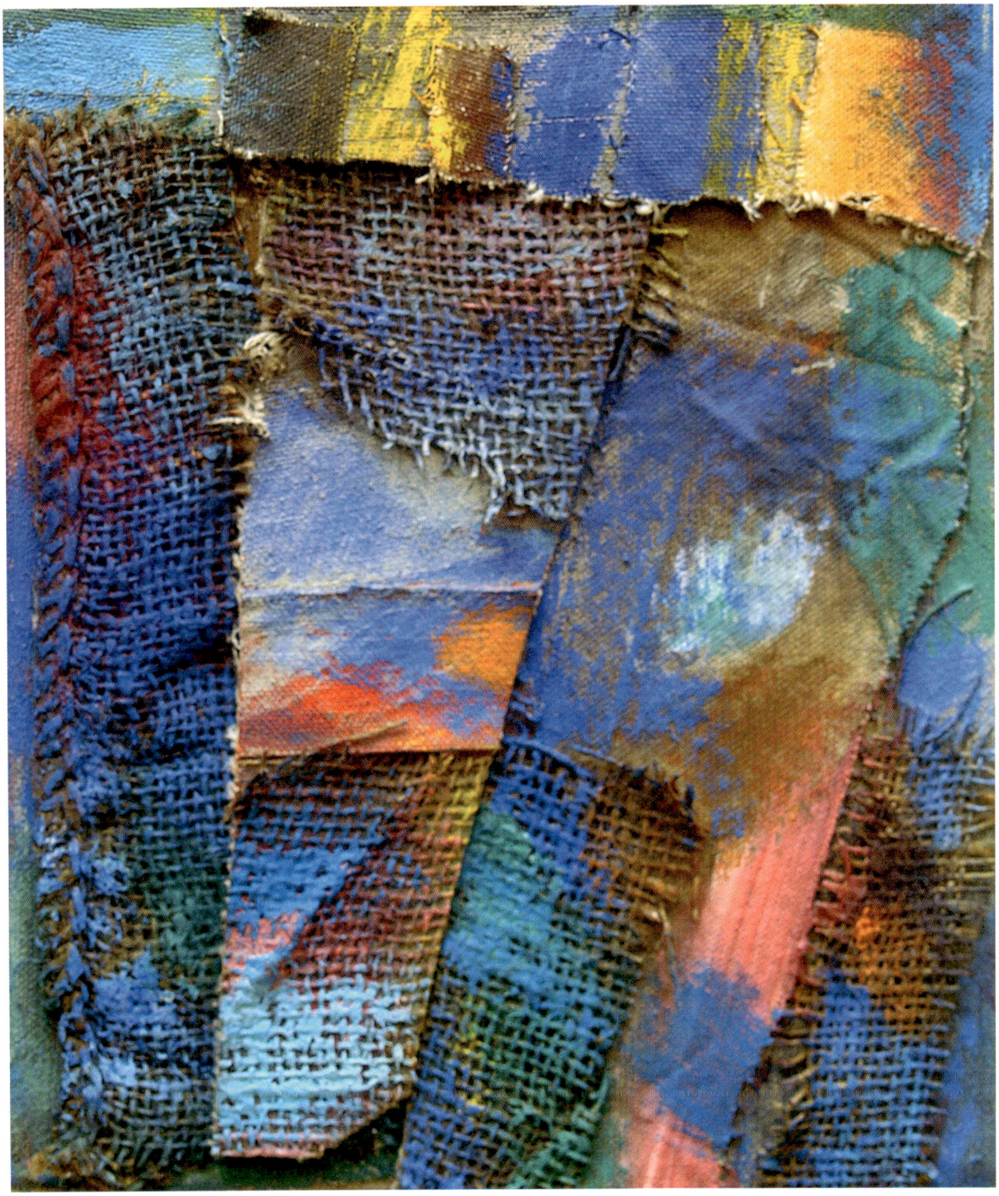

To the Lighthouse, 2002

'For the great plateful of the blue water was before her; the hoary Lighthouse, distant, austere, in the midst; and on the right, as far as the eye could see, fading and falling, in soft low pleats, the green sand dunes with wild flowing grasses on them, which always seemed to be running away into some moon country, uninhabited of men.'

Virginia Woolf: *To the Lighthouse*

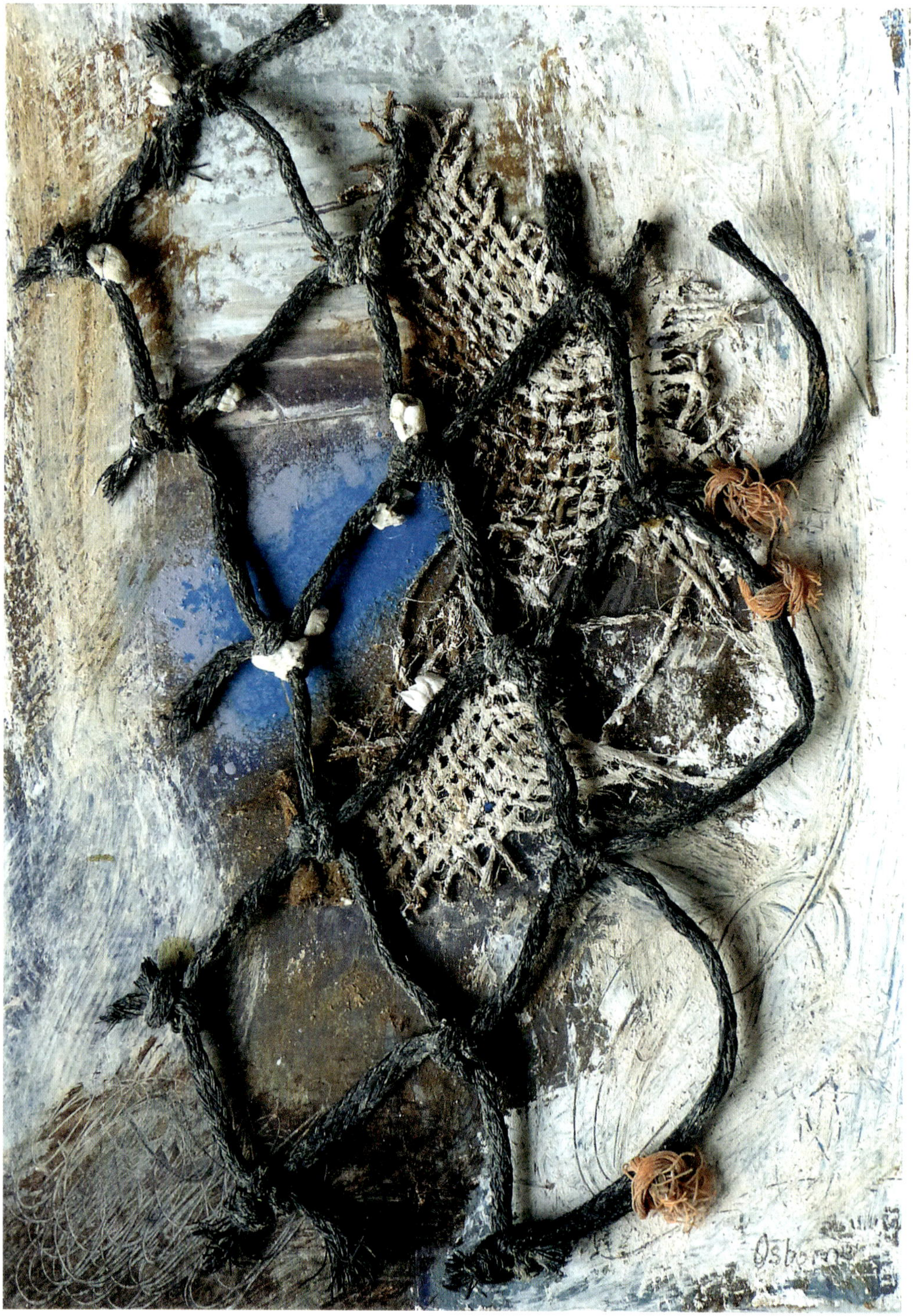

Carbis Bay, 2001

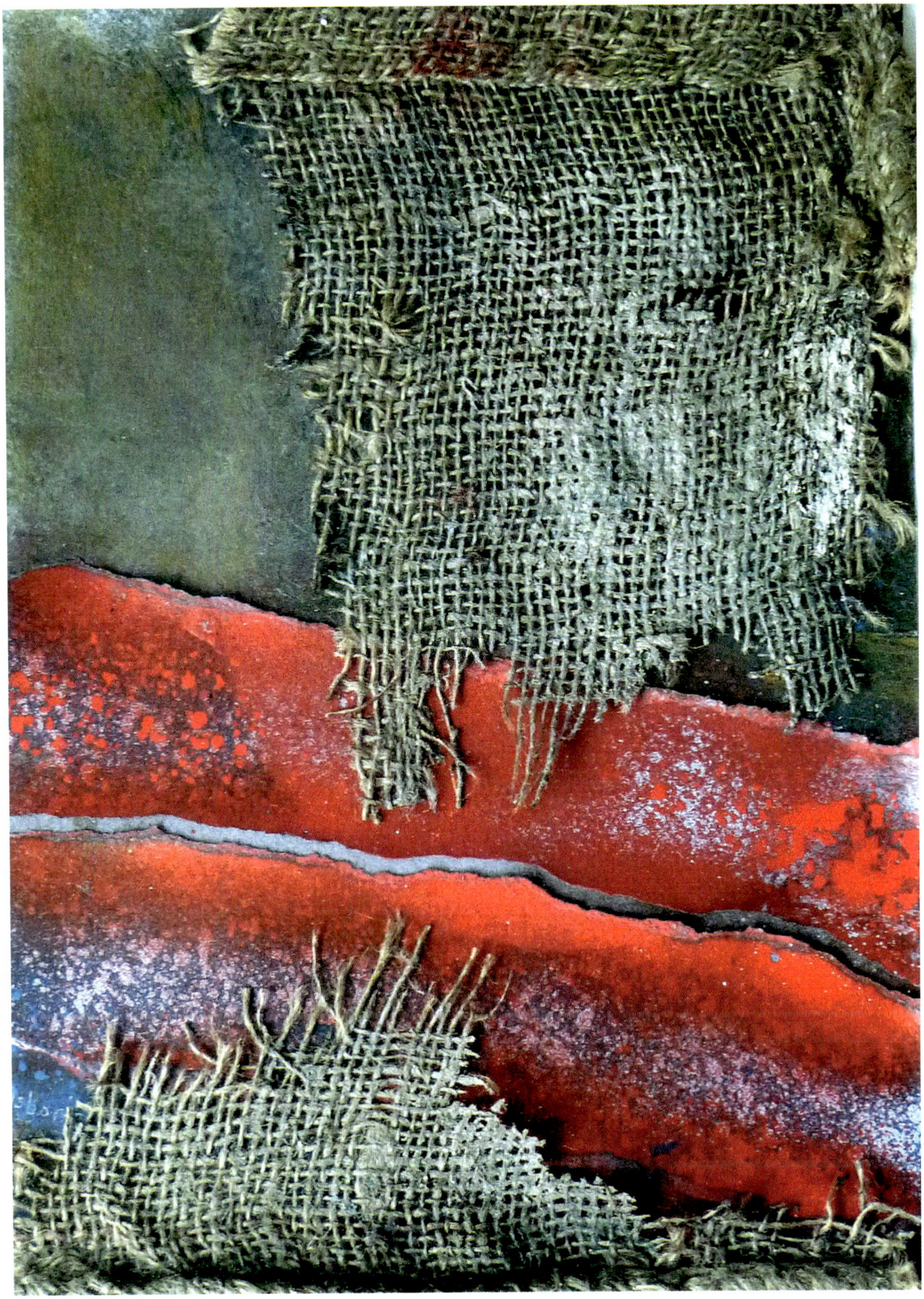

Making Ends Meet, 2001

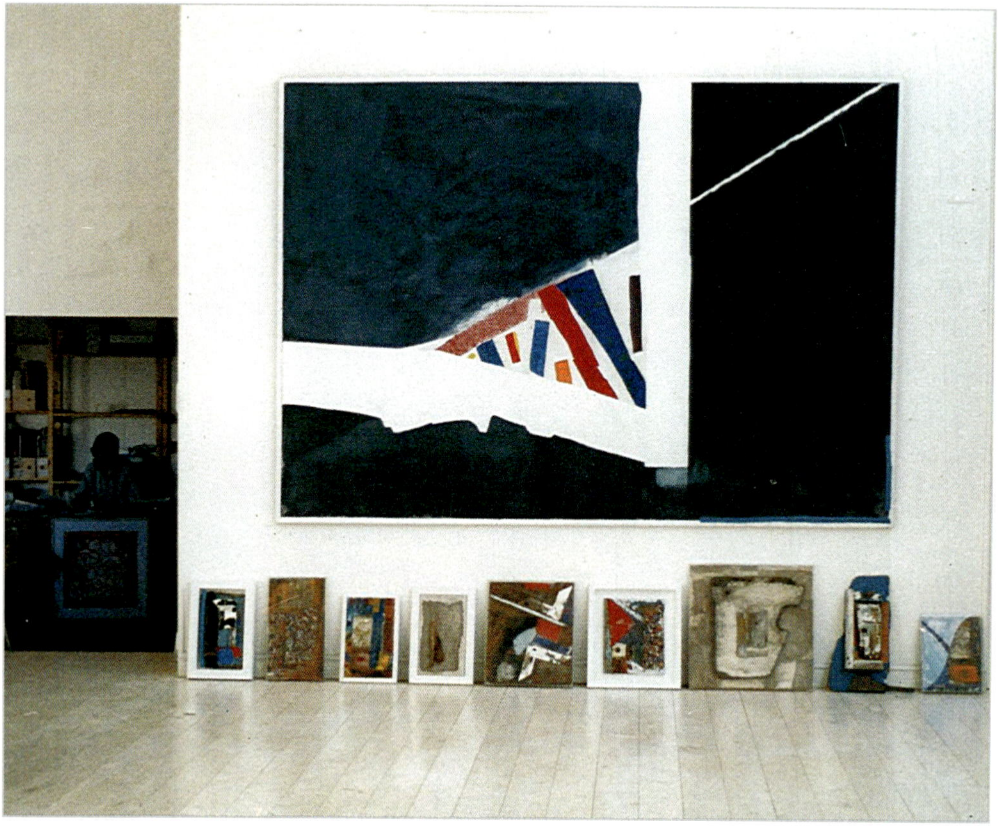

In 2001 Sandra Blow moved into a new studio at Bullans Court in St Ives. Osborne's constructions are lined up in front of her large collage Brilliant Corner 2 (1993) ready to be photographed before a shared exhibition at The New Ashgate Gallery in 2002.

TORN PAPER COLLAGES

Torn paper collage is invariably a process of addition and accretion. It recycles newsprint, shards from advertising hoardings and photomontage elements from magazines and is often urban, though it entertains natural and organic processes such as weathering and environmental damage. It lends itself to speed of execution and exploits the chance or accident as an aesthetic or even moral virtue. Its cultural marginality is paradoxically underscored by its social immediacy and 'democratic' imagery. Collage is something anyone can do–be it child or visual illiterate–and can also be both a noble aesthetic and one of scavenging or theft on the social edge.

One of its leading British proponents, the Cornish-born but London-based artist Gwyther Irwin was a 'Situation' group exhibitor in the early 1960's and shared with colleagues like Robyn Denny and Gillian Ayres an urban orientation and antithesis to St Ives pastoralism. In a later, more pluralistic period Osborne transcends the urban/rustic divide to reach his own post-modern synthesis.

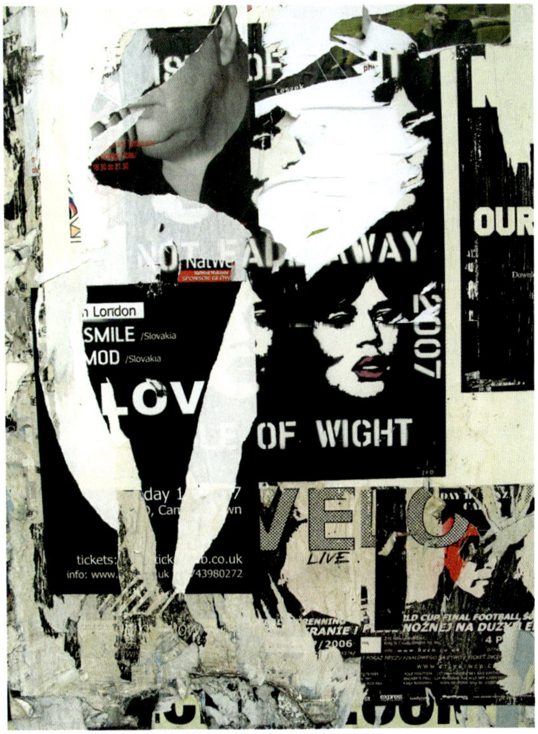

Recomposed fly posters,
Chiswick High Road, 2008

Following Picasso's precept of art as a series of creative destructions, Osborne constructs *affiches lacérés* using the random tears of fly posters and torn materials. ***Shepherd's Bush***, for example, uses the jagged papers of a fairground poster taken from Shepherd's Bush Green in his native West London. Osborne taps into the ethos of art on the edge where the media of fly posting, graffiti and other fugitive but direct and public means of communication come into their own. The slapstick quality of the advertising workman randomly pasting large sheets to public hoardings also appealed to a basic proletarian instinct in which a man in dungarees unwittingly becomes a collage artist and a Situationist drifter.

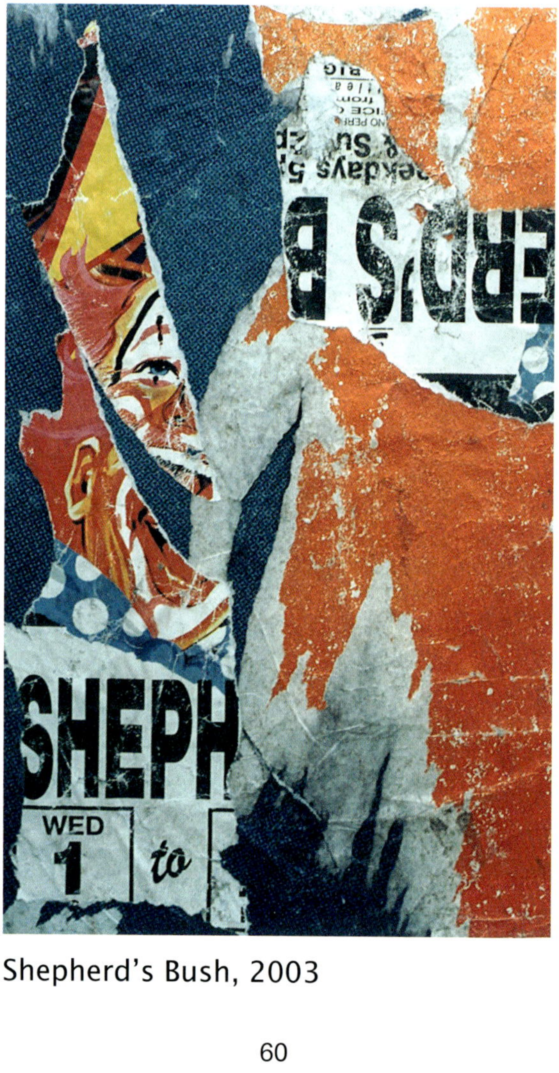

Shepherd's Bush, 2003

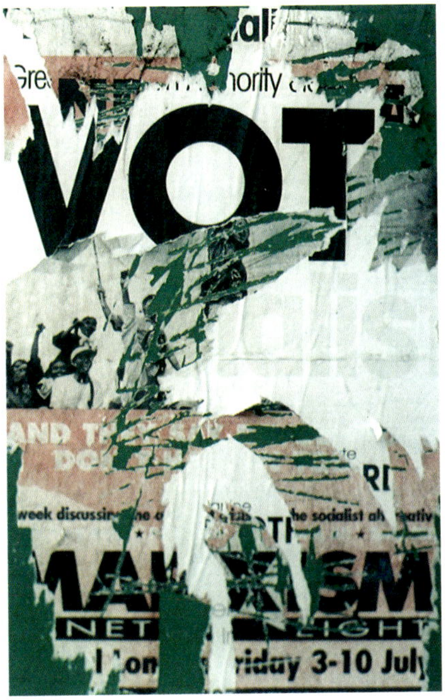

The lettering in ***Shepherd's Bush*** confirms that often in collage the visual and the literary exist in expressive counterpoint. This dichotomy is central in early Robyn Denny and is also apparent in Osborne's box constructions, which range from a Victorian narrative symbolism, literary in nature, to a more plastic and abstract manner where the intrinsic qualities of materials, namely their colours and forms, speak for themselves. As an early 1970's literature student at UEA, Norwich – with Essex University one of the two most politically radical campuses of the time – Osborne was aware of the Structuralist ideas of French thinkers such as Claude Levi-Strauss and other post-Sartrean philosophers. Such an intellectual climate encouraged Osborne's subsequent experiments with the interface between visual and literary meaning. The *affichistes* of the French *Nouveau Realist* movement, notably Jacques Villeglé, made pictures from torn advertising and political posters. In terms of their jagged randomness and asymmetric colour planes such work took collage into a realm compatible with automatist painting movements like Abstract Expressionism (e.g. Clyfford Still) in the United States and *tachisme* in France.

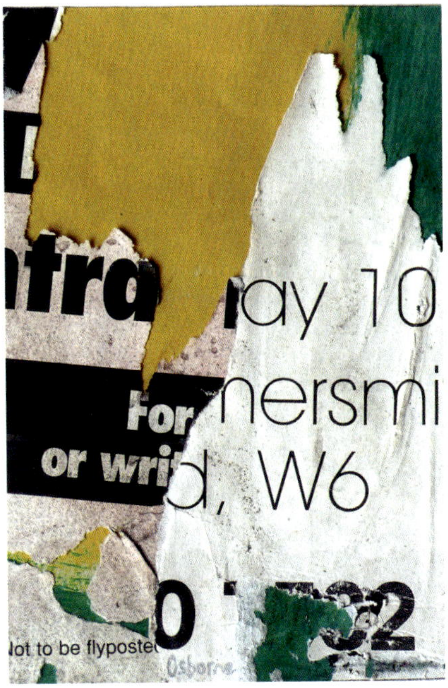

Top: Marxism, 2003
Bottom: Hammersmith, 2003

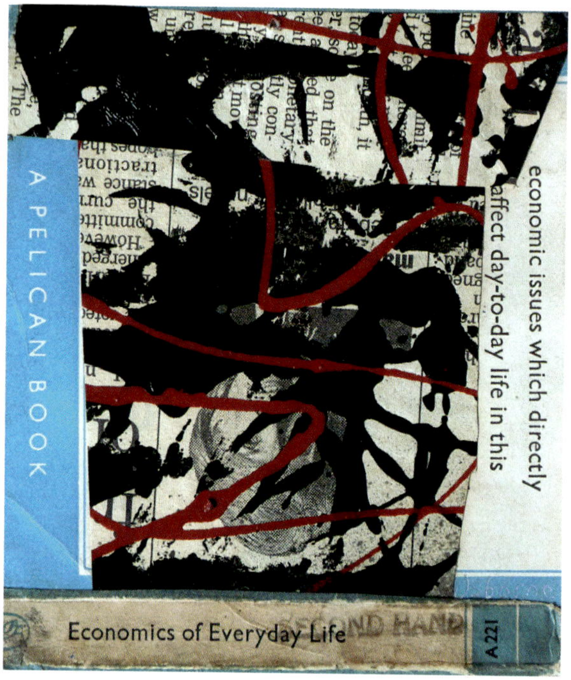

Economics of Everyday Life, 2001

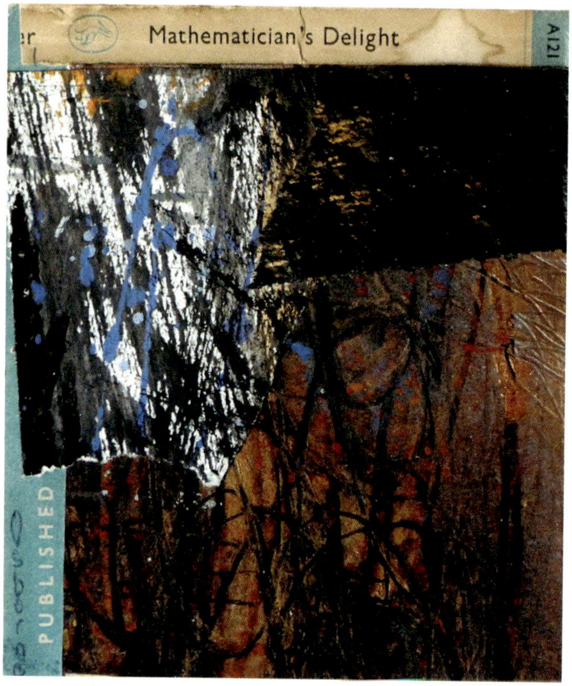

Mathematician's Delight, 2001

Across the River and into the Trees, while employing a literary title taken from an Ernest Hemingway novel, represents this more abstract, visual approach, in which imagery still emerges courtesy of vertical corrugated card 'tree trunks' set against a dark 'sky', with a truncated orange semi-circle symbolising a sun partially eclipsed by the tree.

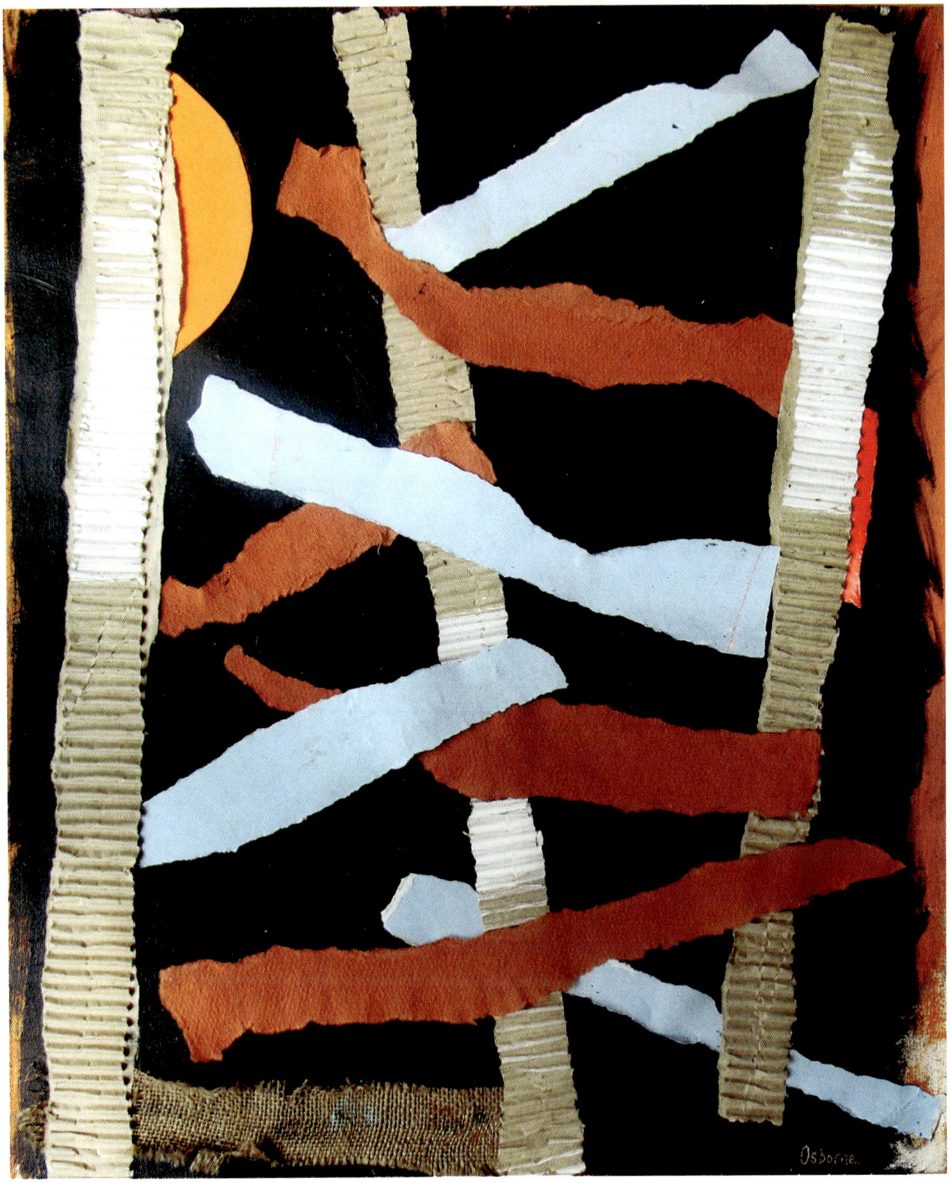

Across the River and into the Trees, 2001

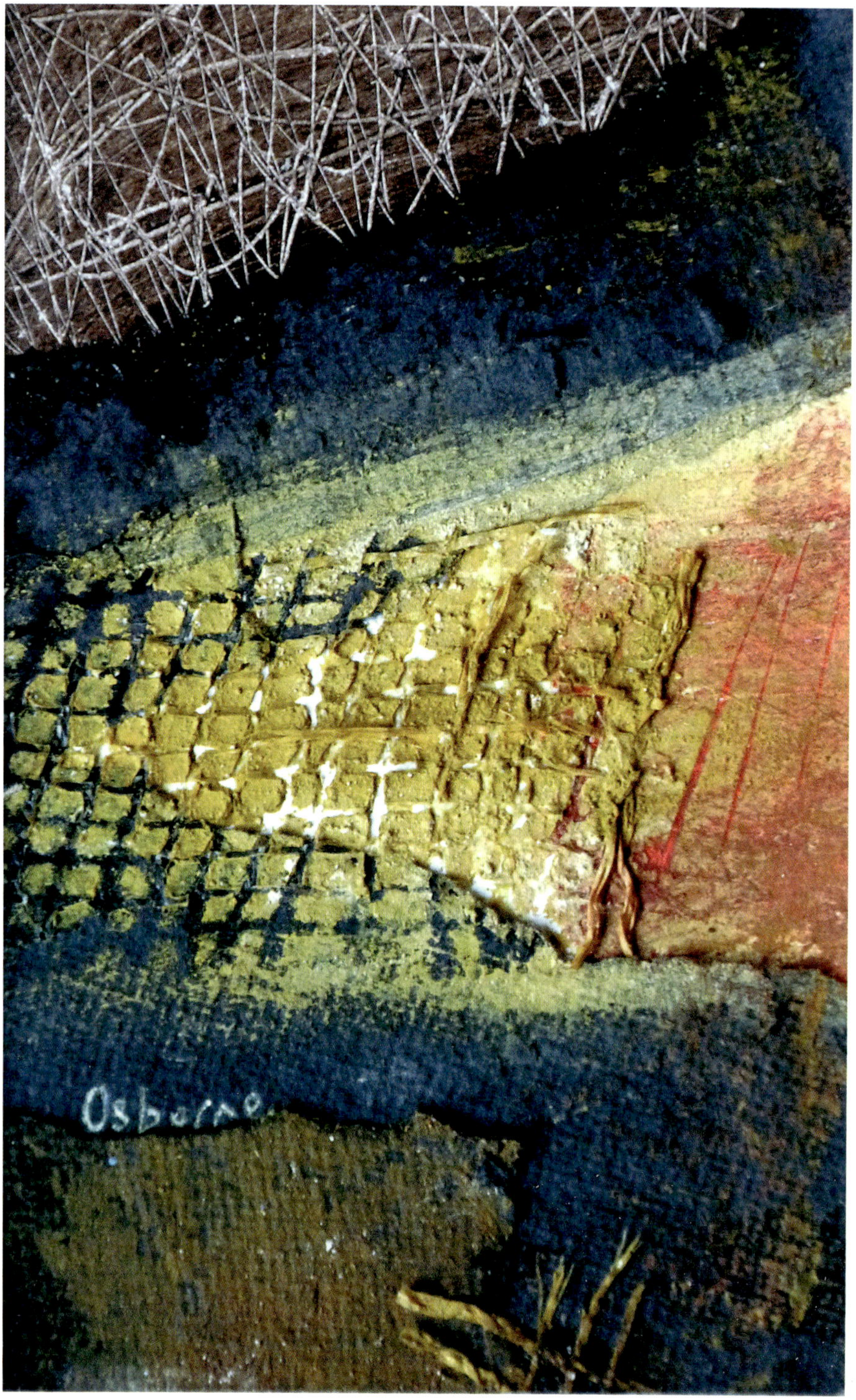

Scratching the Surface, 2001

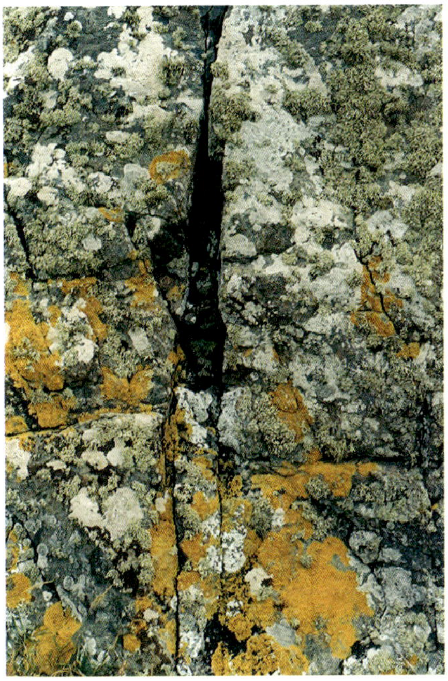

Gorse on Zennor stone

photograph: Bob Osborne

Zennor, 2002

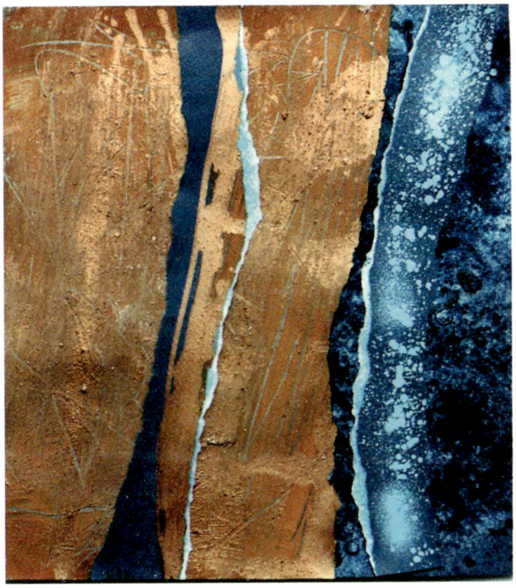

Coastline, 2002

'At Zennor one sees infinite Atlantic, all peacock-mingled colours, and the gorse is sunshine itself. Zennor is a most beautiful place: a tiny granite village nestling under high shaggy moor-hills and a big sweep of lovely sea beyond, such a lovely sea, lovelier even than the Mediterranean . . . It is the best place I have been in.'

D.H. Lawrence (1916).

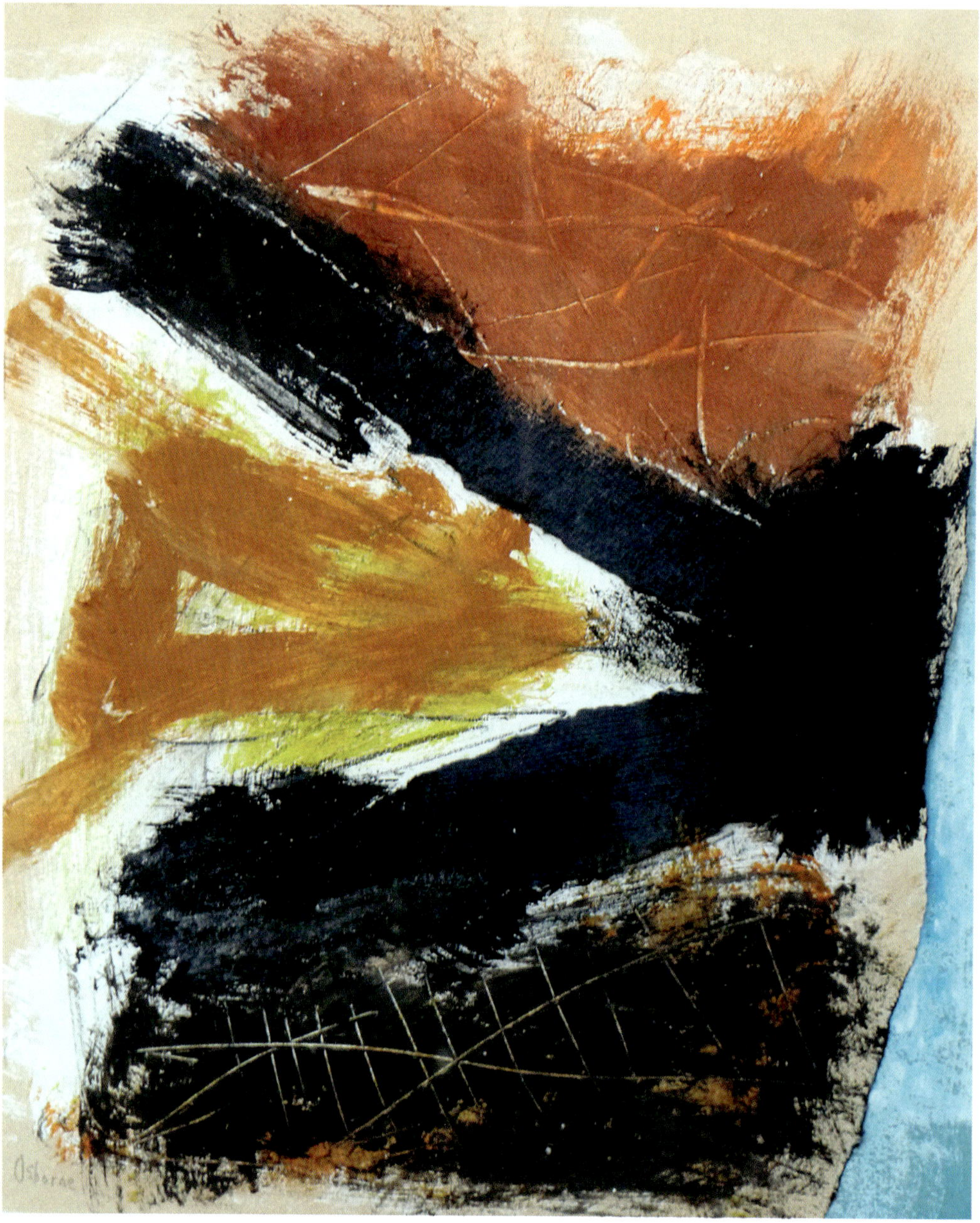

Back to Zennor, 2001

SLOT MACHINE CONSTRUCTIONS

Among Bob Osborne's early works between 1998 and 2001 were constructions adapted from broken slot machines and fairground ephemera. These are Duchampian ready-mades, not only in the sense that they have been found whole, or in part, and transformed into the elevated aesthetic arena of art, but also because they have been stripped of previous function and metamorphosed into contemplative objects of intriguing shape, colour, texture and material.

The artist also knowingly taps into the heady, irreverent and satirical tradition of the found object, being directly aware of the peculiarly British folksy, pop art nostalgia of Peter Blake - a near neighbour in Chiswick - by the more conceptual and rationalist American art of Jasper Johns and Robert Rauschenberg, and also by the Marcel Duchamp-inspired French *Nouveau Realist* movement.

The theatricality of Joseph Cornell's room-like 'Boxes' and Kurt Schwitters' collage environments are also emulated, particularly in terms of the interplay between two and three dimensional imagery, macabre surrealism and concrete design. Cornell is particularly invoked in Osborne's ***Lauren Bacall Clock,*** a 'found' broken clock filled, Arman-style, with assorted worthless 'prizes' and a black and white photograph of the Hollywood actress, who also features in Cornell's *Penny Arcade Portrait of Lauren Bacall 1945-46,* a hauntingly surreal homage depicting the glamorous icon, whose beauty is preserved from decay by being 'trapped', both in time, and in the artist's own invented world.

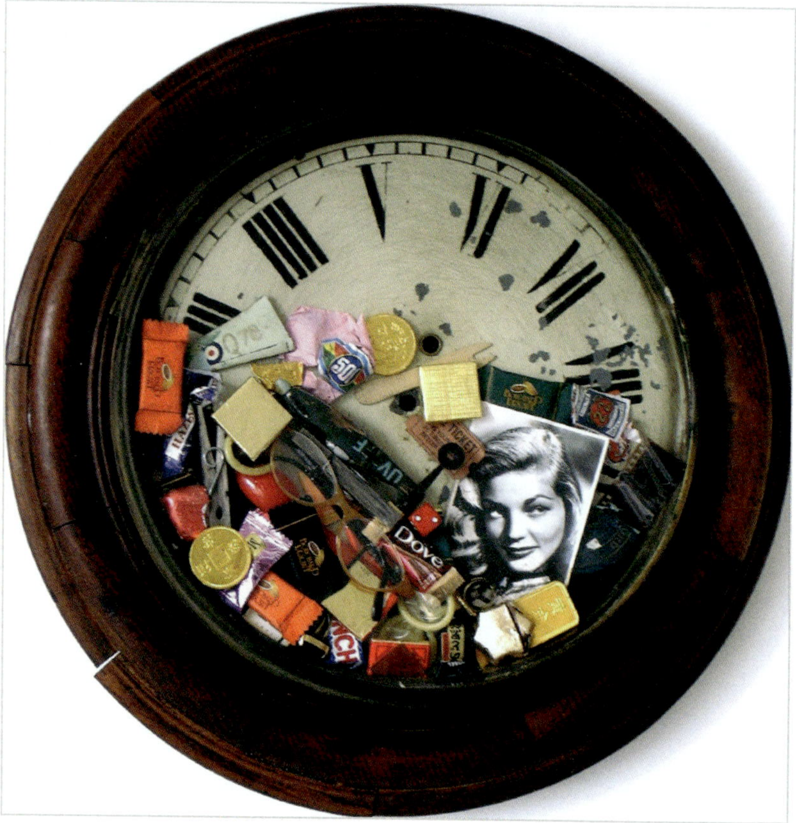

Lauren Bacall Clock, 2006

The interiors of Osborne's Slot Machine constructions, opened up as if sliced in half like an Arman musical instrument or Damien Hirst animal, often hide a neo-Constructive or art deco beauty. And an unlikely though effective marriage ensues between the 'high art' geometry of Constructivist art and the colourful downmarket symbolism of folk-inspired Pop Art. Since his prototype ***Margate***, a framed box containing postcards, sweets, cigarette packets, a laughing sailor and copper coins, the spate of story-telling constructions have similarly played formally between pictorial and sculptural elements and thematically between theatrical and real life imagery. A carefree holiday humour, seaside sauciness and end game eroticism, inspired by the legendary postcards of Donald McGill, animates these hybrid dioramas of the imagination.

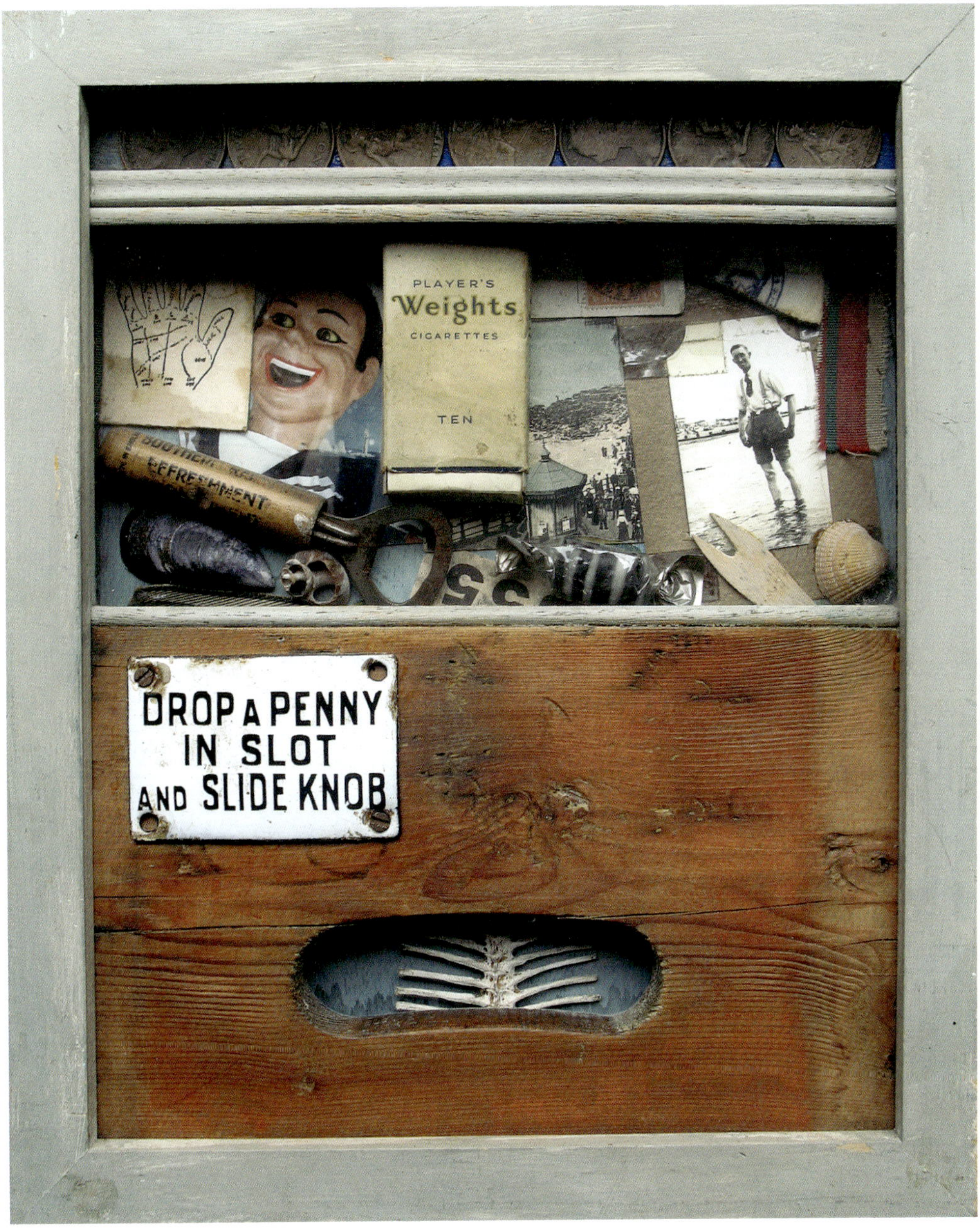

Margate, 1998

In ***Broken Slot Machine 1*** and *2* Osborne makes minor adjustments to the intricate interiors of these worn and beaten up fairground objects in which metal spirals, rings or red, blue and yellow diagonal plastic strips create elegantly mechanical relief-like compositions. Rodchenko inadvertently meets Kenneth Noland or Bridget Riley. These slot machines remind one of Jean Tinguley's Kinetic sculpture contraptions gone to sleep, their former recreational function now presented in stasis and silence for our post-industrial contemplation.

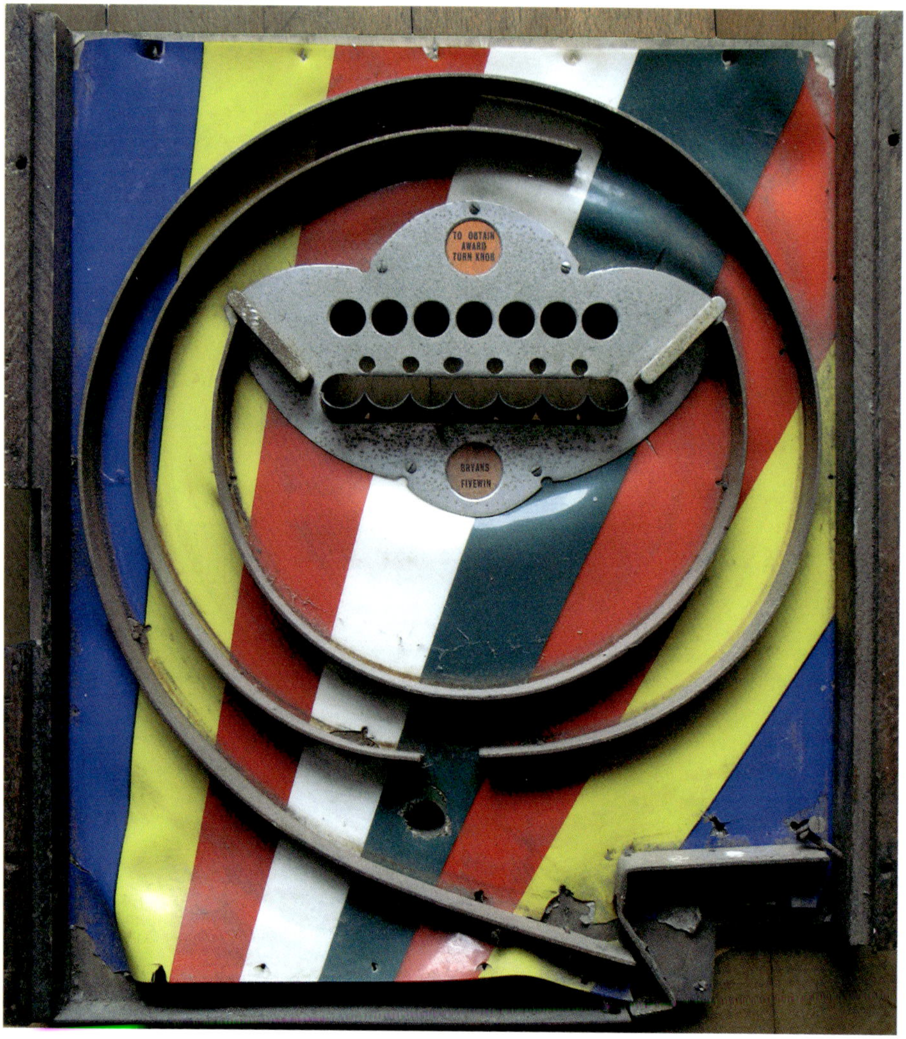

Broken Slot Machine 1

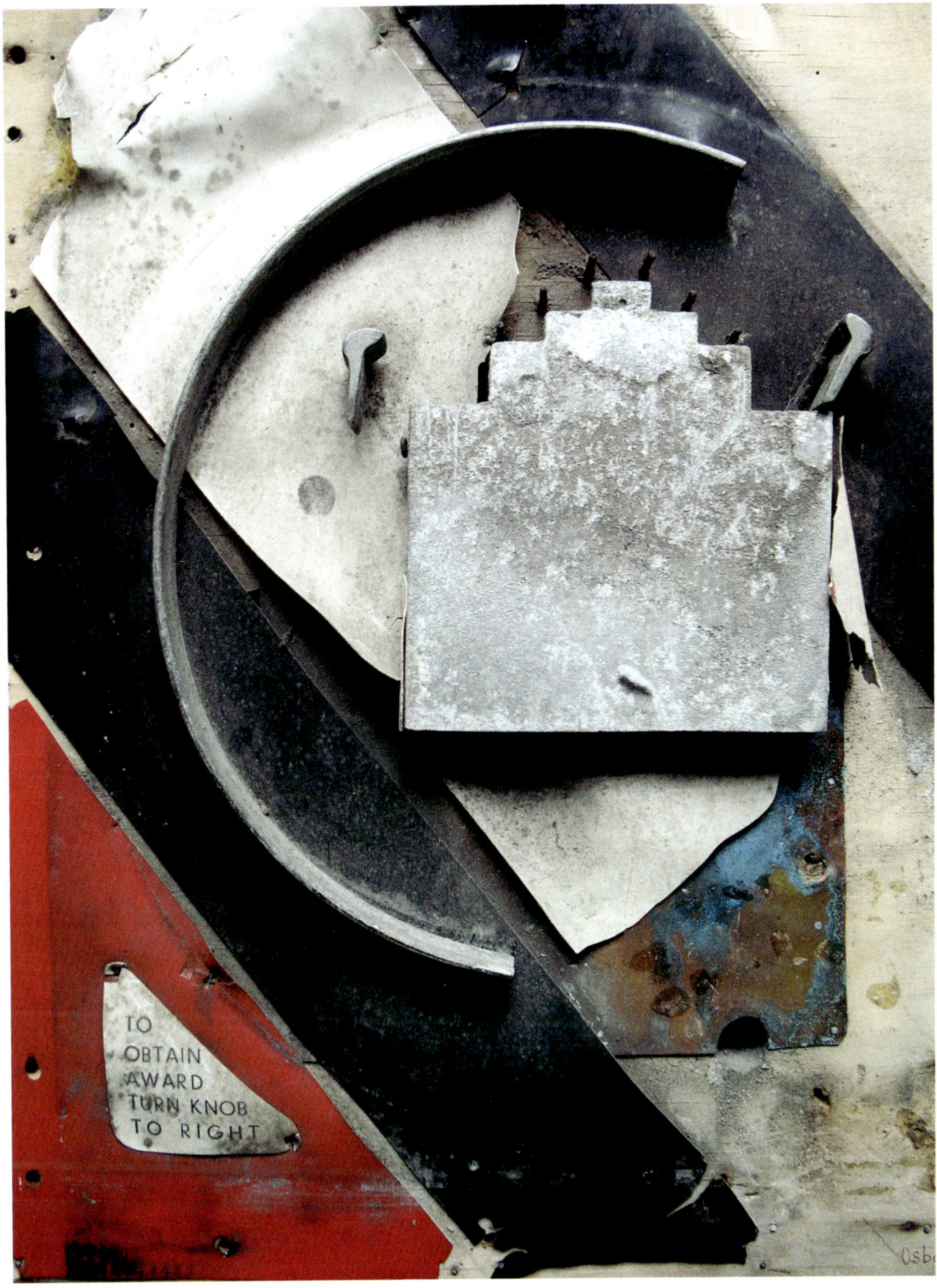

Broken Slot Machine 2

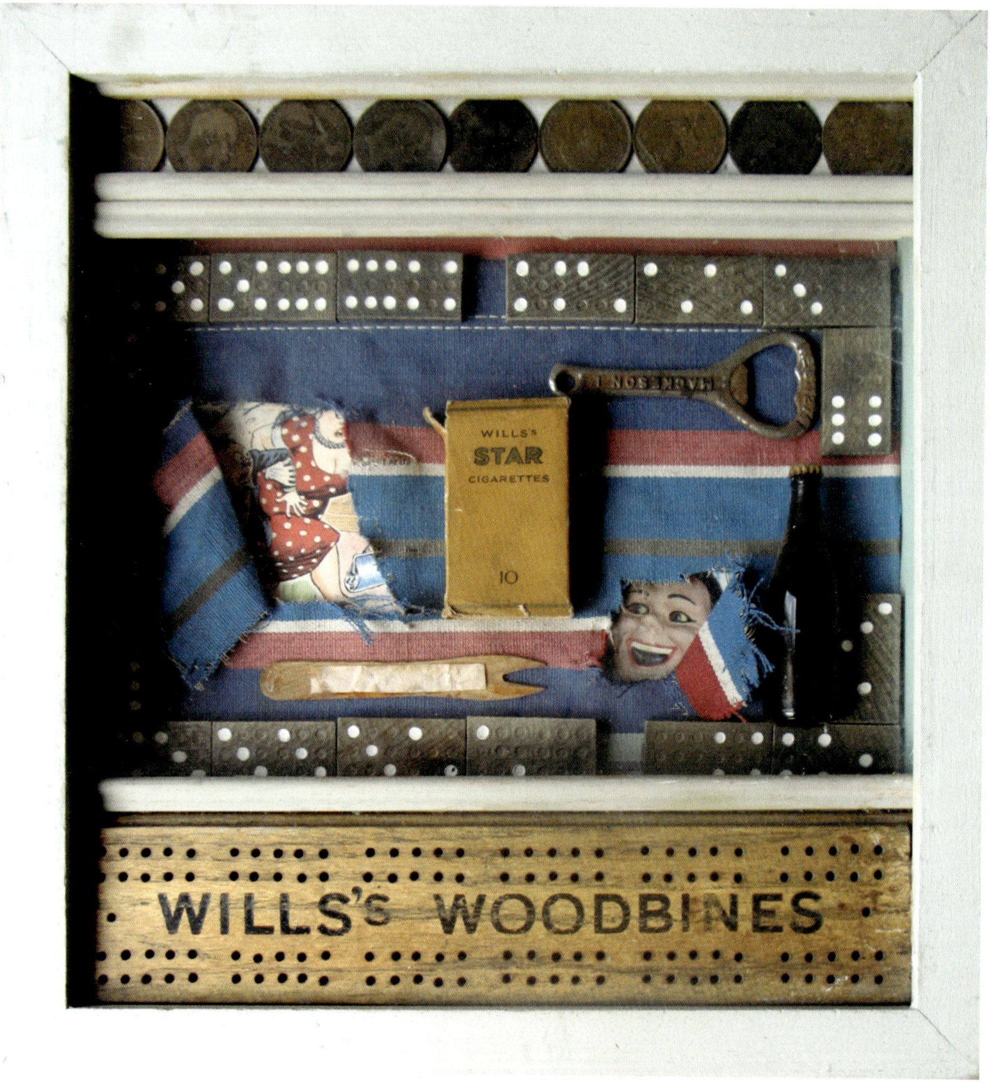

Wills's Woodbines, 1998

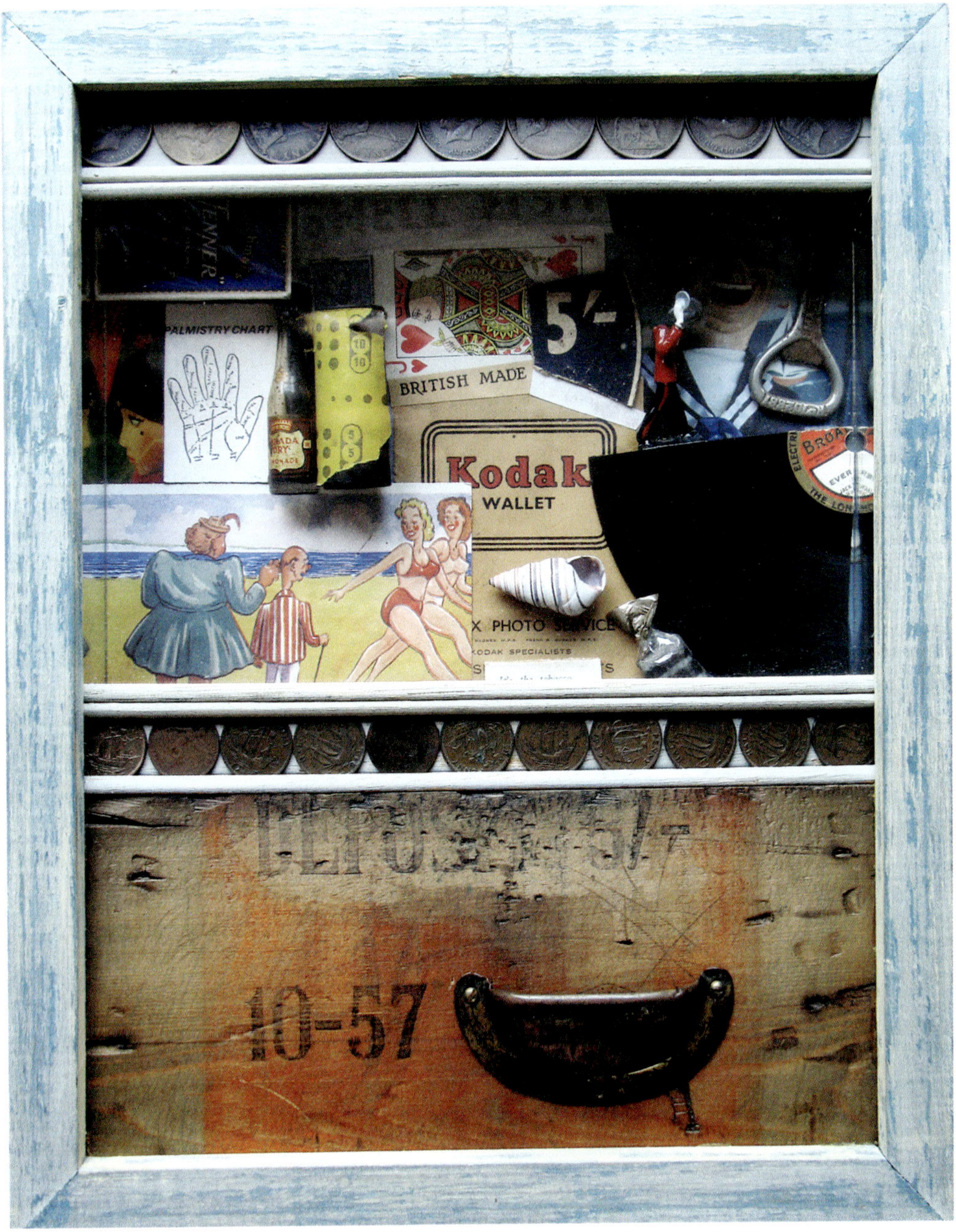

Deposit 5/-, 1998

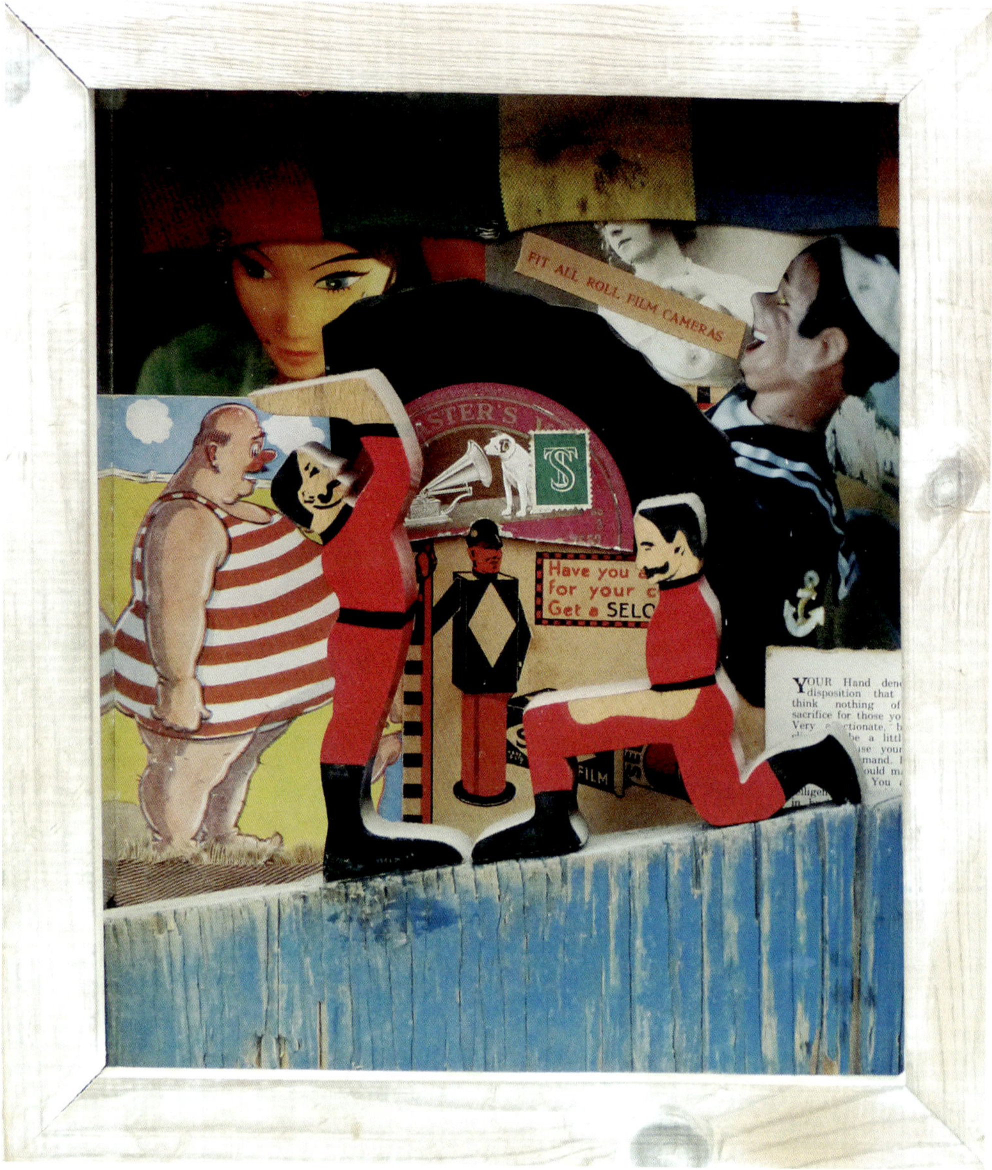

Acrobats, 1998

The fairground sources provide a quintessential repository of items from folk and popular culture. Concerning the aesthetic aspects of such content Osborne has written:

'The use of bright primary colours and bold lettering on English penny arcade machines proved a visual counterpoint to a largely drab and monochrome post-war Britain and predicated the vibrant brashness of pop art design that lit up the 1960's. The romantic connection to gipsy mythology and fortune telling, combined with a bawdy innuendo and an air of the unexpected, created an atmosphere where sunlight streamed in to a world that also contained sinister and criminal undertones, as captured by the film Brighton Rock (1947), with a screenplay written by Graham Greene and based on his 1938 novel, featuring the author's anti-hero running a slot machine racket.

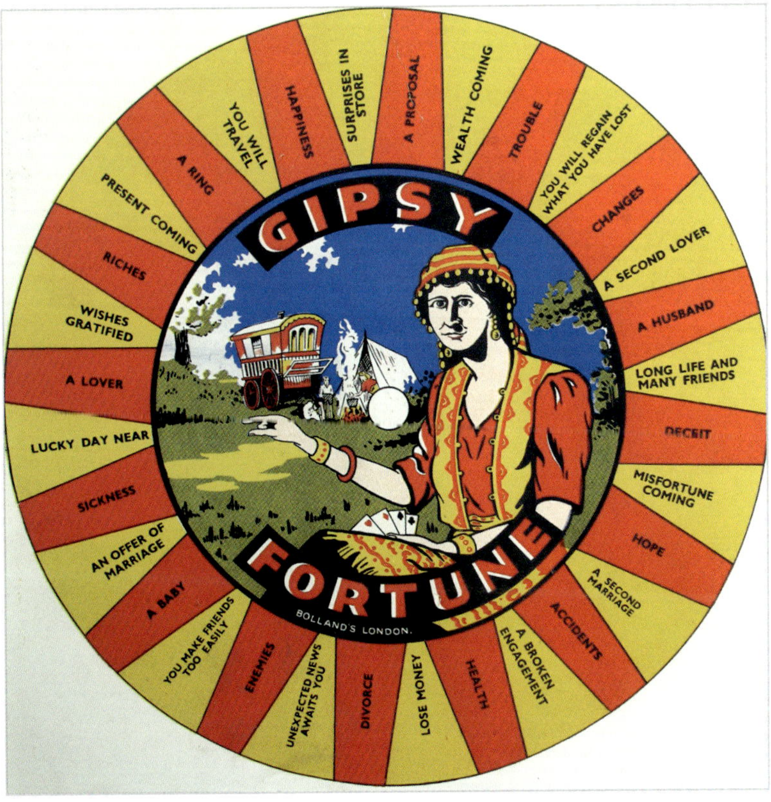

Fairground ephemera from Osborne's collection

I have always been fascinated by the tawdry eroticism of the 'What the Butler Saw' genre of penny arcade machines. Some of my slot machine constructions engage the spectator in the act of looking and this becomes a vital part of the artwork. The viewer who is 'outside' becomes an unwitting voyeur by observing the drama of the trapped images within the box through small windows of glass. This 'peeping tom' conceit is enhanced by the use of mirrors, often cracked or broken, or tears in post-war deck chair ticking where the spectators can catch glimpses of themselves in the act of looking.'

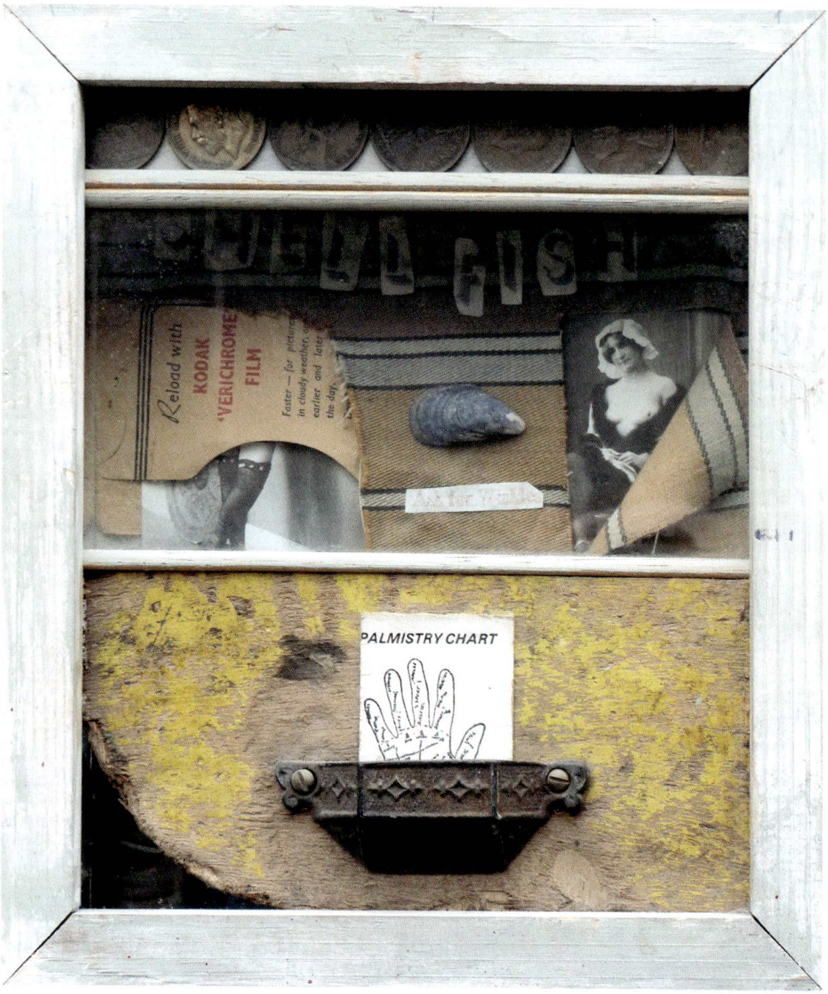

Palmistry Chart, 1998

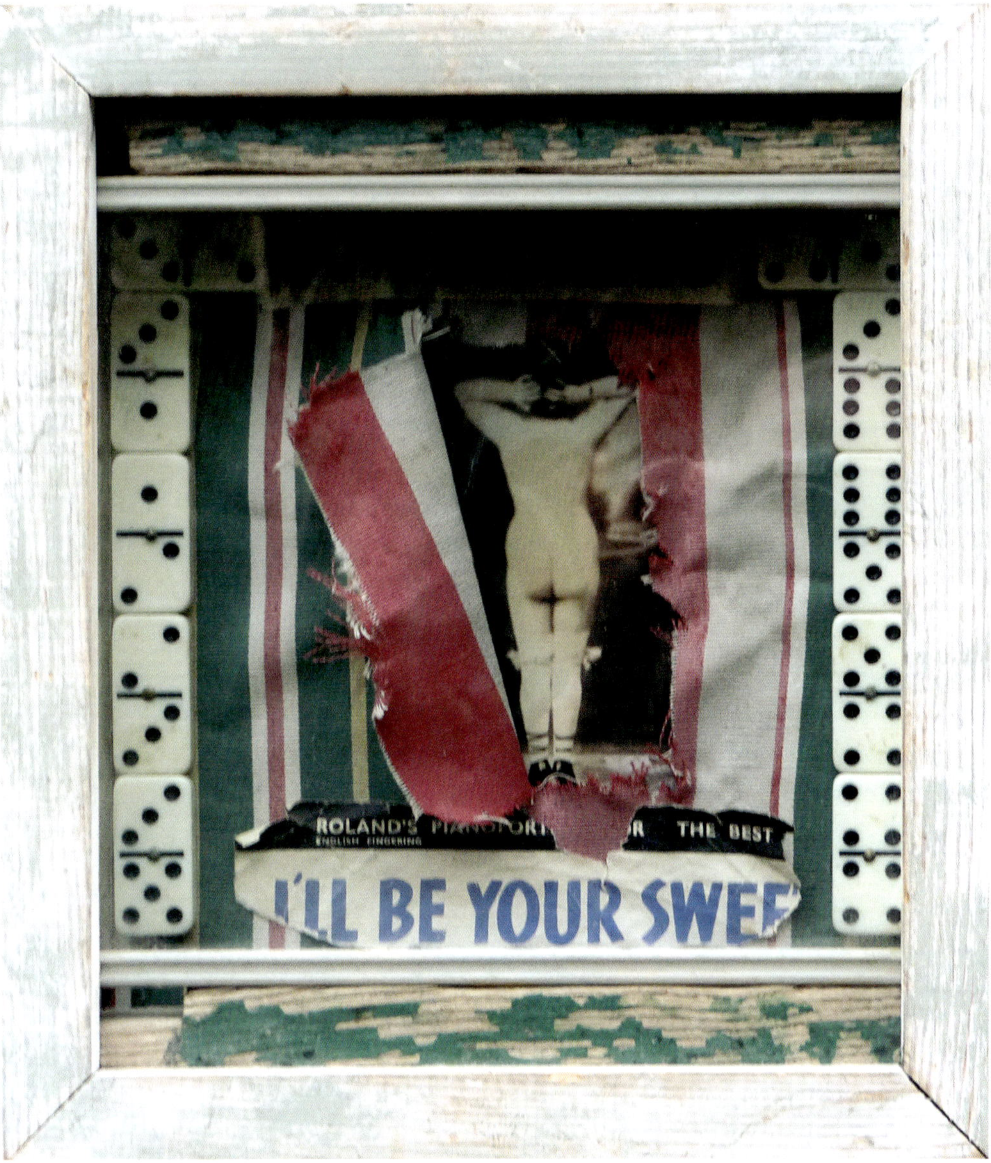

Domino Dream, 1998

'A dirty joke is a sort of mental rebellion.'
George Orwell

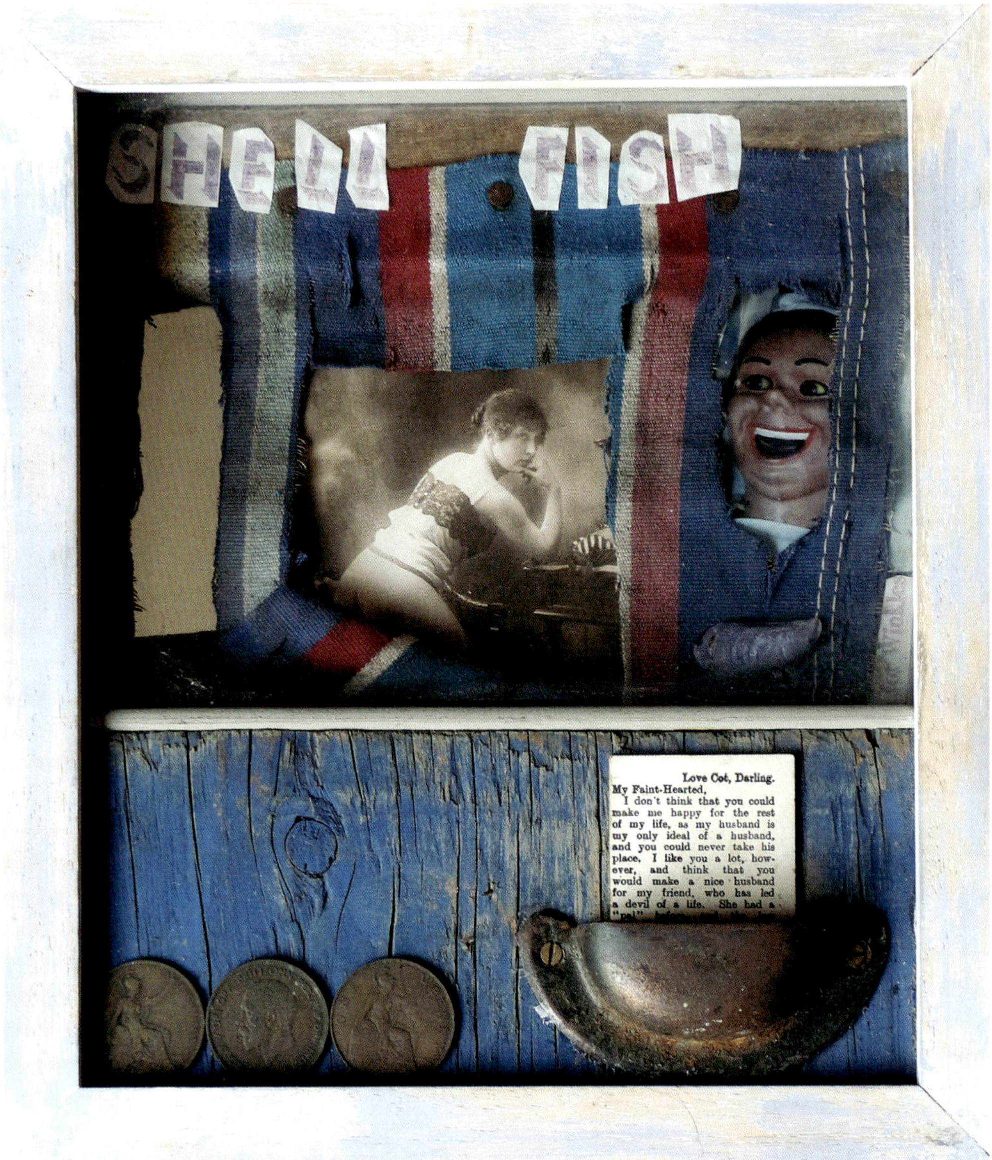

Deck Chair Dream, 1998

DECONSTRUCTED BOOKS

Osborne's love of literature and, by extension, books as concrete objects came about because - rather than in spite - of his ancestor's lack of formal education. From an early age Osborne collected books and postcards, newspaper cuttings, football programmes and stamps. A lifelong love of games with their associated slang and humour has informed much of the collaged scrapbooks provisionally stuck to the fading surface with now brittle, yellowing glue or sellotape.

From 1958 onwards Osborne has been a habitual Queens Park Rangers supporter at their atmospheric Shepherd's Bush stadium. The collages ***Juventus and Real Madrid*** draw on period football imagery, the posed team photos 'doctored' with the superimposition of heads of cats and dogs. This ironic subterfuge is as endemic to Osborne's work as is the frequent erotica, the feline or canine masks instilling both an air of menace and mocking satire.

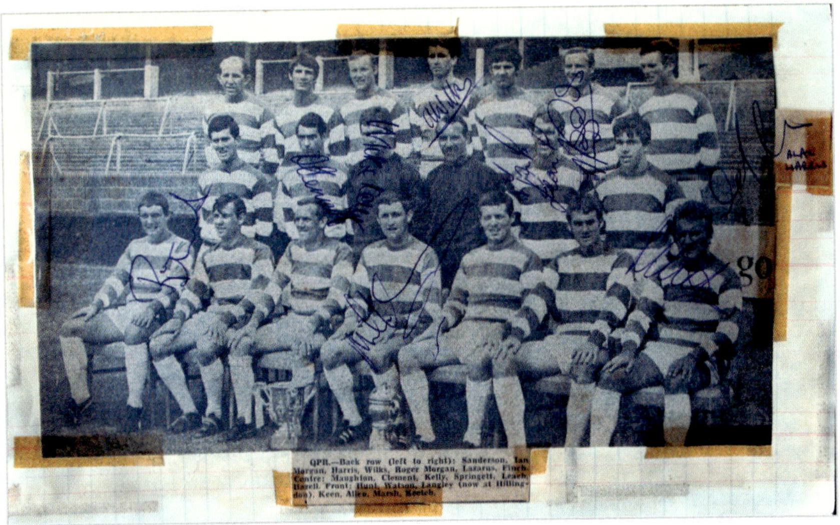

Osborne's autographed QPR scrapbook, 1968

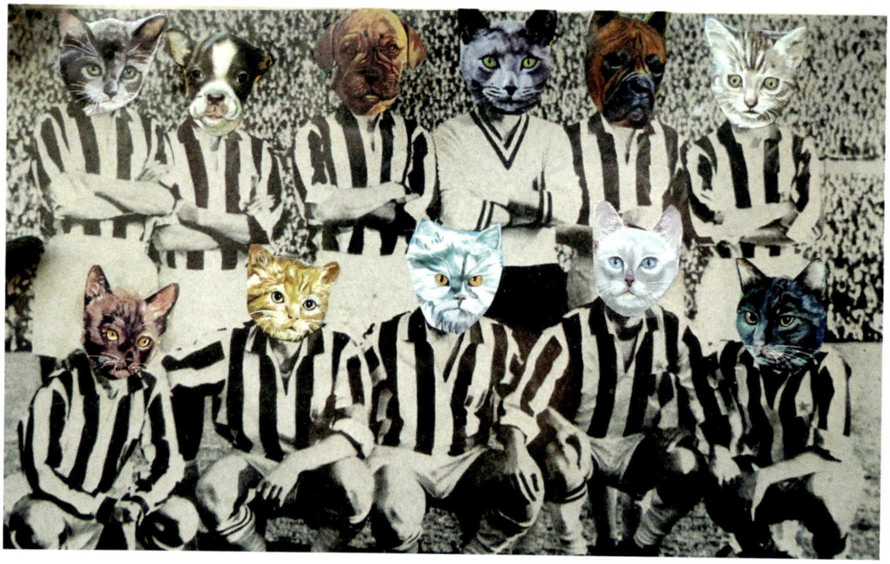

Juventus, 1999

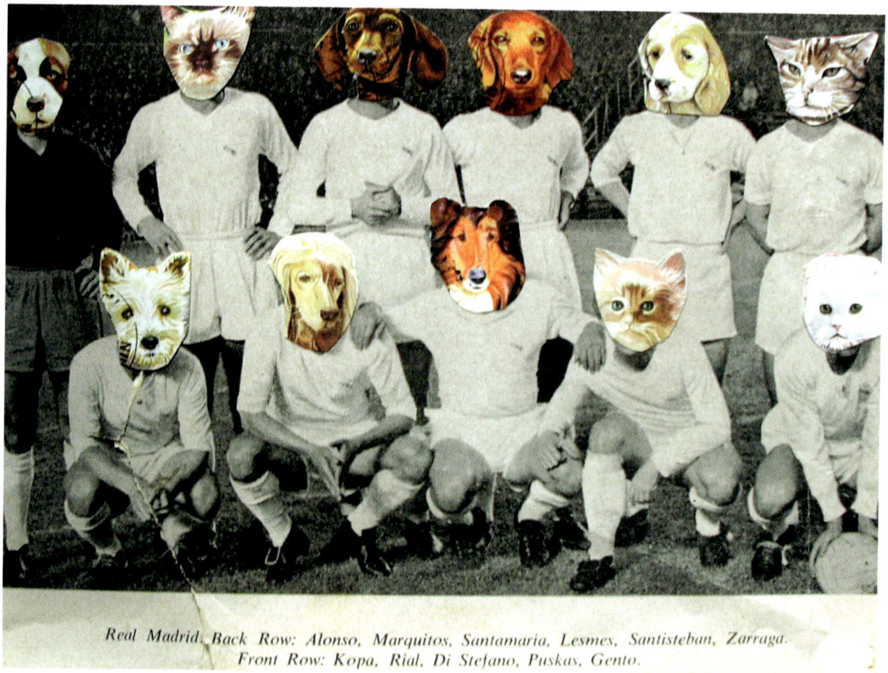

Real Madrid, 1999

'All that I know most surely about morality and obligations I owe to football.' – Albert Camus

The book as object moves on from literary content to fulfil bibliographic concrete drives. Versed with modern literature from his time as a student tutored by novelists Malcolm Bradbury and Angus Wilson at the University of East Anglia's legendary English and American studies department during the early 1970's, Osborne knows the cultural connotations or symbolic significance of specific books. One is reminded of playwright Joe Orton's criminal bibliographic vandalism in replacing illustrations in public library art books with collaged pornographic images or of avant gardist John Latham's edgy *Art and Culture (1966),* a conceptual piece that, after its early notoriety, found its way into the acceptable annals of the Tate Gallery's permanent collection. Latham was sacked from St Martin's School of Art after the theft of critic Clement Greenberg's *Art and Culture* from the library. His students chewed up the pages of the seminal tome and Latham represented them as a vial of fermented pulp juice in an artwork, the implicit conceptualism of the piece bearing iconoclastic and anti-art meanings. The Greenberg target was tantamount to throwing down a post modern, anti-formalist gauntlet, a provocative gesture with faintly sinister undertones of the Nazi 'degenerate art' book burnings.

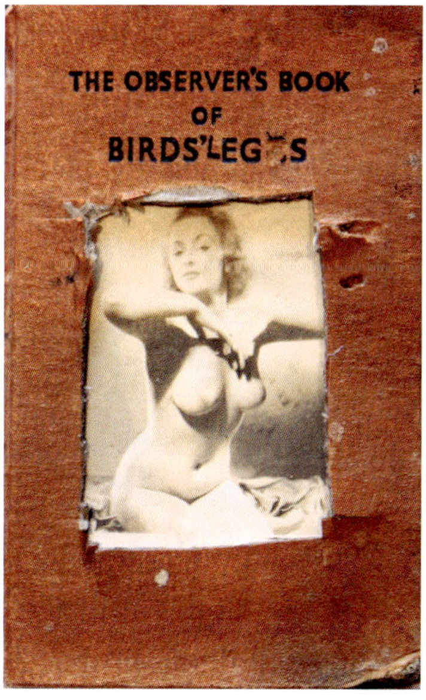

Bird's Eggs, 2009

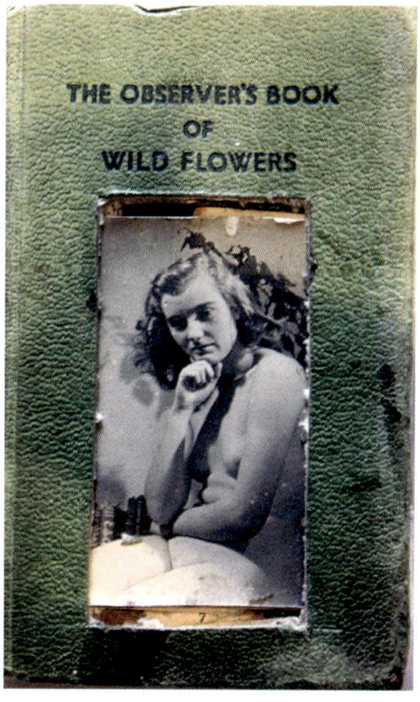

Wild Flowers, 2009

The book as solid object therefore transcends the literary content within its pages; Osborne invariably prefers a mixture of the verbal and visual. This is true of a rich vein of box collages from the late 1990's, among which ***Rediffusion, Service Action*** and ***Rime of the Ancient Mariner*** are prime examples. The wood fragment of a 1960's television screen in the former bears classic features such as switches, knobs and grooved patterns. The simple lettering and post-art deco stylisation offers a pre-computer graphics clarity and conciseness. The inherent element of nostalgia is complemented with a period football image. This replaces the moving picture compartment within with a static photographic image of Bobby Charlton placing a goal-bound header. Similarly, ***Service Action*** uses netting across tennis imagery and a bottle of Brilliantine in a plight of what Osborne describes as "deconstructing the past". In ***Rime of the Ancient Mariner*** Osborne cuts into the book to hollow out an enclave fitted with a Magrittan pipe and bird's eggs. The vivid Yves Klein Blue paint makes a further oblique art historical reference.

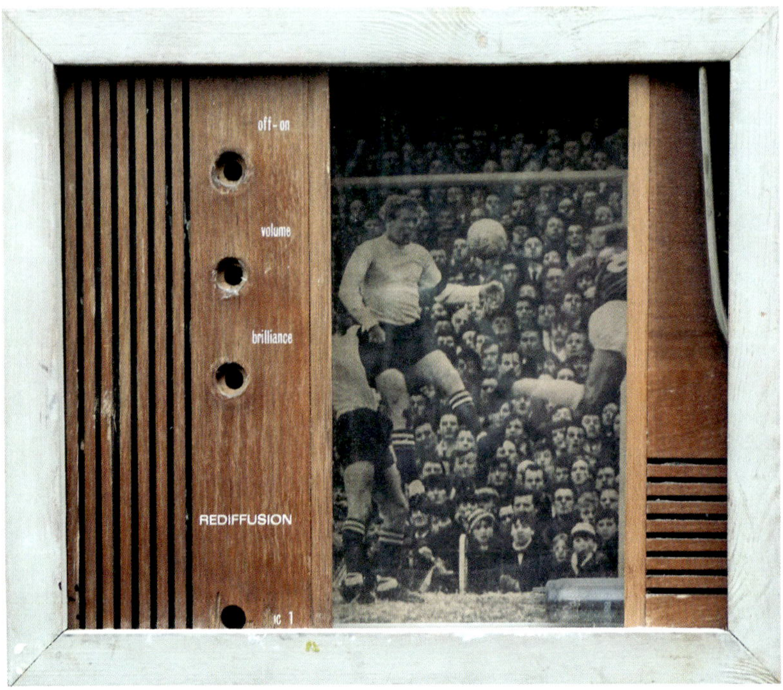

Rediffusion, 1999

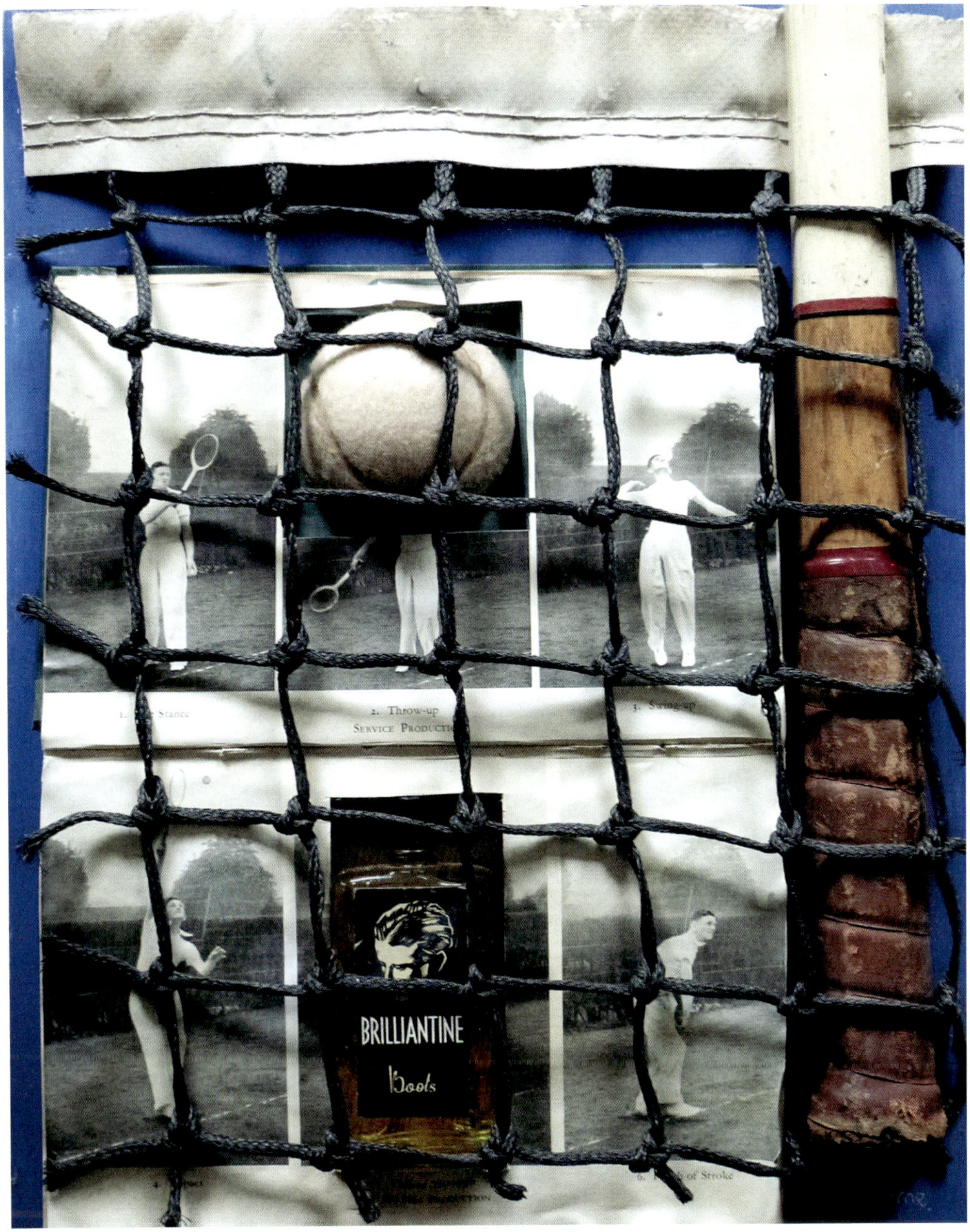

Service Action, 1999

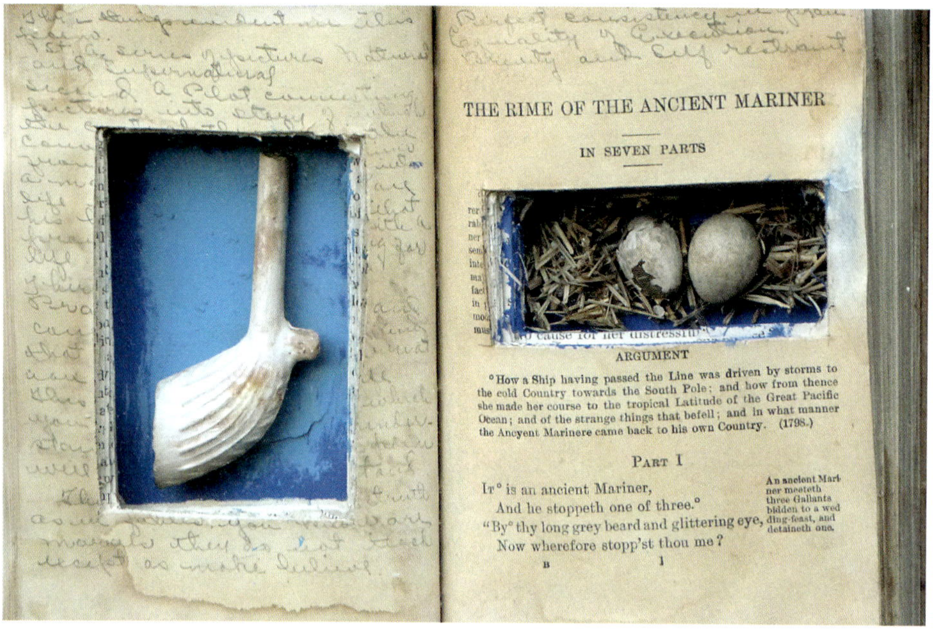

Rime of the Ancient Mariner (detail), 1998

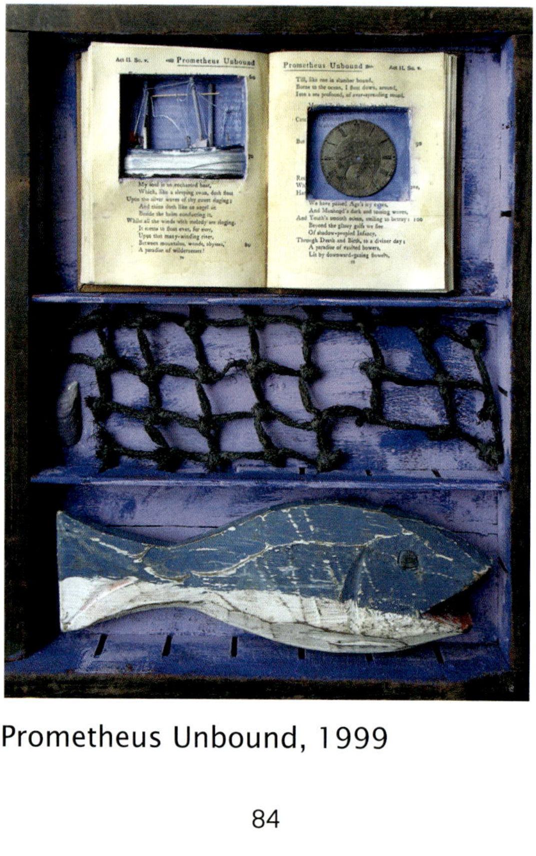

Prometheus Unbound, 1999

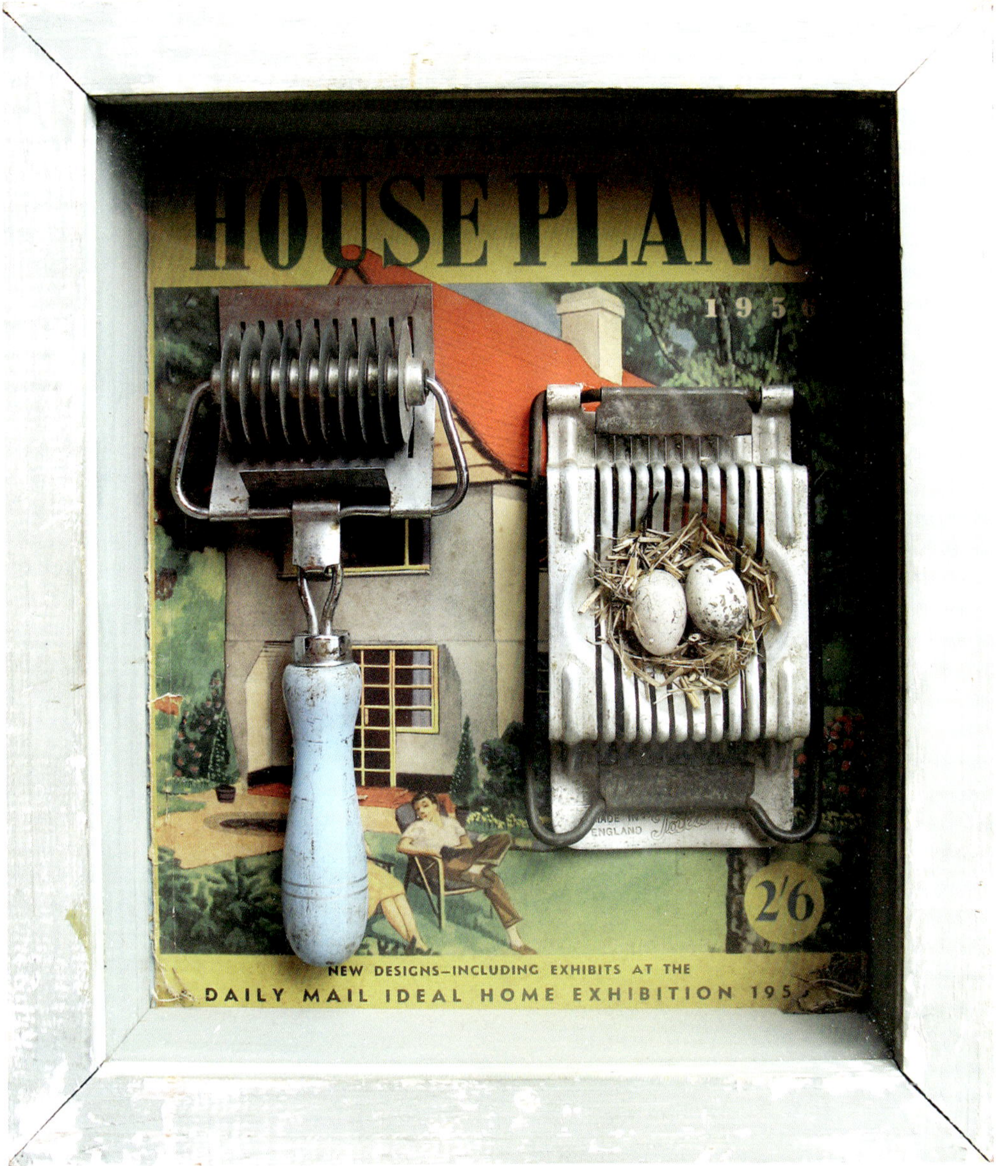

House Plans 1956, 1999

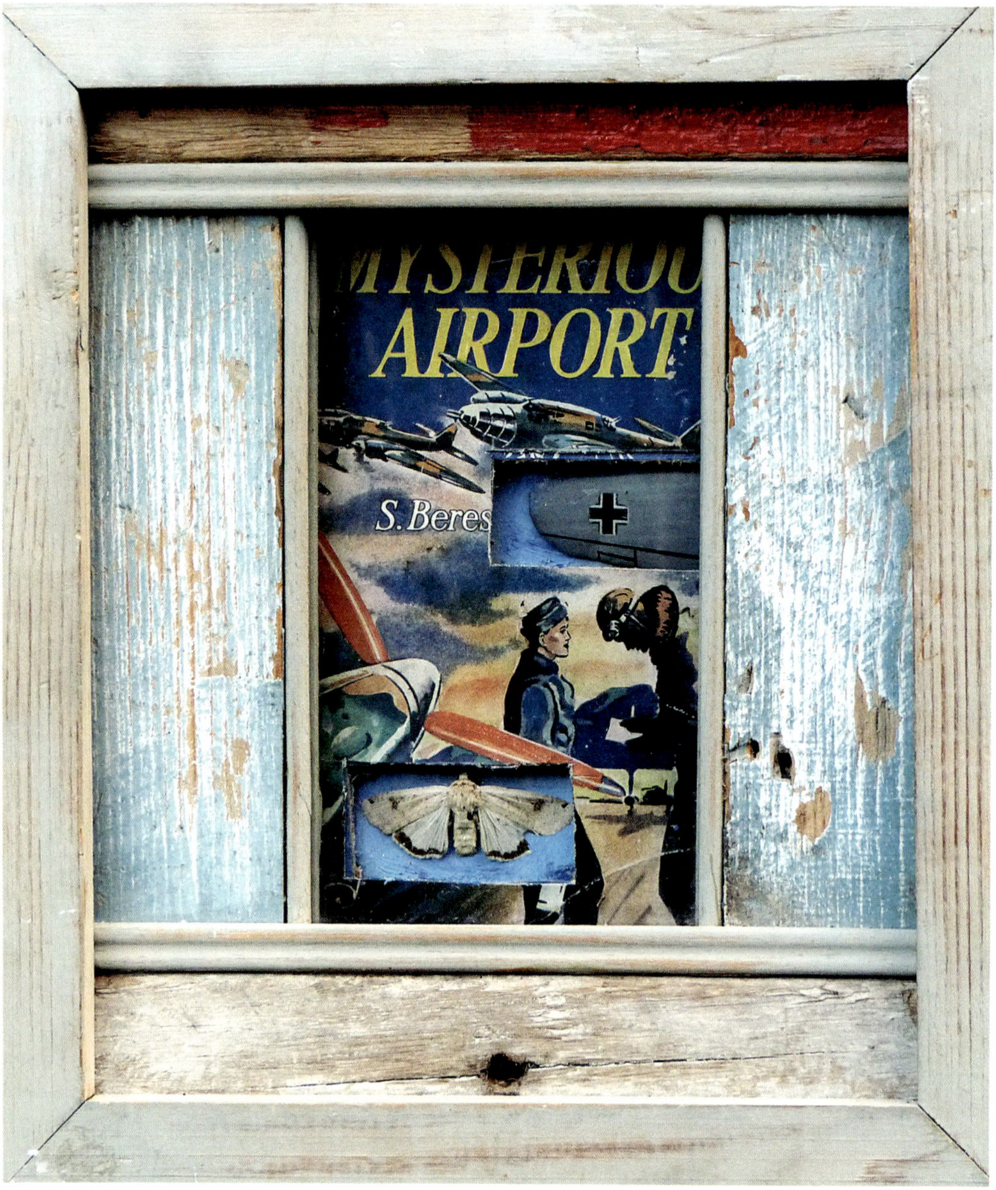

Mysterious Airport, 1999

POSTCARD COLLAGES

Like stamps or coins, postcards became collectable items replete with nostalgia, their current-day obsolescence replacing former function with the new role of social history relic, aesthetic 'icon' and sentimental keepsake. Here, what had once been personal memos now become cultural ephemera of a generic kind. From today's perspective these often grubby or faded objects, with their traditional typographic design, contain images of landmarks or popular resorts that have become barely recognisable through subsequent development and tourist industry modernisation.

By re-casting these postcards into a new art context, where they are marshalled into modular Warholian sequences, Osborne transforms them into visual and literary objects for contemplation, their ready-made aspects further subverted through the accident of weathering or of the administration of distressing agents such as bleach. This results in a random abstraction, the now only partially recognisable imagery giving way to the textural irregularity and autonomy of an Italian fresco, or of an *art brut* or Abstract Expressionist painting surface.

These effects are clear in ***Cathedrals*** and ***Postcards from the Isle of Wight***, the former containing a dozen part obliterated cards of celebrated ecclesiastical sites, the latter a series of phantom-like Edwardian figures emerging from misty, historically distant, backgrounds. The free association and automatic procedures of Surrealism are at play here. Since Surrealism was primarily a literary movement, albeit one that lastingly impinged on the plastic automatism of informal painting, Osborne's deployment of random postcards, with their handwritten notes, possesses pertinence mid-way between the visual and literary. Osborne's background as a published poet (*A Moon in Leo: Collected Poems 1975-76*) indeed squares this particular circle perfectly.

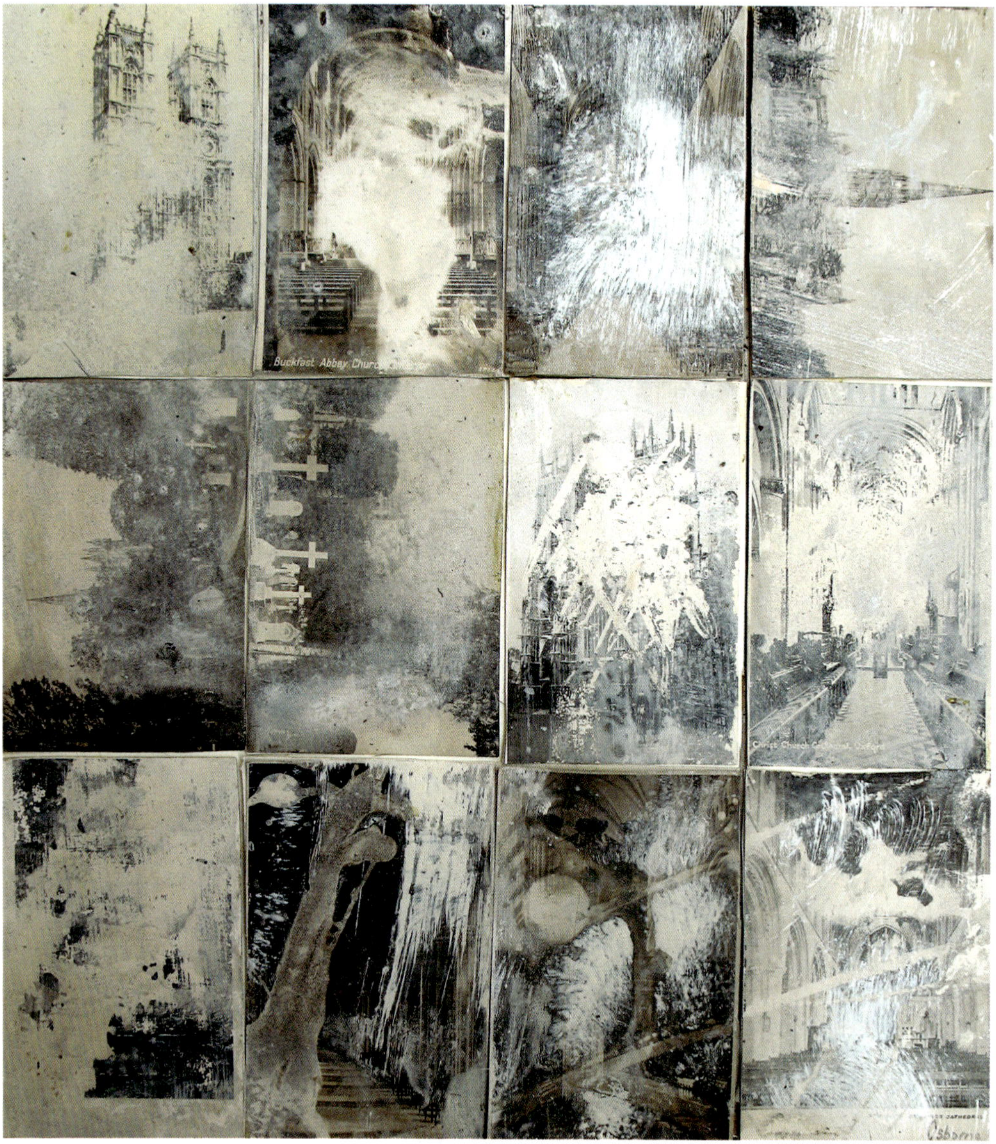

Cathedrals, 2006

'Death has a hundred hands and walks by a thousand ways.'
T.S. Eliot: *Murder in the Cathedral.*

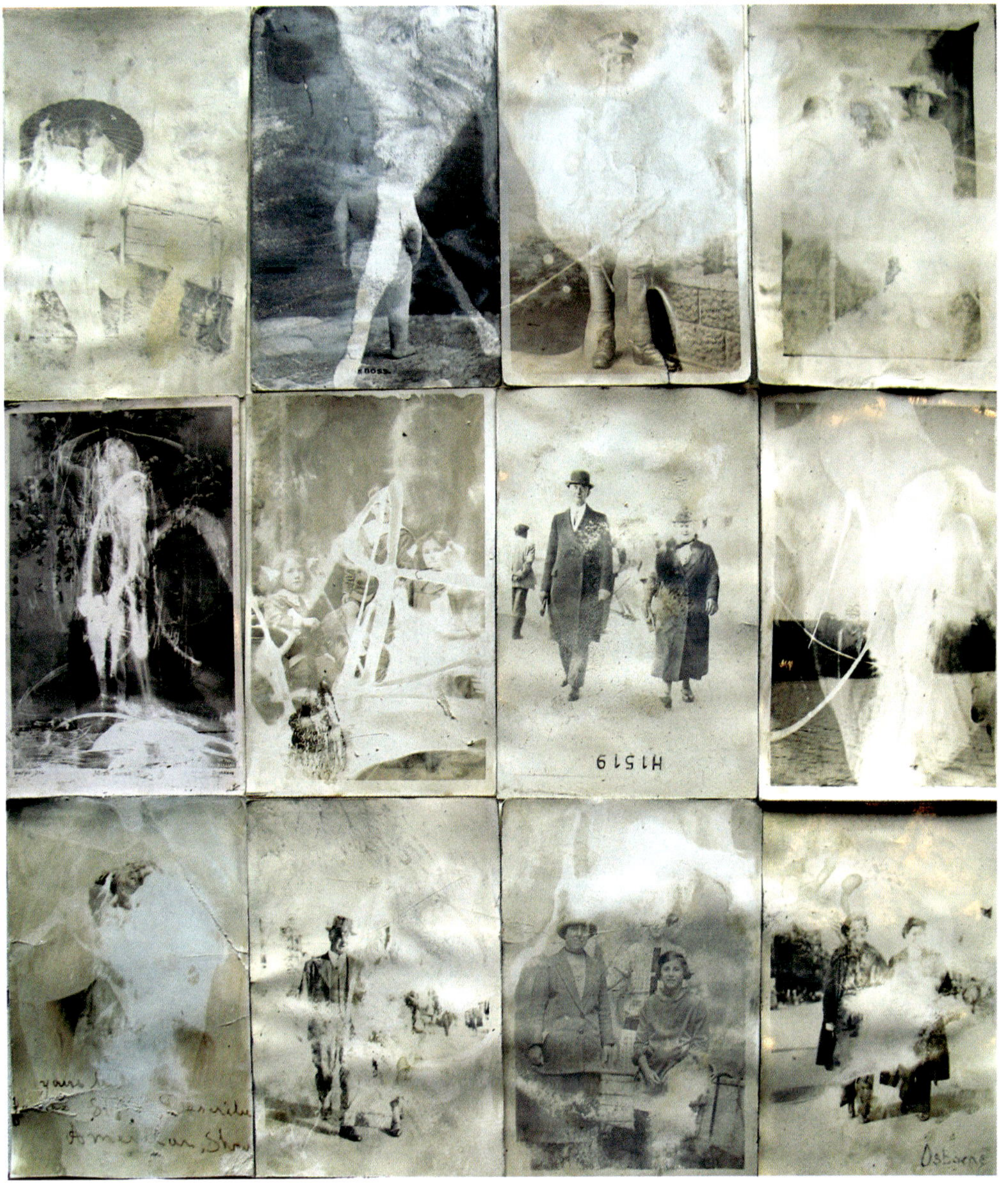

Isle of Wight, 2007

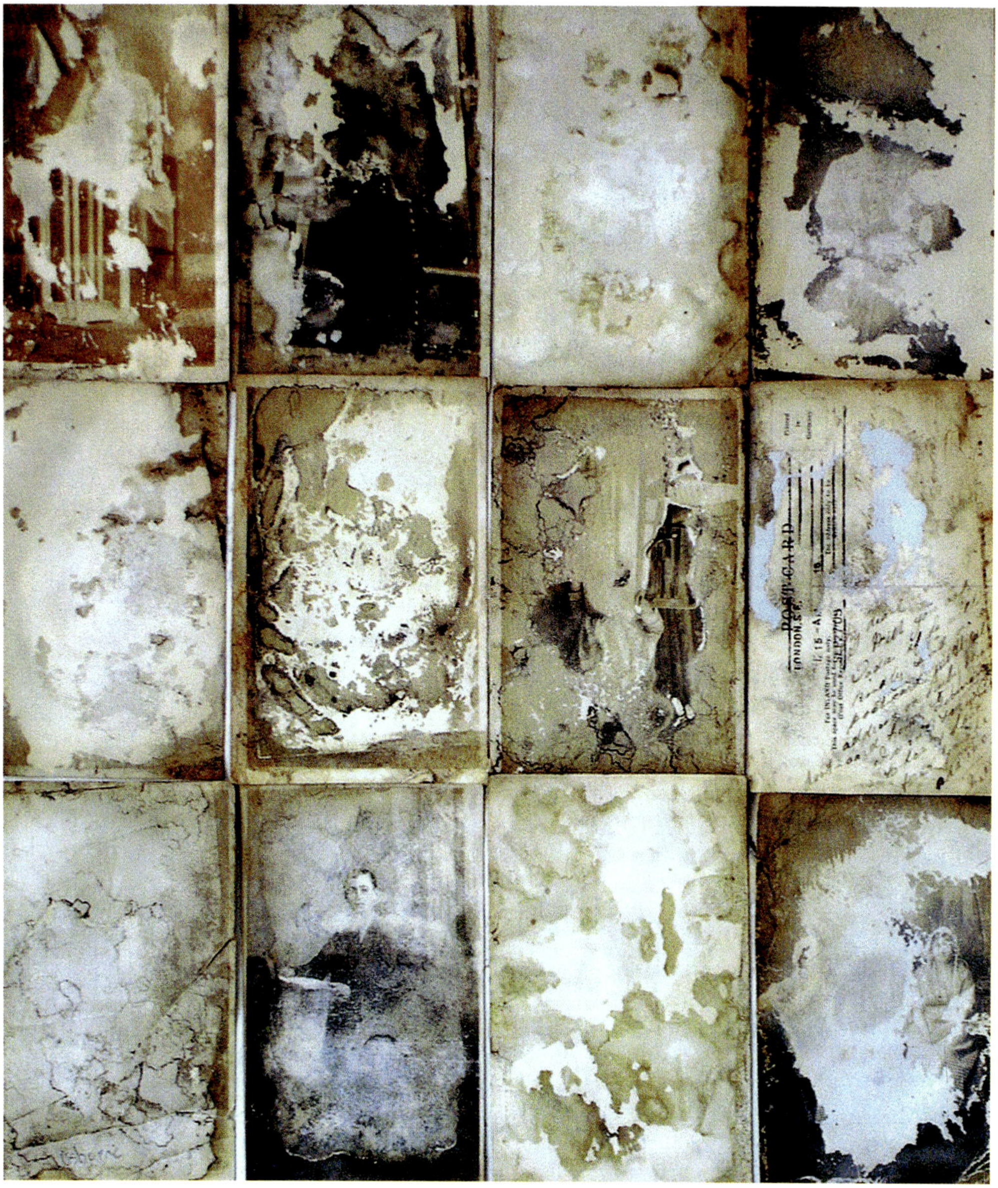

Ghosts, 2006

'The past is a foreign country: they do things differently there.'
L.P. Hartley: *The Go Between.*

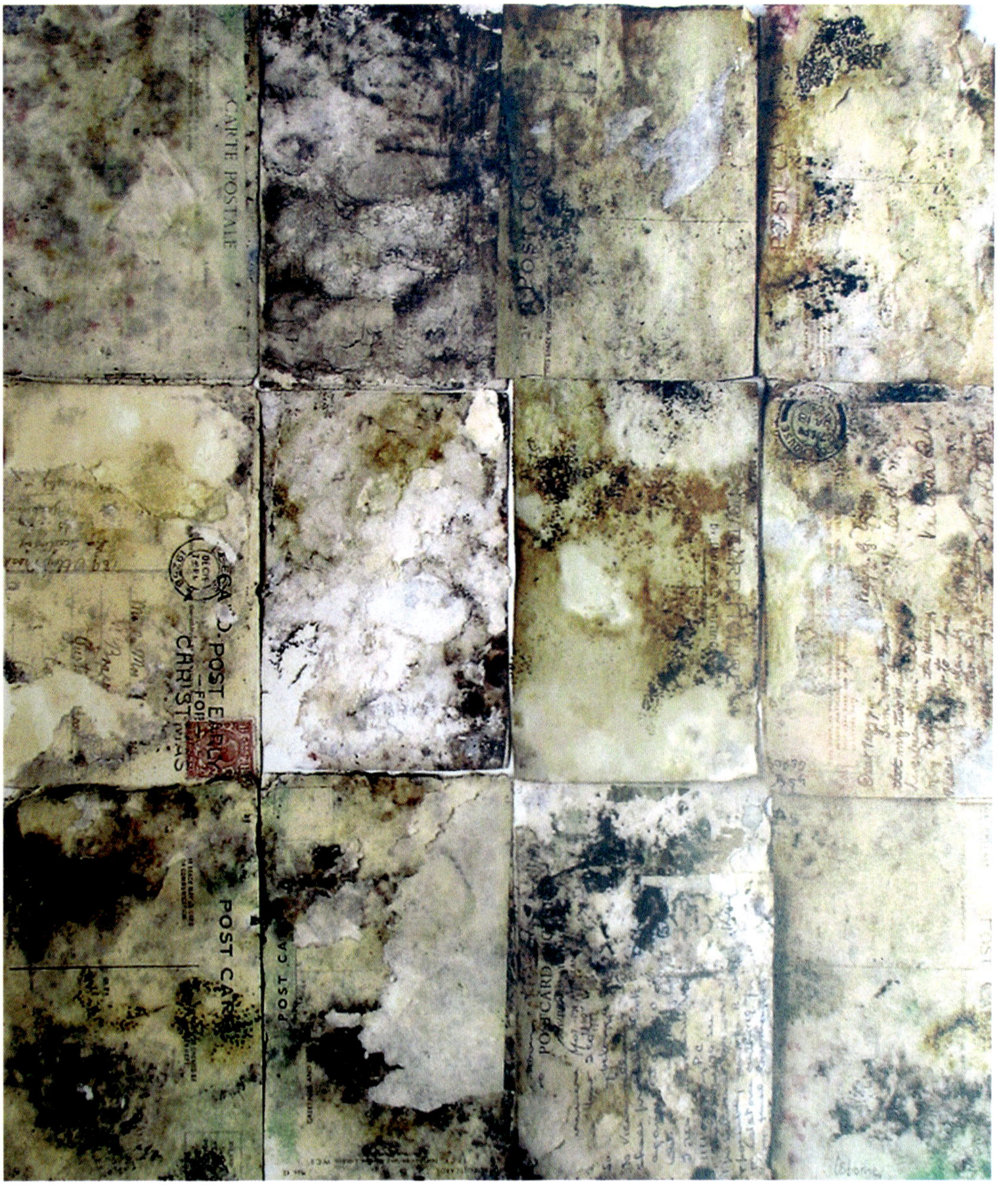

Decomposed Postcards, 2006

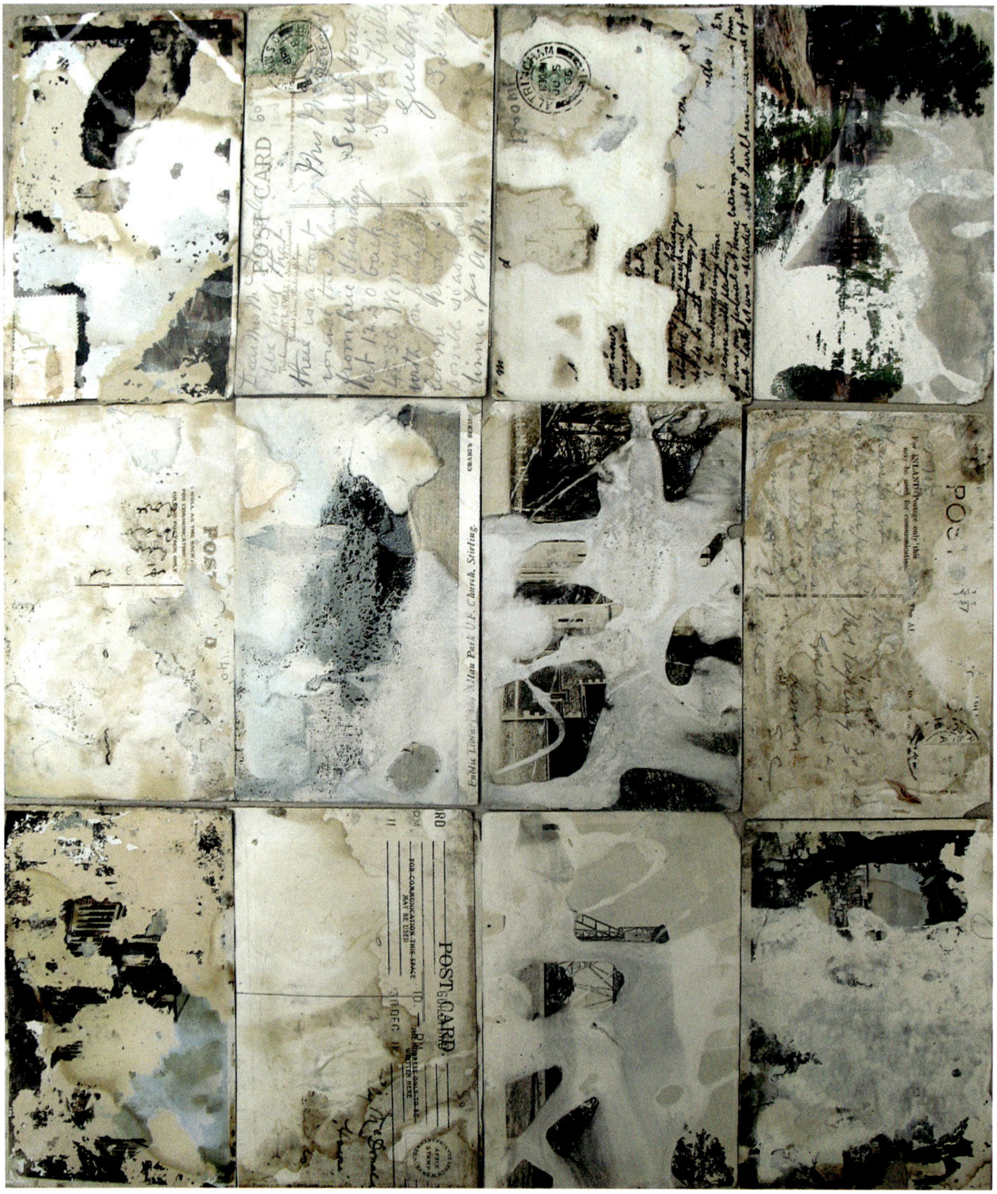

Decomposed Postcards, 2012

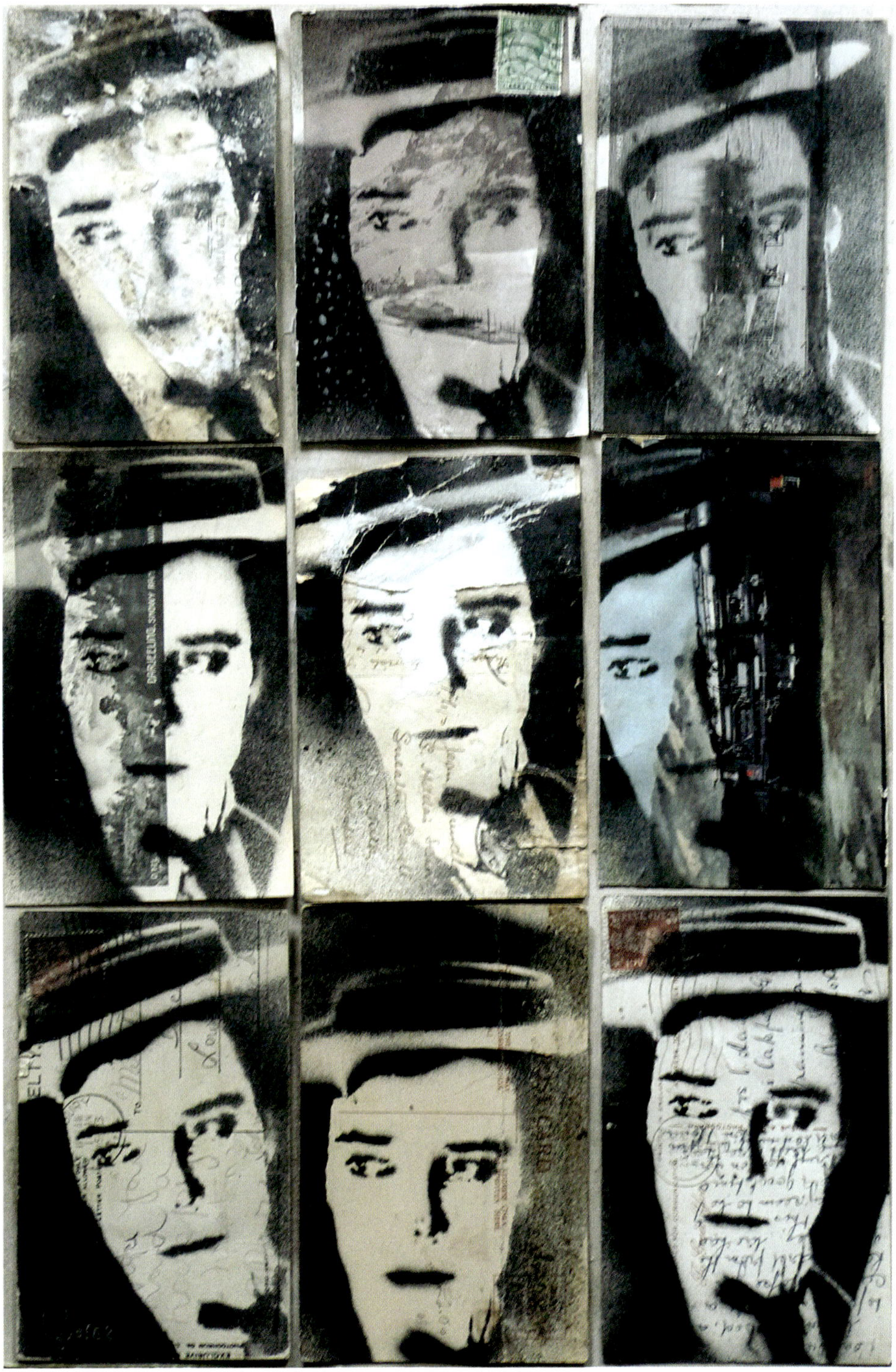

Buster Keaton Postcard Collage, 2007

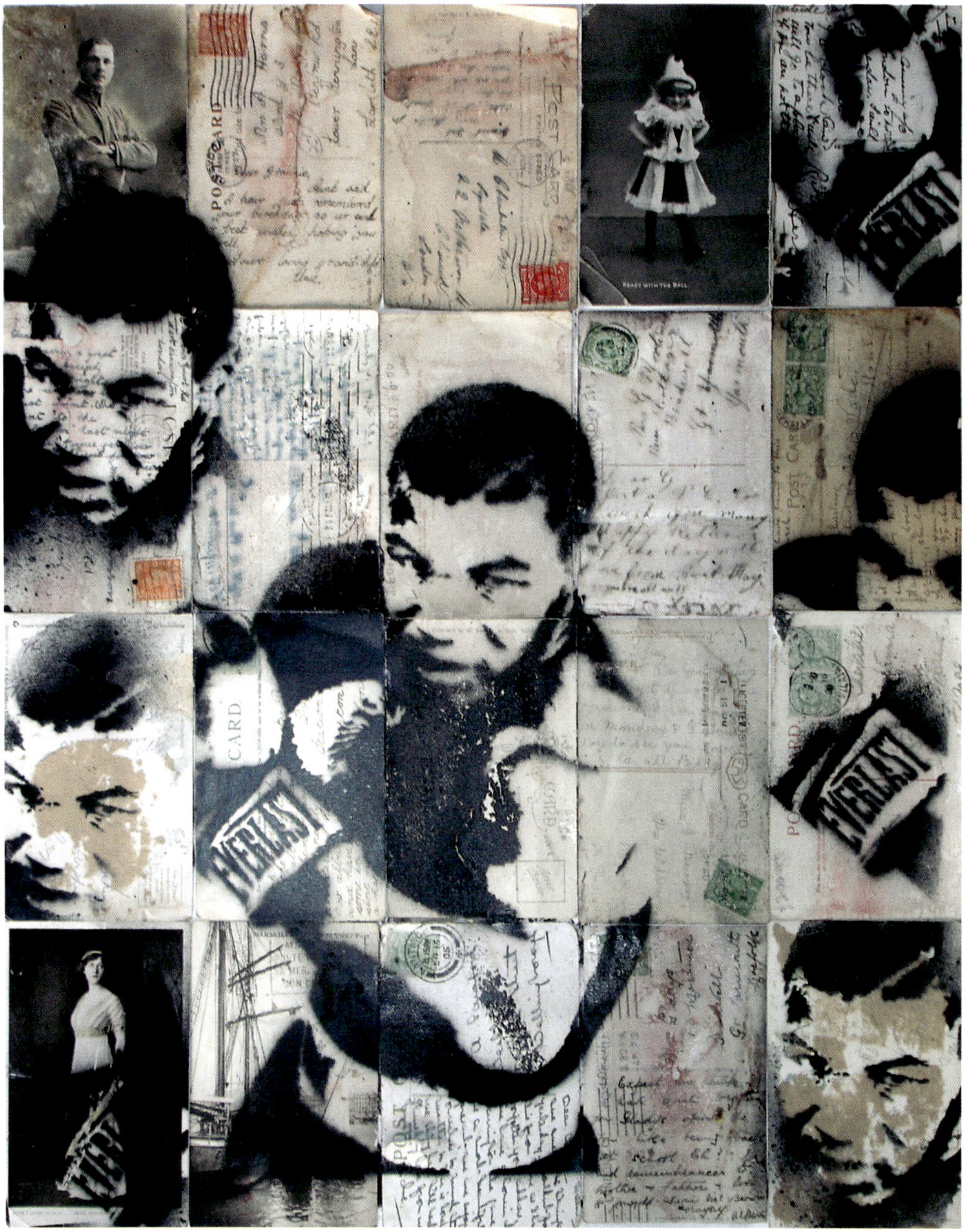

Mike Tyson Postcard Collage, 2010

SPRAY CAN PAINTINGS

Meeting the Marble Arch based abstract painter Denis Bowen in 2000 was a revelation for Osborne, leading to a close working relationship and friendship lasting until Bowen's death, aged nearly 85, in 2006. Bowen's *tachism* and *gesturalism*, which during the 1950's had been promoted both through the radical New Vision Centre Gallery he founded with Nancy Halescz and Frank Avray Wilson, and through inclusion in the Redfern Gallery's landmark *Metaphysical, Tachist, Abstract* show in 1957, chimed with Osborne's anarchic feeling for random and chance effects.

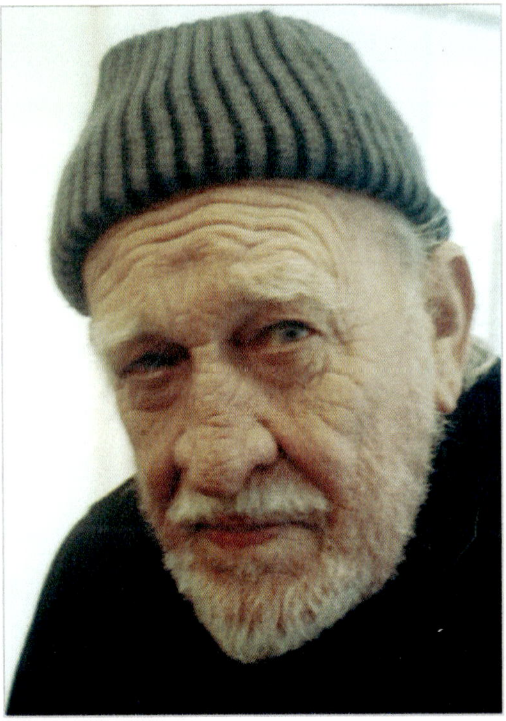

Denis Bowen *photograph: Bob Osborne*

While the younger man's application of these working methods was geared to the semi-sculptural medium of collage and box constructions, Osborne allowed the influence of Bowen to lead him towards experiments with spray cans and metallic car paints. Following Bowen's use of metaphorical out-of-this-world astronomical imagery, Osborne luxuriated in free association *informalism*, in which the physical propensity of paint as an inherently flowing, lyrical medium was fully exploited. Random textural and chromatic effects stemmed from fortuitous stained and sprayed passages. Osborne exhibited alongside Bowen within the *Sharing a View* group, both at the Royal West of England Academy, Bristol, and at the Julia Margaret Cameron Museum on the Isle of Wight.

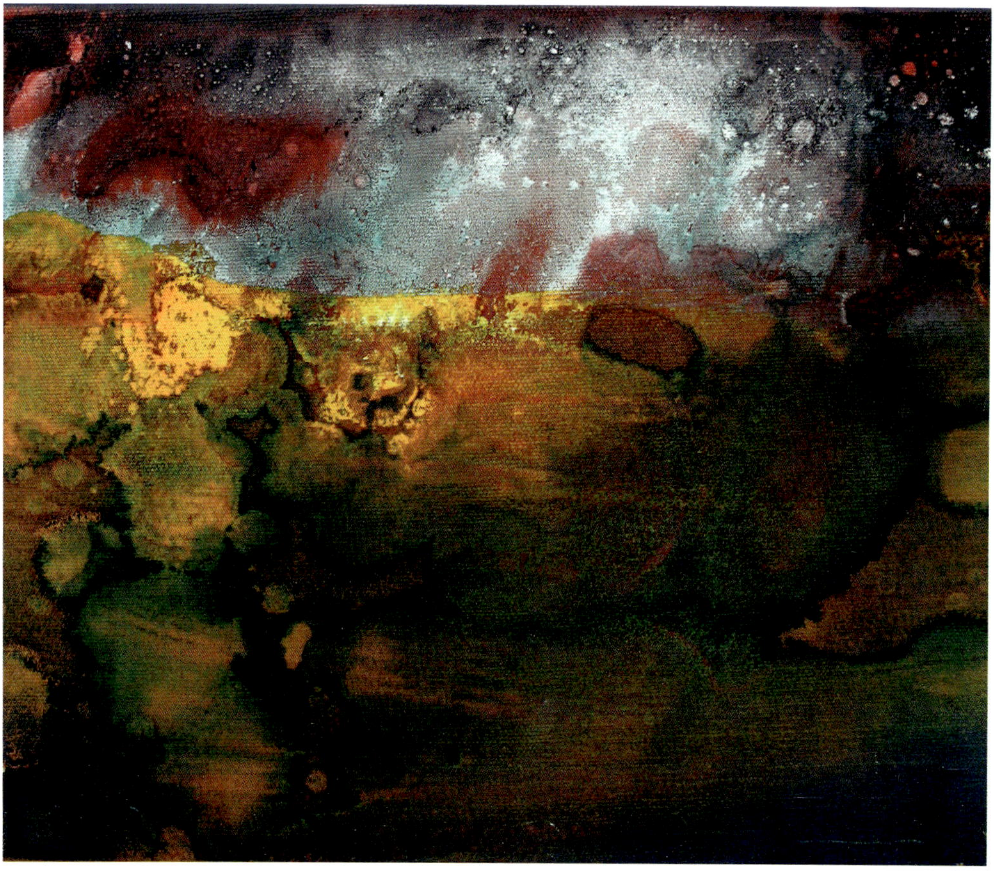

Denis Bowen's Encrustment, 2002

While teaching at Ealing College of Art in the early 1960's, Bowen made experimental paintings whilst listening to the music of Jimi Hendrix and Pink Floyd. The influence of psychedelia and mind-expanding drugs also proved relevant to Bowen's experiments with strobe light effects, with fluorescent or luminous colours and with a creative synaesthesia between different media. Osborne assisted the ageing artist in his London studio and started using spray paint techniques in his own art work.

Discovering Bowen's haphazard and bohemian living and working quarters at Seymour Place, near Marble Arch, confirmed to Osborne the relevance of his own aesthetic instincts. A mutual interest in the poetry of discarded fragments drew the two together during the vital five year collaboration. Bowen's 'Aladdin's Cave' of collected ephemera and works in progress was both inspirational and instructive to the eager, younger artist. Among the objects that made up Bowen's cultural cornucopia - much of it junk elevated to the status of trophy - were a collection of plastic cutlery, random scraps of paper found in the street and, perhaps most important of all, an empty, rusty wartime sardine can that triggered the idea for Osborne's subsequently successful sardine cans construction series that proved popular entries at the Royal West of England Academy Autumn Exhibition and at the Bath Society of Artists Summer Exhibition.

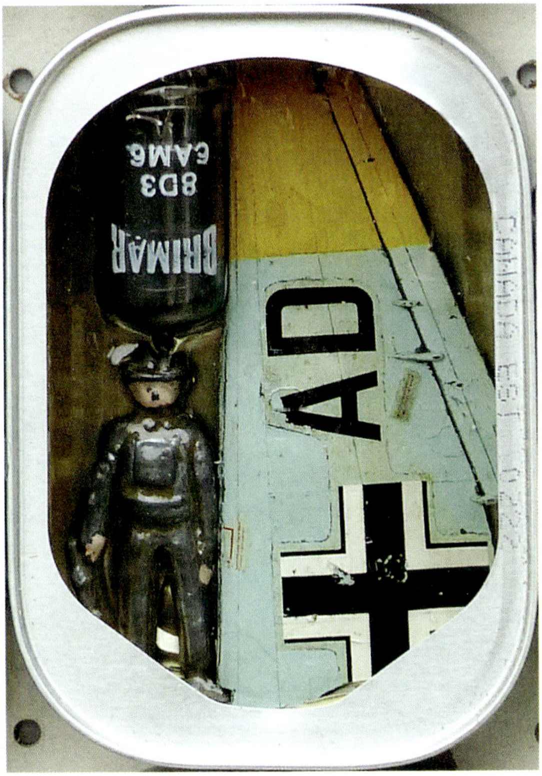

Keep Calm and Carry On, 2010

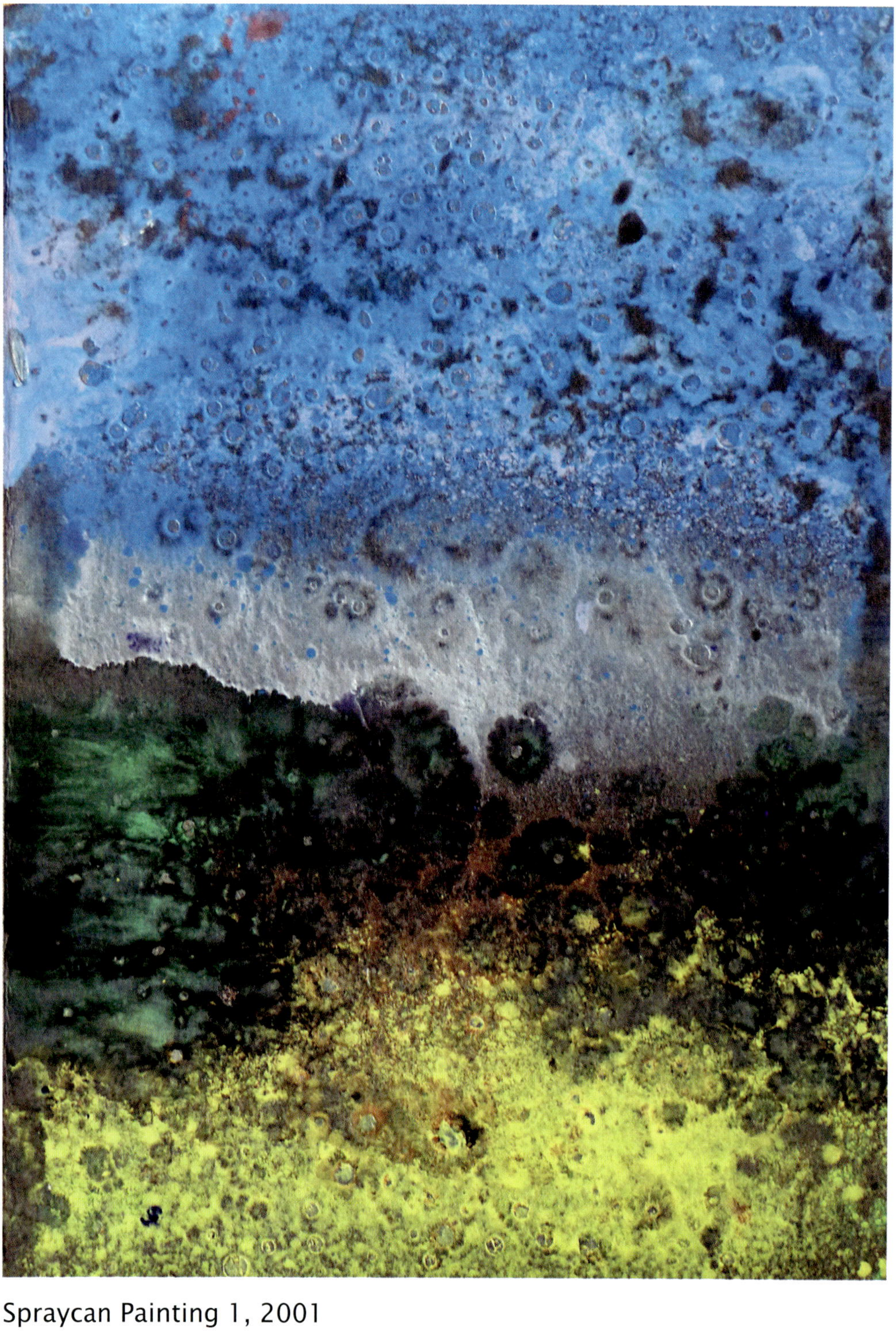

Spraycan Painting 1, 2001

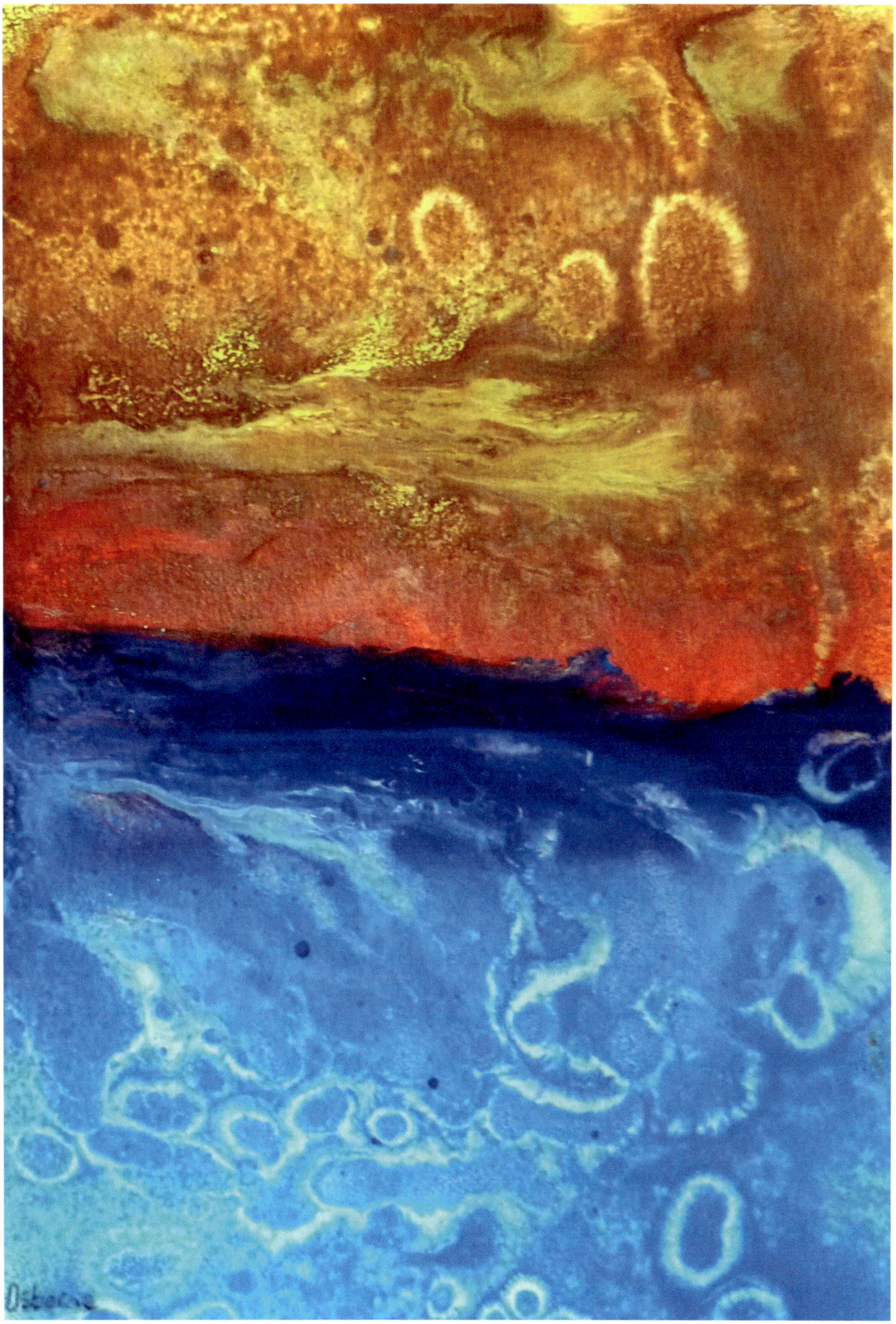

Spraycan Painting 2, 2001

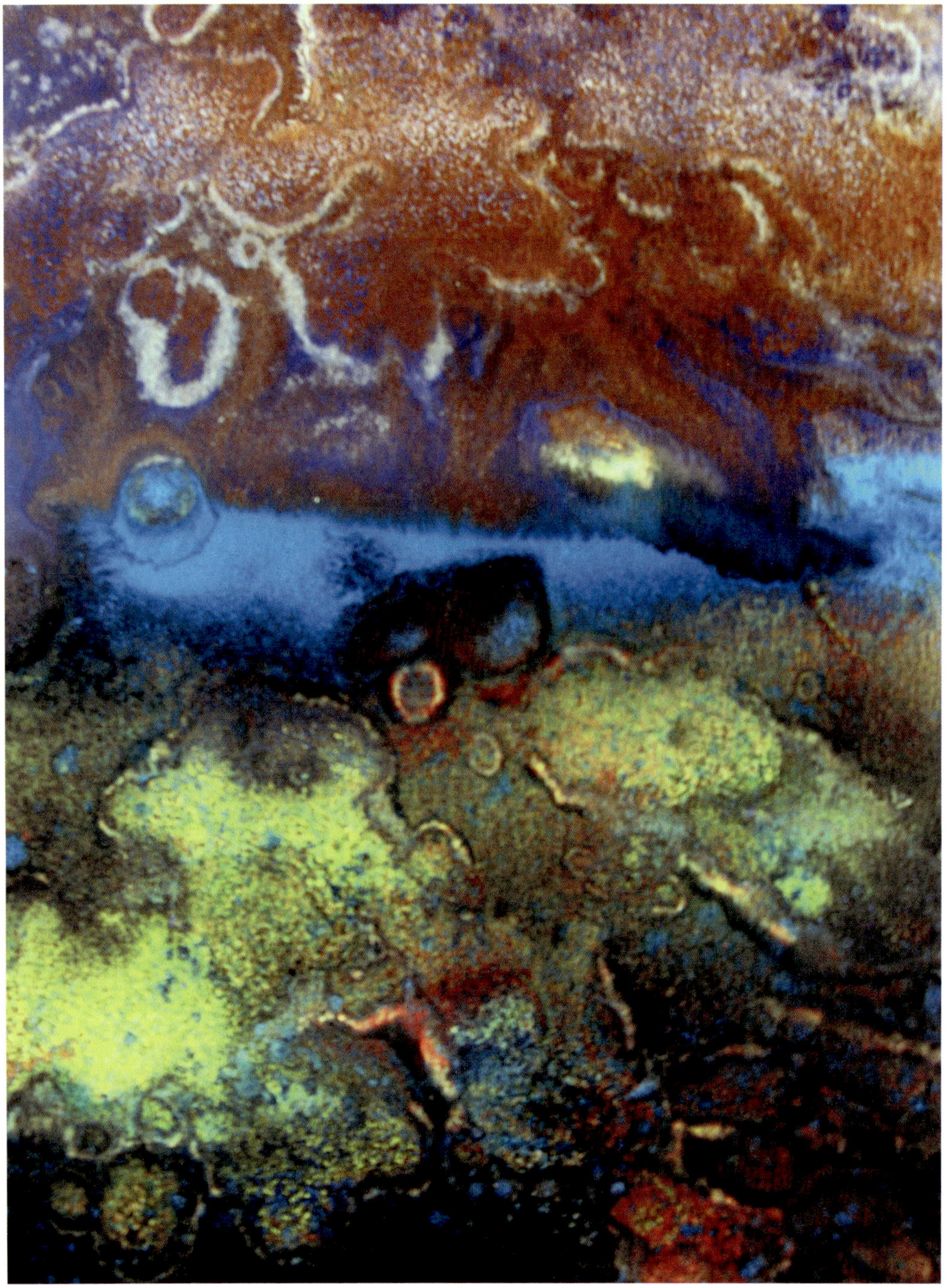

Spraycan Painting 3, 2001

Bowen's use of the spray can to achieve fugitive, almost otherworldly, atmospheric effects stemmed from his teaching after the war in industrial design art school departments. Other informalist influences lay conveniently around the Chiswick corner in the guise of near neighbours Jeff Hoare and Derek Stockley. Hoare's stained abstract landscapes are ciphers of freedom, arenas of free flowing paint dipped into the sea on the Kent coast where the 'seasoned' Strand-on-the Green painter keeps a beach hut studio. Liverpool-raised and St Martins School of Art-trained, Stockley took up painting after serving in the Navy. His trowelled impasto and use of blowtorches to emulate the *fumage* effects of *matter painting* wildly bypassed academic or even avant garde conventions, in a way that equally appealed to Osborne's iconoclasm.

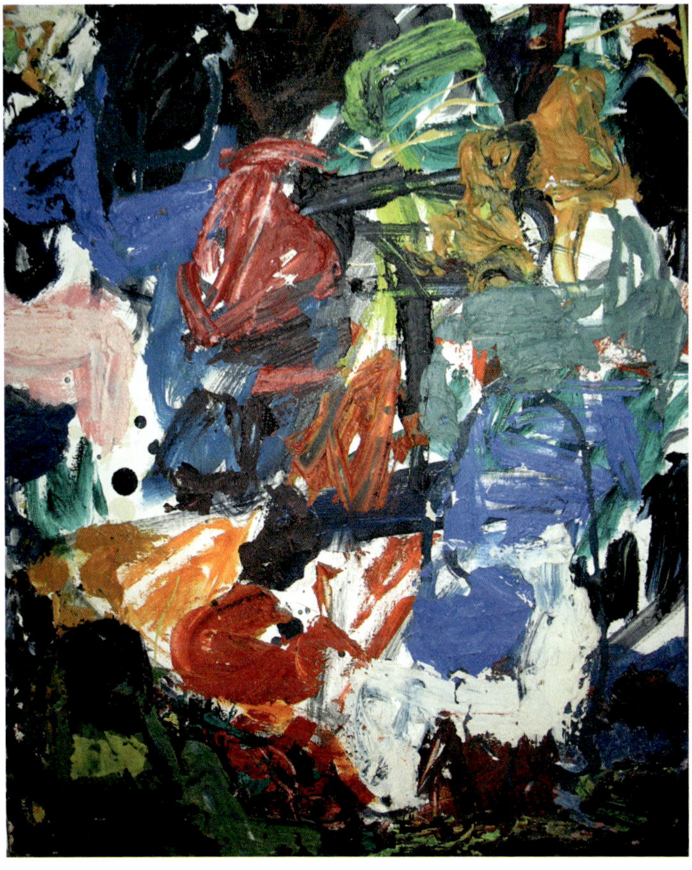

Derek Stockley's Heading Past the Blue, 1994

With his circumnavigation of the cult of craft already half assuaged by the industrial connotations of spray painting, Osborne later made forays as a *plein-airist manqué*, indulging subversive tendencies through a spell of urban graffiti painting using the tag **Defy** after becoming involved with the international street art movement. The celebrated French stencil artist Jef Aerosol has painted a large dancing figure on the studio wall of the English artist's Chiswick house after staying there whilst exhibiting and working in London. Osborne's youngest daughter Rosie, who along with her sister Sophie, grew up surrounded by artists and writers, has picked up the alternative artistic baton and has written a dissertation on the history of French Street Art *Le Street art en France: un phénomène controversé,* which proved a bit radical for her professors at Sussex University.

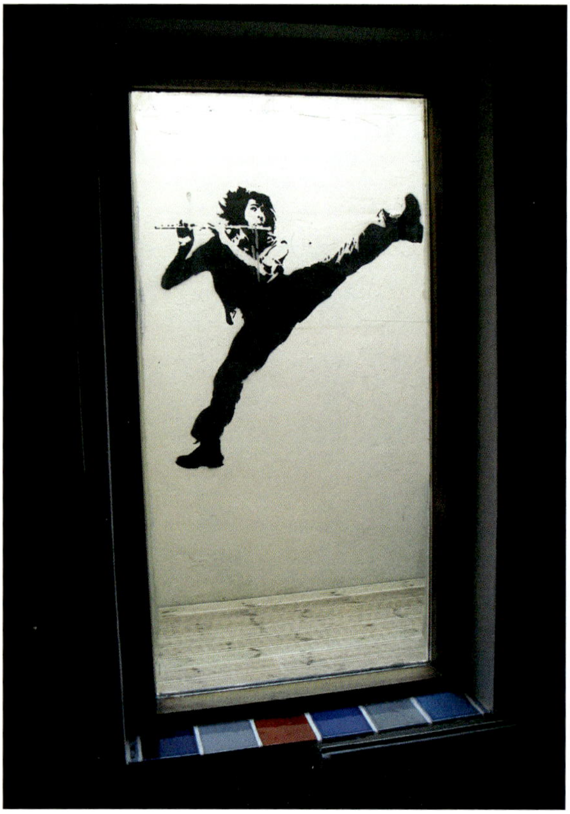

Jef Aerosol's Flautist, 2007

'Bob Osborne is a man of good taste! That's what struck me when we first met: a long-haired bloke wearing a leather waistcoat that welcomes you with a glass of good wine and listens to Pentangle, the Blues and Tom Waits while spray painting collages of Bob Dylan, John Lennon or Mick Jagger. A glimpse at his bookshelves and at the walls of his studio was enough to understand that we belong to the same cultural family and generation. In our veins runs a mixed blood, as red as the blues, as hot as rock'n'roll, as bitter as punk. Bob can do everything, he can switch from poetry to collage, from street art to abstract painting, he's a living "cut up" in perfect beat fashion and every new step he takes has surrealistic flavour and psychedelic fragrance. I'll never forget our painting sessions in the most derelict areas of Chiswick, on a cool moonless night'

– Jef Aerosol.

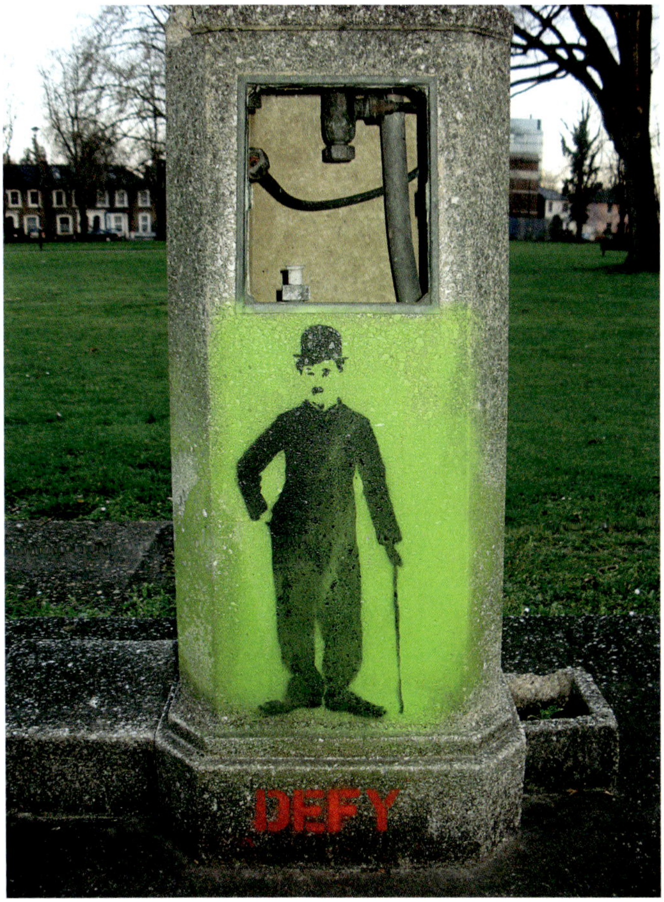

Charlie Chaplin Water Fountain, Chiswick, 2009

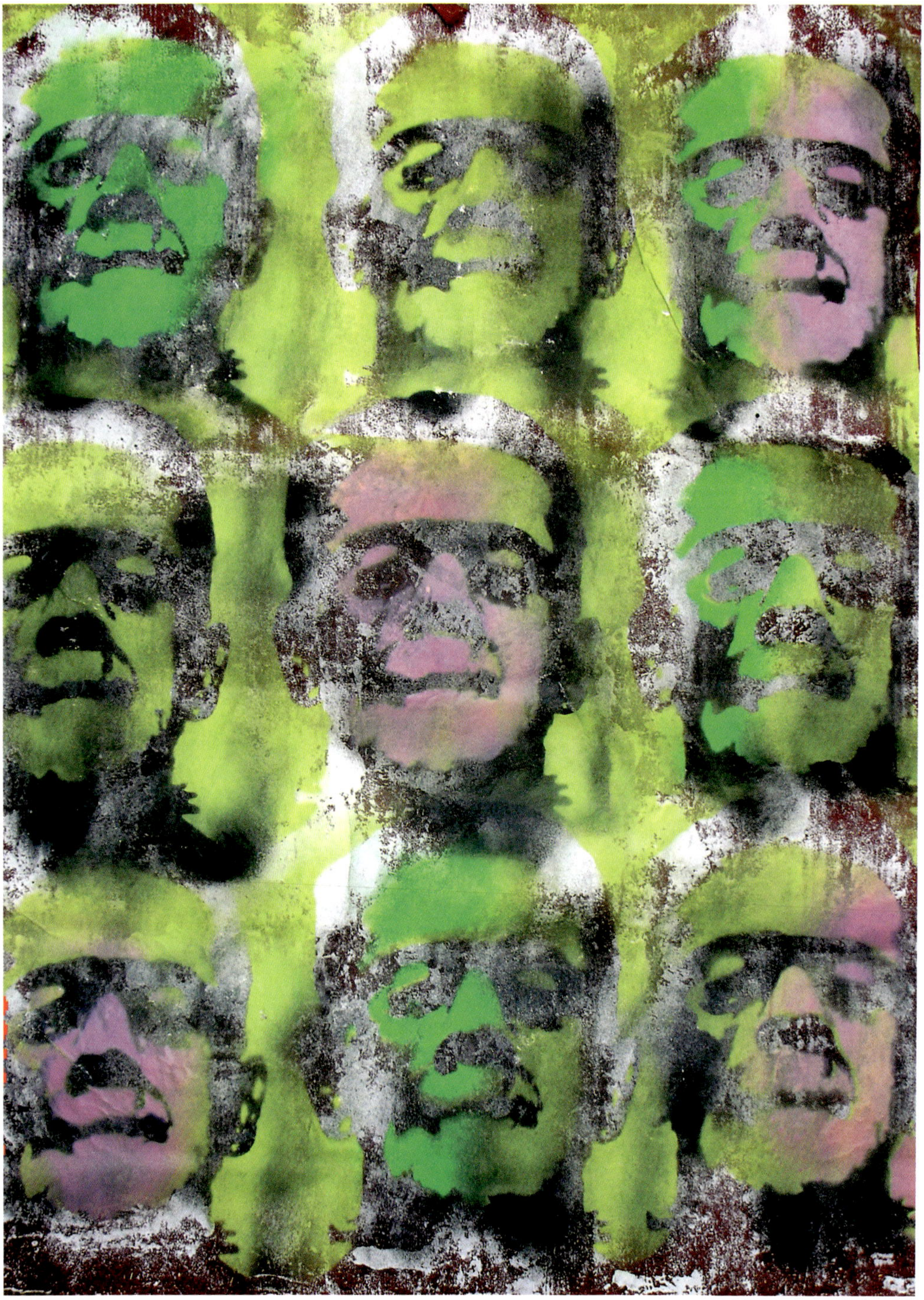

Frankenstein, 2007

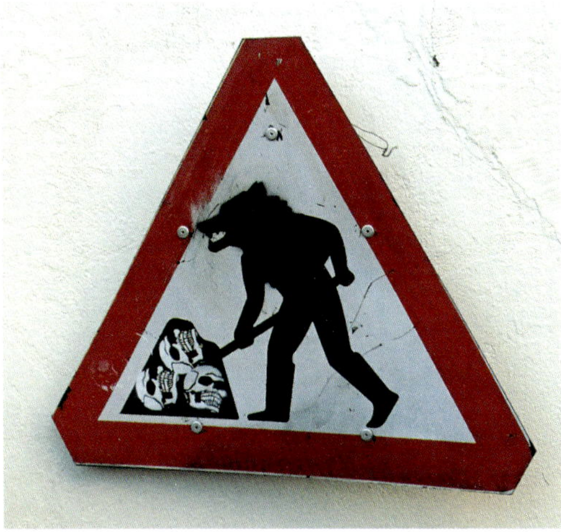

The dumped and forlorn caches of sandbags unearthed by Osborne in a suburban Ealing street in 2006 were crudely hand painted with cryptic messages and evoke fading collective memories of the London Blitz. These sacks have an arty resonance reminiscent of Barry Flanagan's rope and sacking installations. The stencilled lettering is again 'doctored' or forged' to imply both humour and menace. The use of statements from philosophical tracts as titles, such as Sartre's ***On Being and Nothingness*** and Stalin's sinister military ***Five Year Plan,*** add a satirical and mischievous dimension to the mundane subject matter and play with juxtapositions of the profound and banal. Referring to the sandbags as 'left' rather than 'found' objects, Osborne rescues them from inevitable decay and worthlessness by returning them to the street after giving them the newly immortal identity of a photographic record, which then becomes both momento and surviving artwork. In this respect he followed Andy Goldsworthy's photographic retrieval of ephemeral nature sculptures. The wartime association of sandbags appealed to Osborne's interest in the Mass Observation movement, public announcements and outbreaks of psychological hysteria and paranoia.

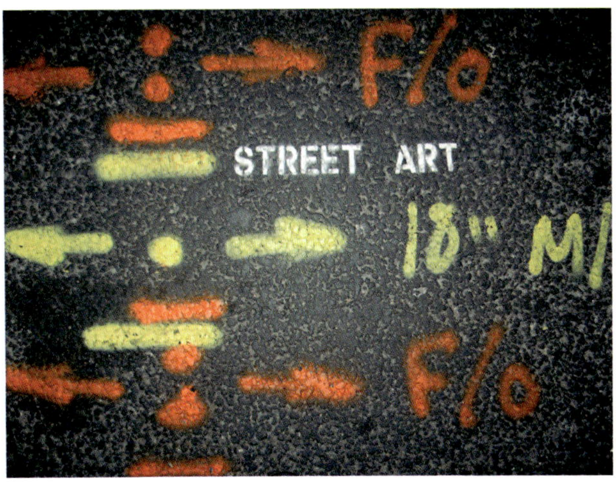

Top: Werewolf at Work, 2007
Bottom: Road markings, 2007

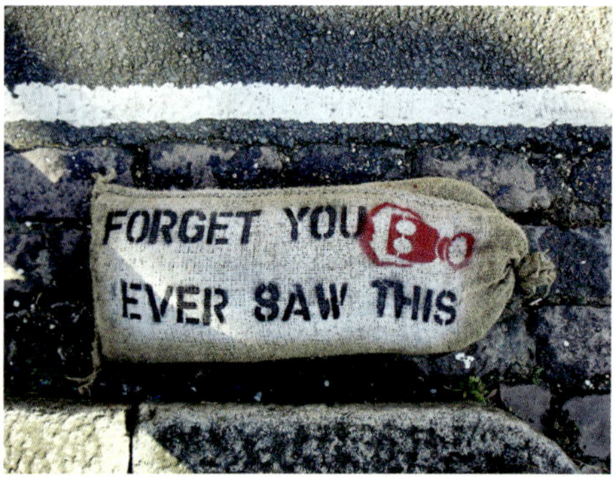

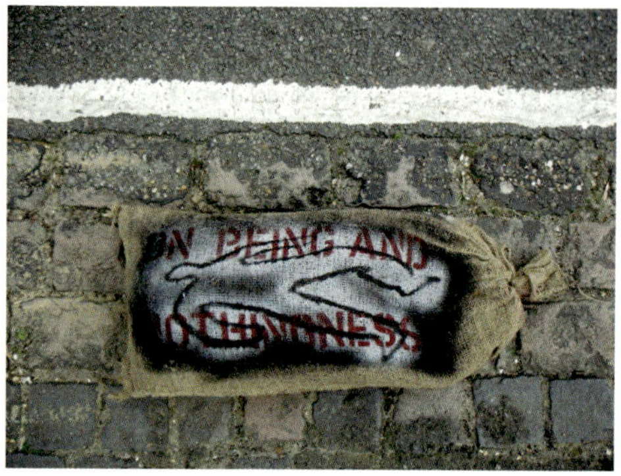

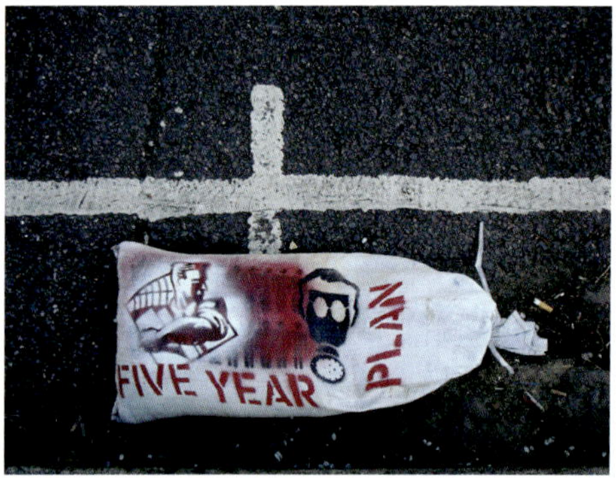

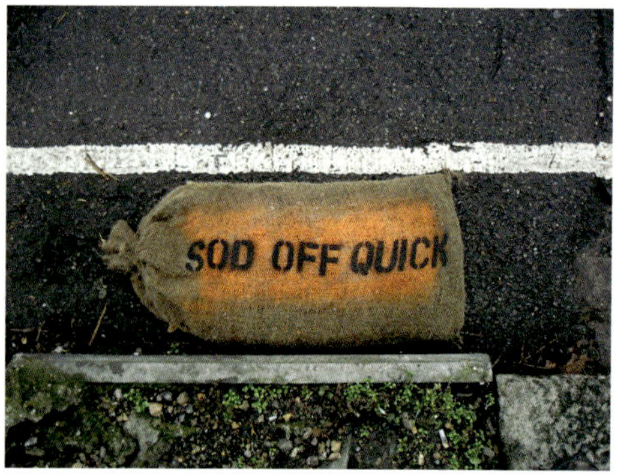

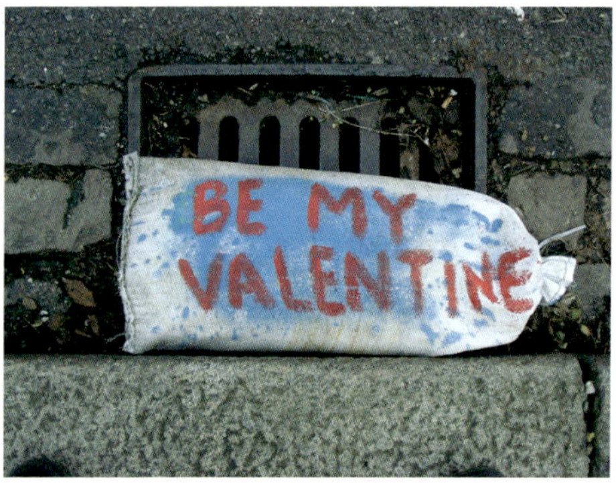

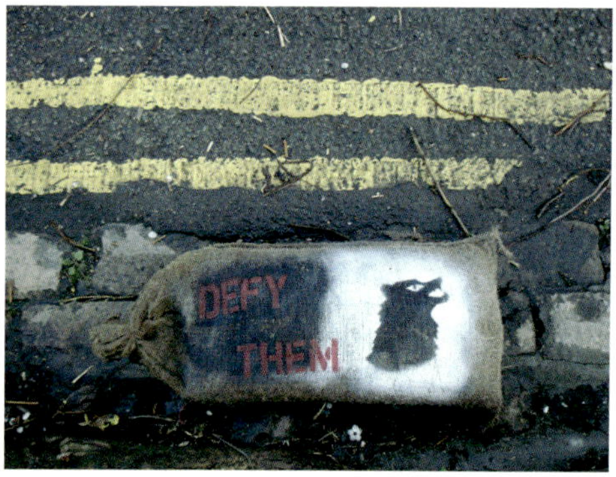

Sacks 1 - 6, 2007

BROKEN TOYS

By adapting material from junk shops, among which are children's toys, Osborne has struck up a synthetic interplay of a pictorial and sculptural kind. The two and three dimensional vie for our attention so that the art work once again accommodates surrealistic symbolism and intrinsic abstract qualities. The recurring literary and visual interface endows the work with a vital tension, or paradox, calling into question the functional role of the plastic arts at large within the broader cultural context. Old questions concerning aesthetic autonomy (art for art's sake) or social utility and function (art for society's sake) are thereby touched on.

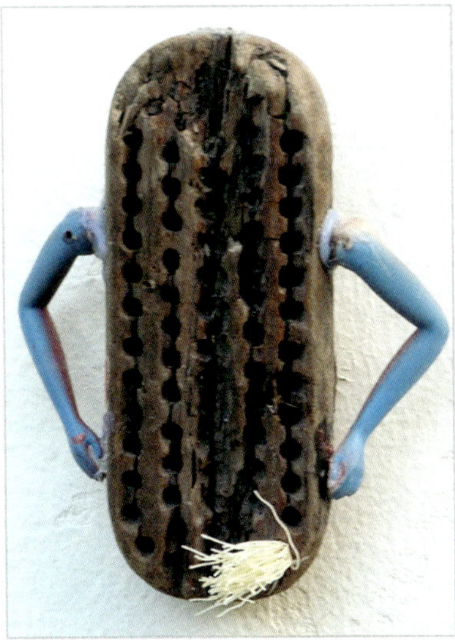

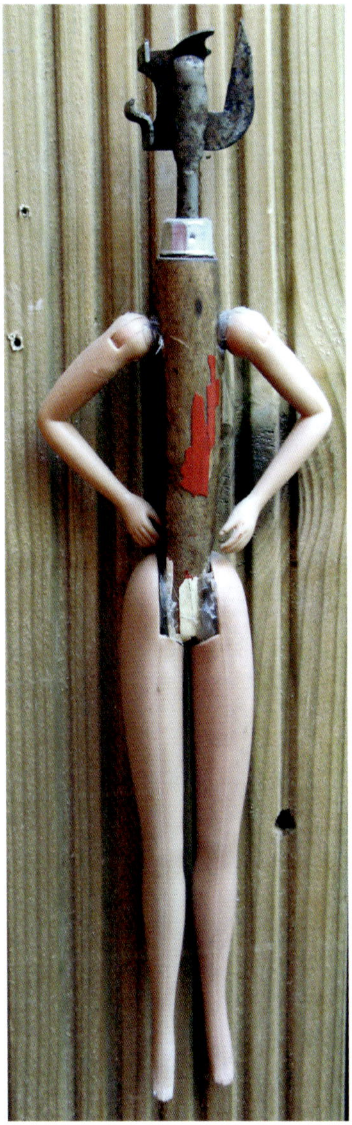

Left: Brush with the Law, 2009
Right: Tin Opener, 2009

The subject of the doll, used by the celebrated surrealist artist Hans Bellmer, has fascinated Osborne and influenced important modern British sculptors, such as Bernard Meadows, Reg Butler and Ralph Brown, as well as more recently the limp figures of YBA artist Sarah Lucas. The American conceptual photographer Cindy Sherman has also used doll imagery. For Osborne, the use of the doll is perhaps less overtly sculptural, than a discreet extension into the third dimension of the satirical photomontage and *art brut* textural collage that had hitherto exercised his imagination. The slightly disturbing, even macabre, associations of a child's plaything subjected to distortion, or damage, adds a further conceptual twist, touching on the raw nerve of black humour and surreal psychological dysfunction.

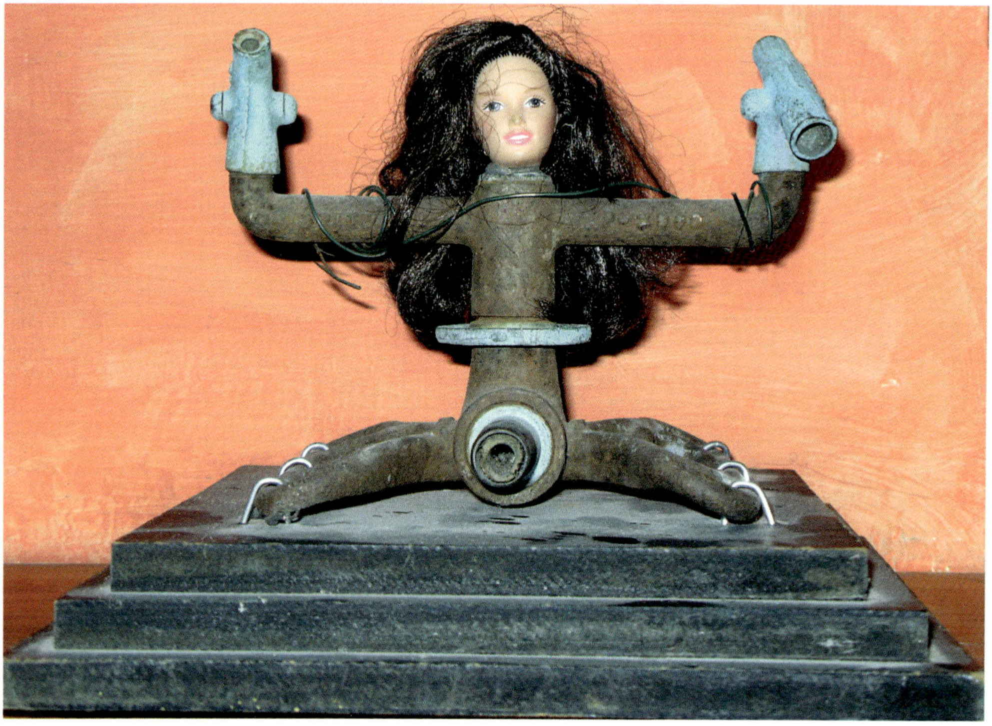

Garden Sprinkler, 2009

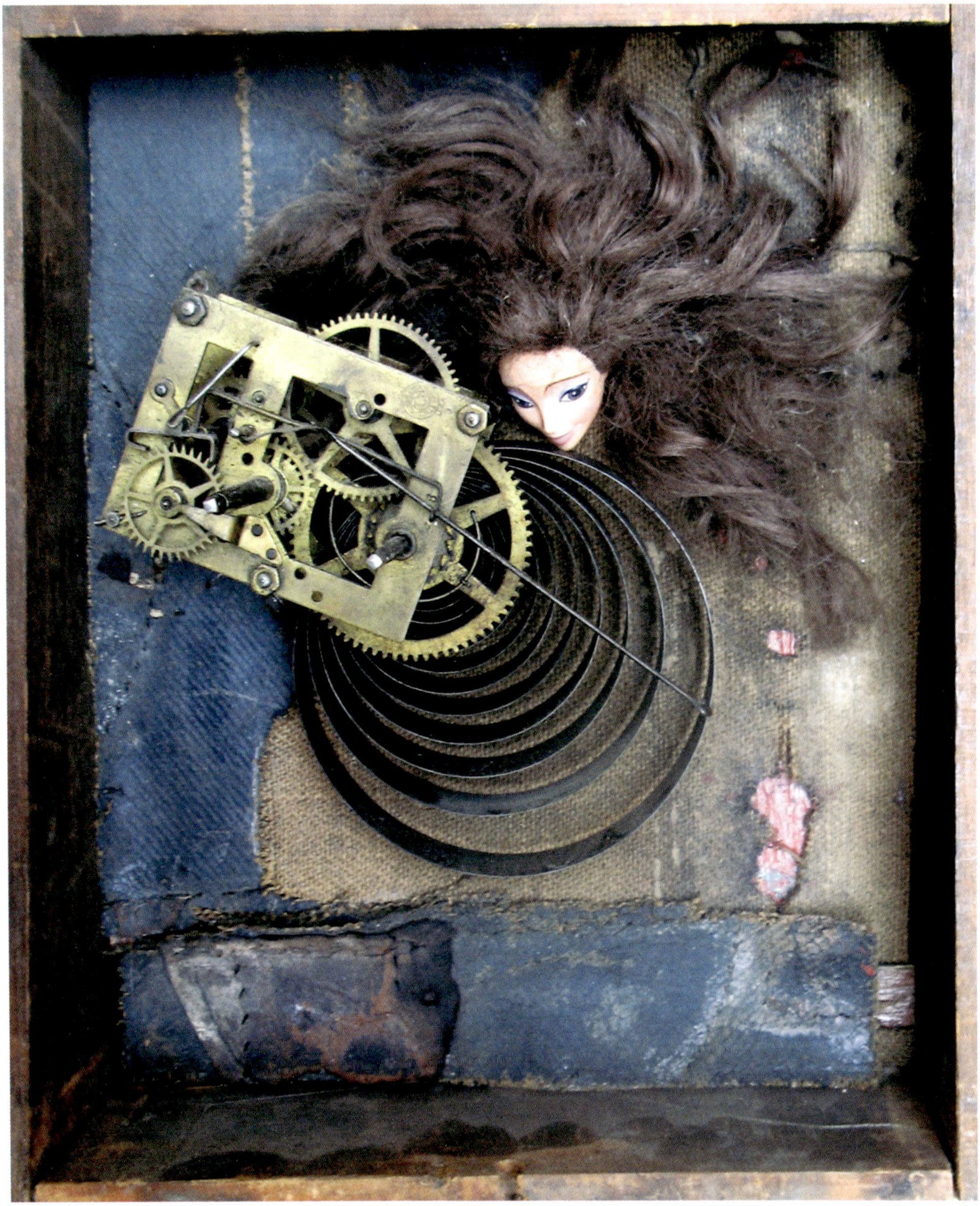

Caught in the Machine, 2006

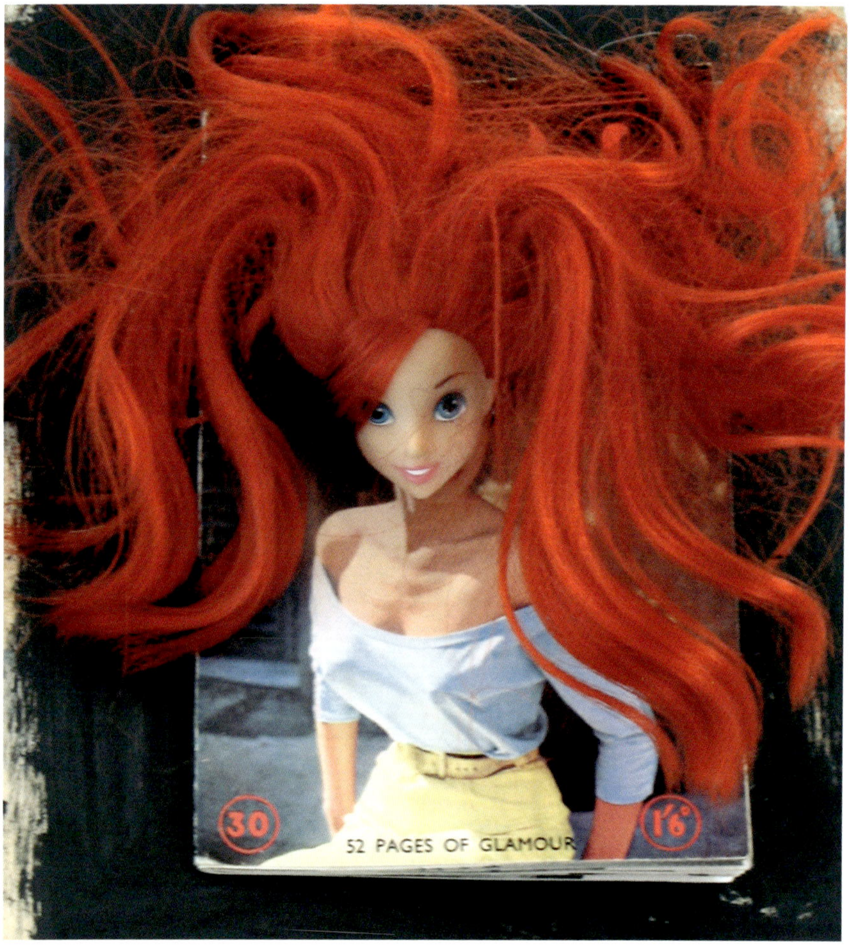

52 Pages of Glamour, 2009

From the earlier phases of Surrealist and Italian metaphysical painting de Chirico used mannequins as subject-matter. Bellmer's use of dolls in his sculptures was influenced by Freud's theory of 'The Uncanny' *(Das Unheimliche 1919)* which prefigured Jung's concept of Synchronicity. Two artists from the contemporary London art scene, Richard Niman and the 'pop' sculptor Clive Barker have made witty transformations of commonplace objects that appeal to Osborne, who has himself worked with defunct machinery and broken kitchen implements. Niman's sculptures using buckets and mannequin limbs have a satirical humour that challenges norms of taste and conventional perception.

'I frequently work with dolls, mannequins, shop window installations and other ready mades. I regard such subjects in their original state as aesthetically dead. I have always tried to administer some form of surprise to shock the viewer, but in order to do this I have to bring the dolls to life, This I do by transforming them-by decontextualising, stripping them of certain things and bringing in other parts or objects that don't normally fit with them. I believe my function is to make the incredible believable.'

– Richard Niman:
Voodoo Hoochie Coochie and the Creative Spirit (2009)

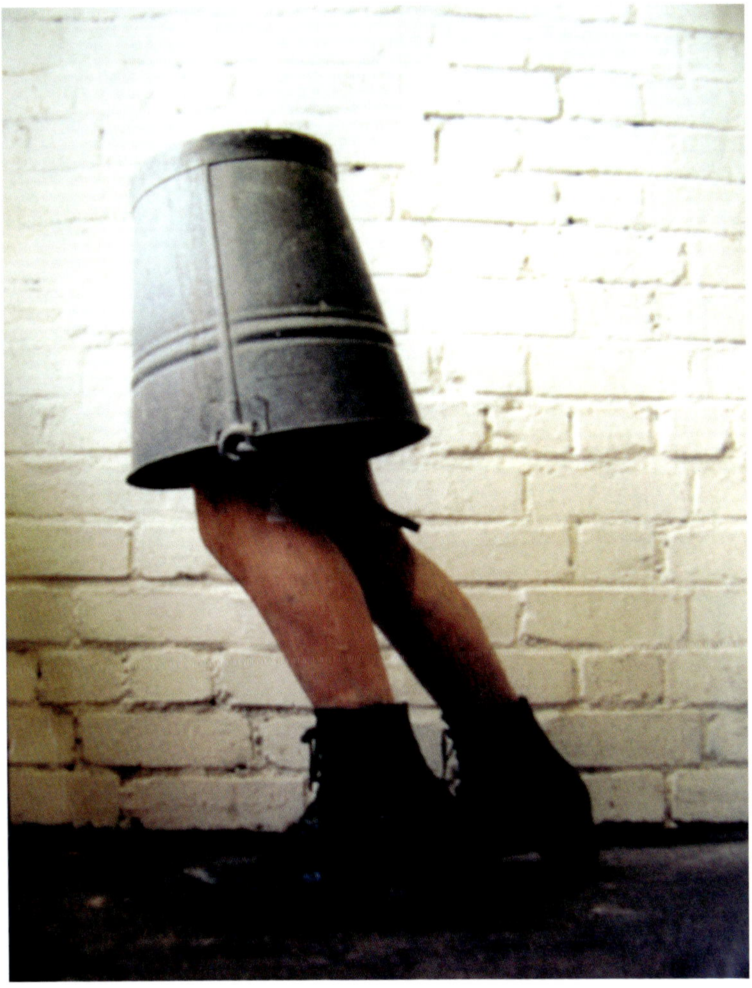

Richard Niman's Head in the Clouds, 2000

photograph: Anna Niman

A visit in 2004 to see Tony Penrose at Farley Farm in Sussex–one time home of surrealist Roland Penrose and his American wife, the photographer Lee Miller – impressed on Osborne the manner in which the satirical and outlandish extremes of surrealism were effortlessly accommodated in everyday life. In particular, Osborne was taken with the remnants of Picasso's 1950 visit, notably a spontaneously made ceramic tile now cemented as a key decorative feature in the kitchen wall.

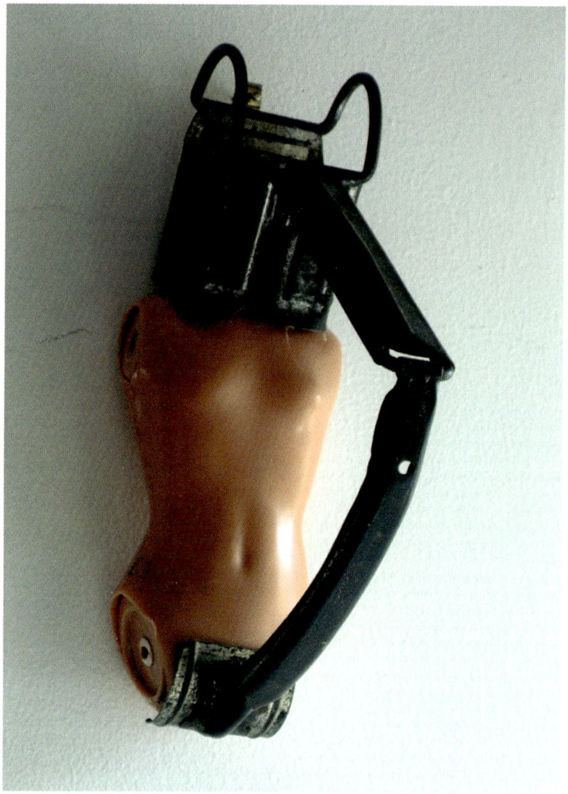

Moulis Grater, 2009

'Intellectual uncertainty; so that the uncanny would always, as it were, be something one does not know one's way about in. The better orientated in his environment a person is the less ready will he get the impression of something uncanny in regard to the objects and events in it.'

– Ernst Jentsch: *On the Psychology of the Uncanny* (1906).

Another near neighbour from "arty" Chiswick, the well-known polymath Barry Martin, once played chess with Marcel Duchamp's wife 'Teeny' on Duchamp's own designed chess board and set. Osborne also plays chess and, like Martin, enjoys sports and games - whether of a physical or intellectual kind - and both were active members of the Hogarth Health Club, which was a favourite watering hole for 'resting' actors and dancers during the 1980's. The ancient toy-like symbols of chess and the situational randomness of a contest makes the chess board akin to a surrealist playground, a scenario characterised in the mysterious early tableaux of sculptors William Turnbull and Eduardo Paolozzi.

In specific terms Osborne's plastic cowboys, soldiers and metal cars take on the semblance of individual chess pieces which can be arbitrarily moved by the whim of the artist or 'player'. Another surrealist influence in Chiswick was the seasoned and celebrated artist Julian Trevelyan, also a chess player, whose riverside studio at Durham Wharf was shared with the painter Mary Fedden and was often visited by Osborne. Trevelyan's aquatint *Washington*, from Osborne's own collection, demonstrates the artist's early surrealist and *faux naïf* qualities, the cars and figural effigies creating flat, random patterns akin to Osborne's toy car or soldier reliefs.

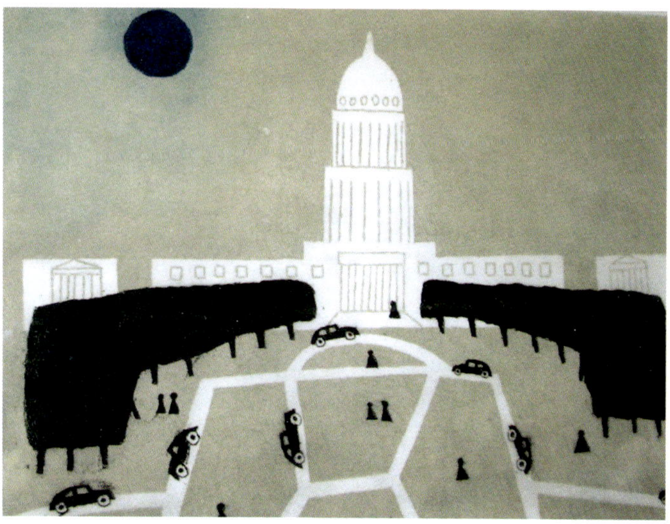

Julian Trevelyan's Washington

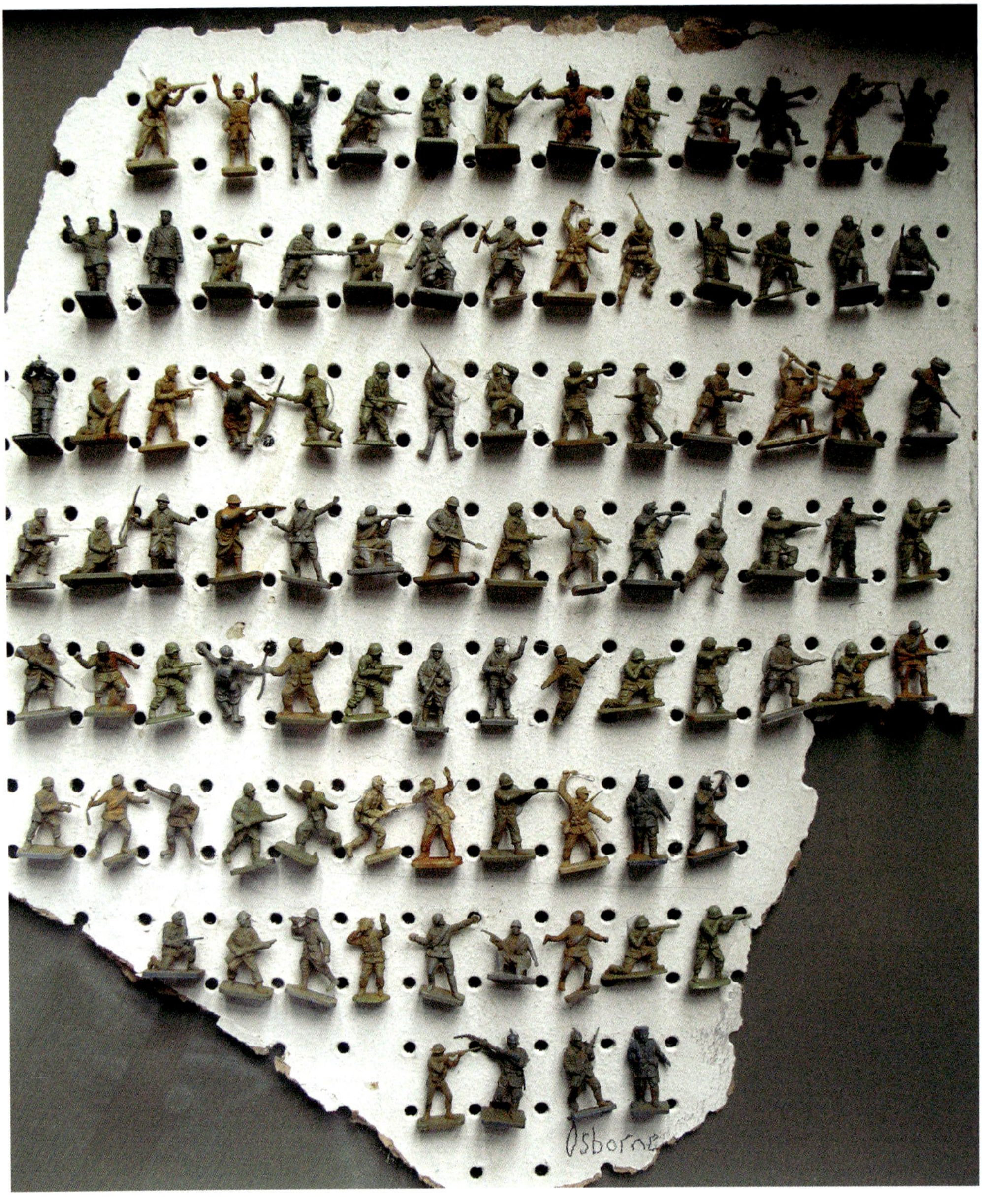

Soldiers, 2009

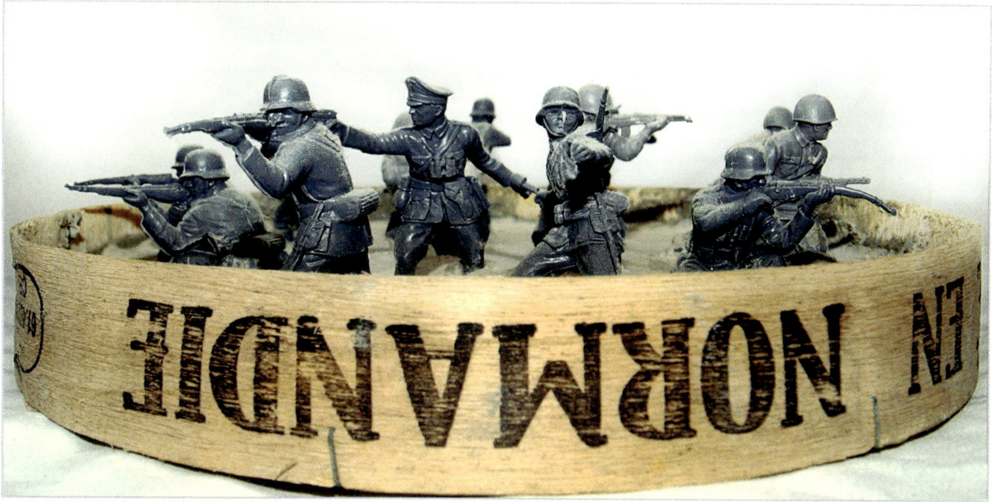

Battle of the Brie, 2010

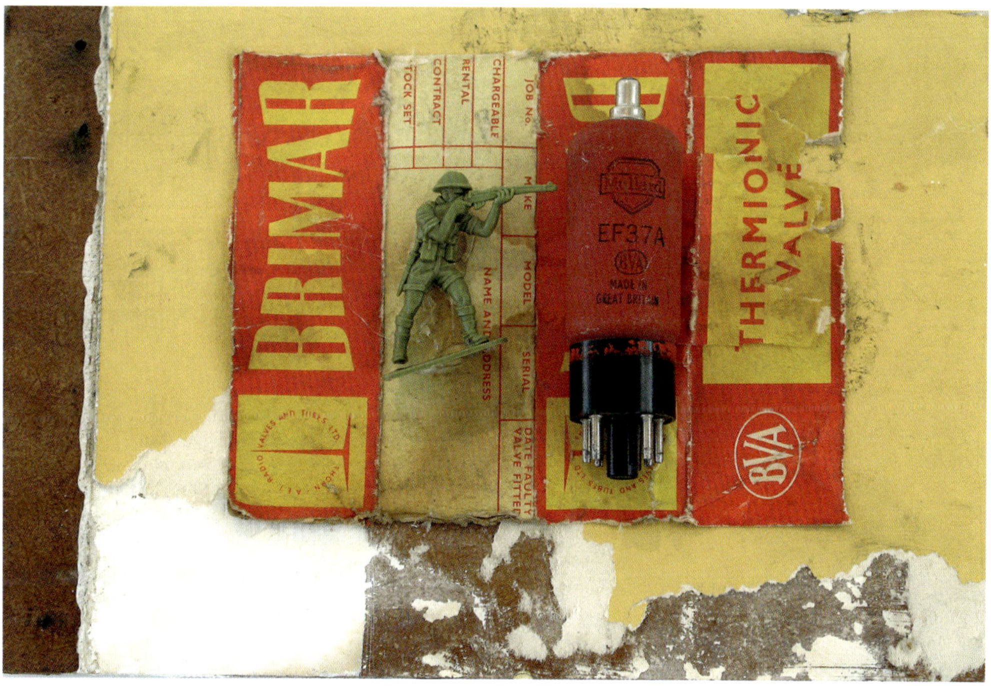

For You the War is Over, 2009

A further development sees the replication into bronze of these plastic cowboys and metal toy cars. The objects become iconic and durable bronze 'sculptures', with or without patination and colouring. Recalling Cézar, Arman or early Jasper Johns-whose bronze-cast painted Savarin coffee tins or collected paintbrush cans call into question the nature of appearance and the borderline between reality and subterfuge- or between the art and functional object.

Osborne's gun-wielding cowboys or stacked dinky car 'totems' take on the semblance of collectable and durable 'high art' sculptural talismans.

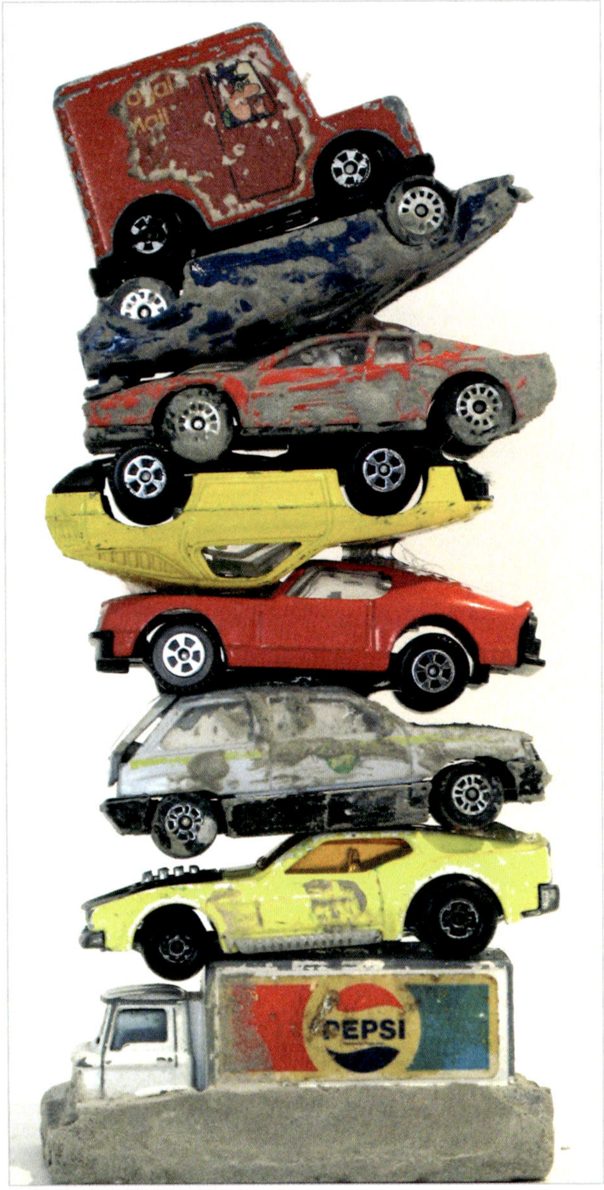

Cars, 2009

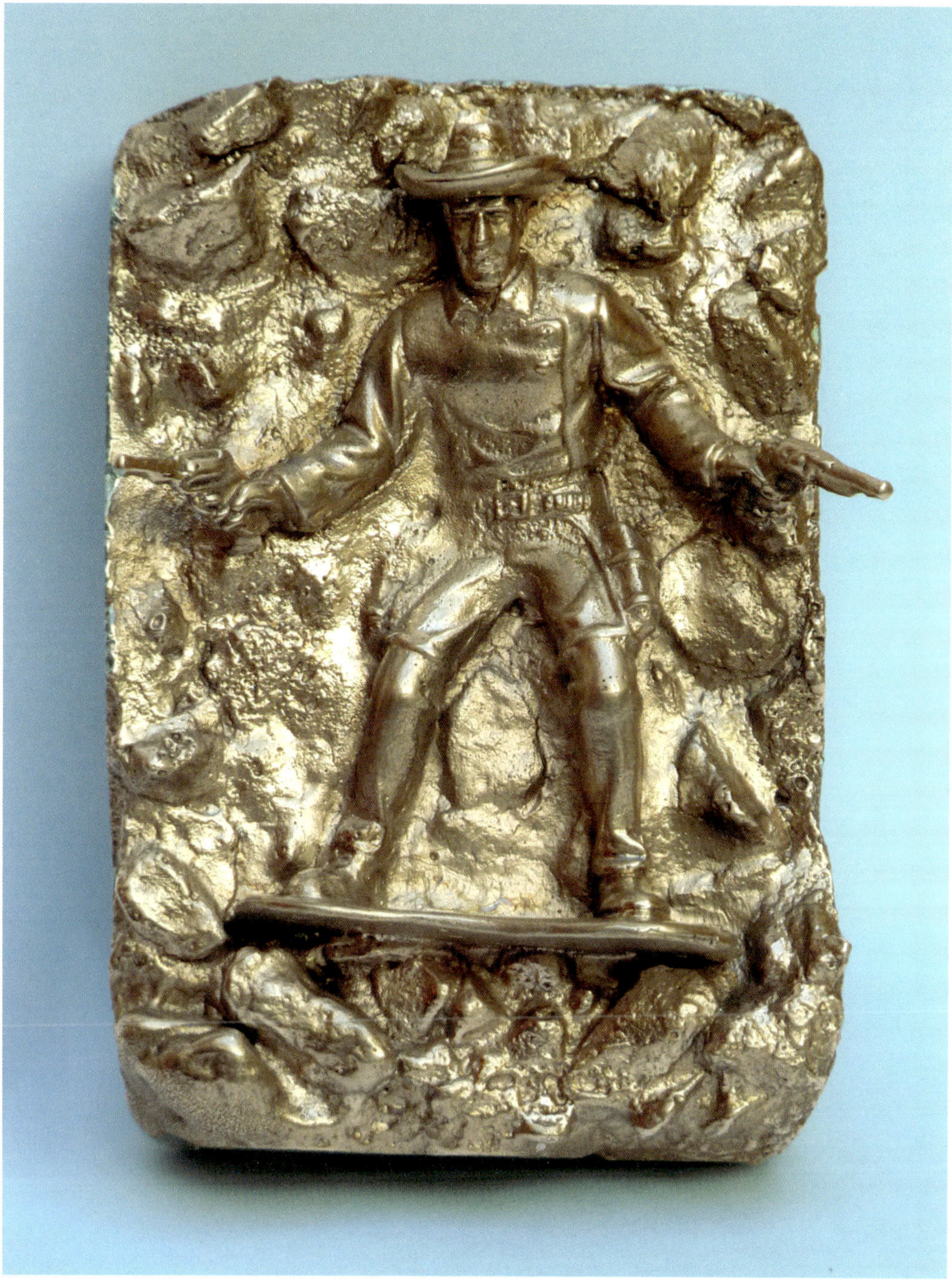

True Grit, 2012 : Polished bronze. Edition of 6

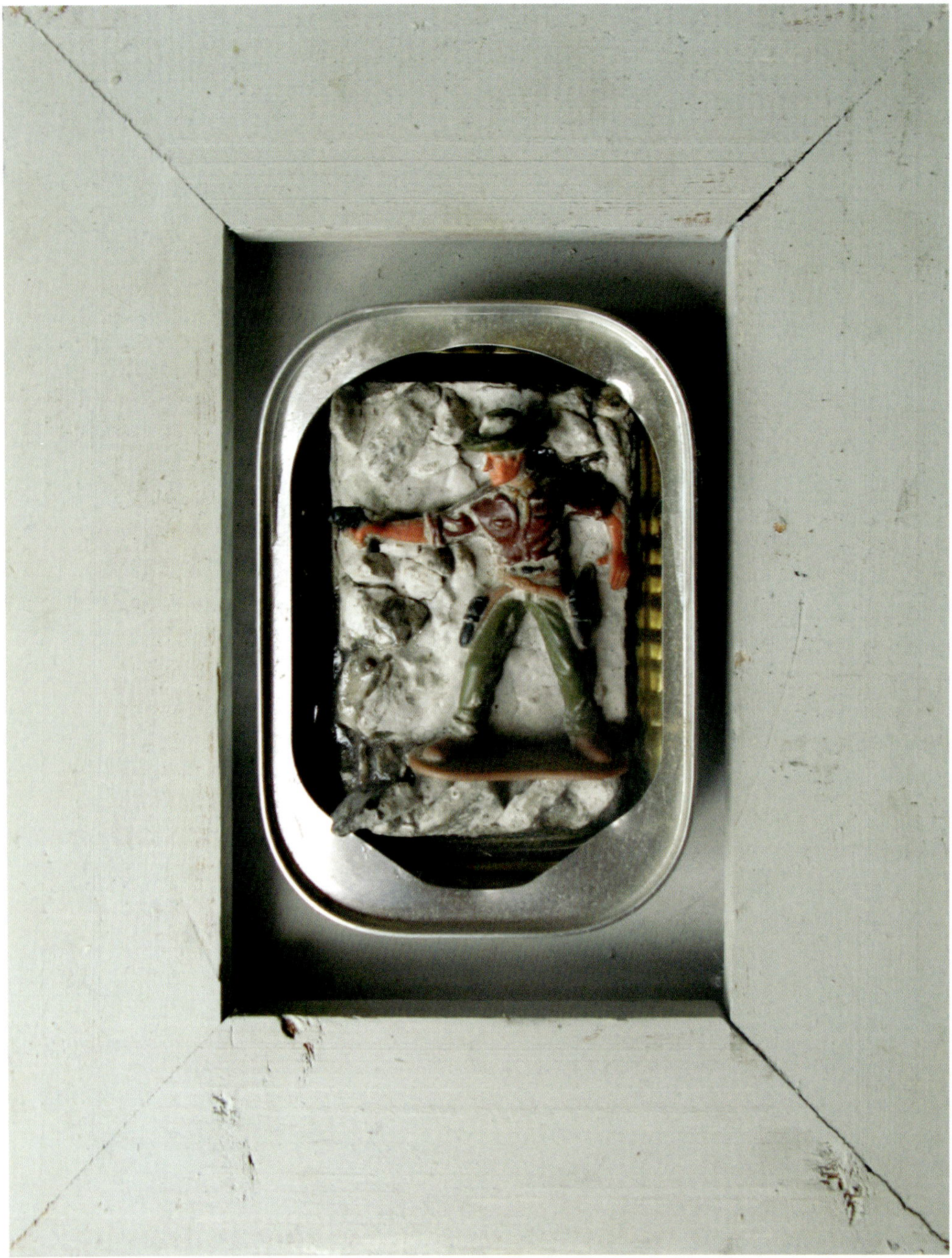

You Will Never Take Me Alive, 2010

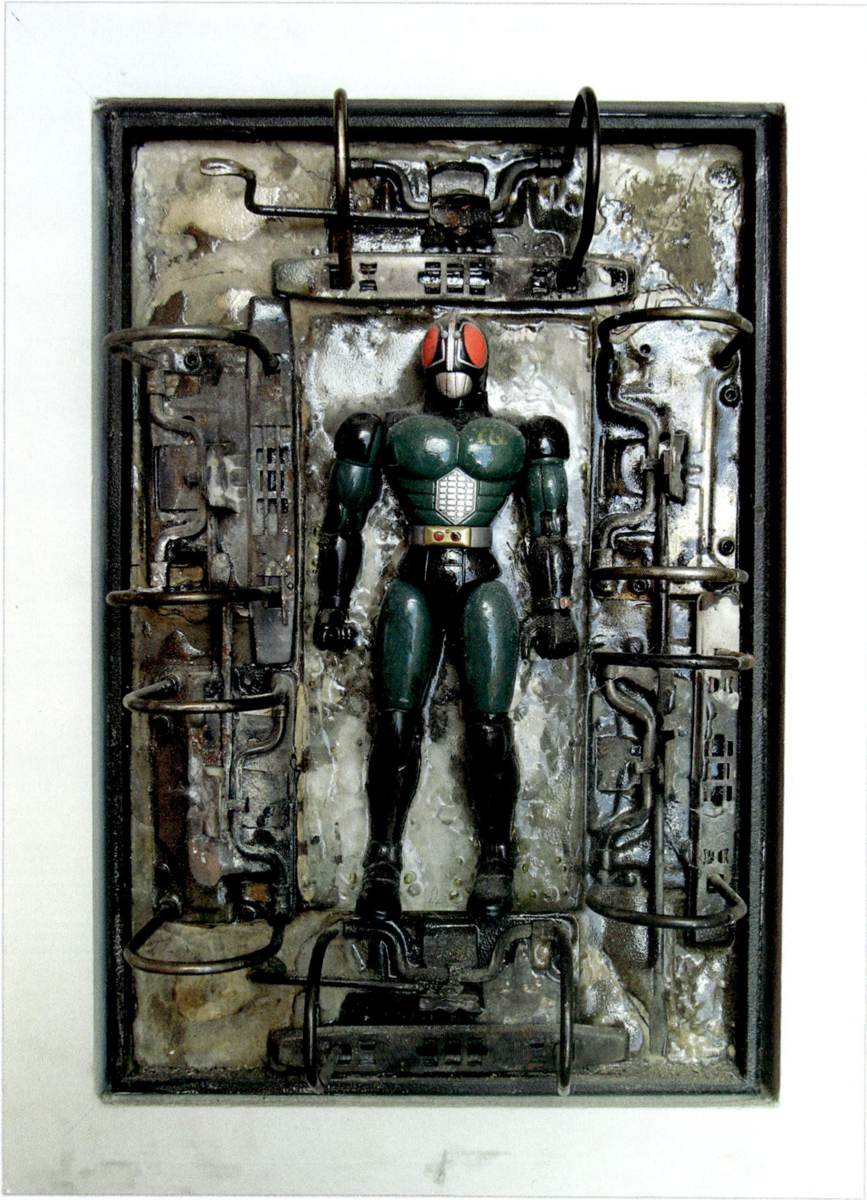

Time Traveller, 2010

'The fact is, the Time Traveller was one of those men who are too clever to be believed: you never felt that you saw all round him; you always suspected some subtle reserve, some ingenuity in ambush, behind his lucid frankness.'

– H.G. Wells: *The Time Machine* (1895).

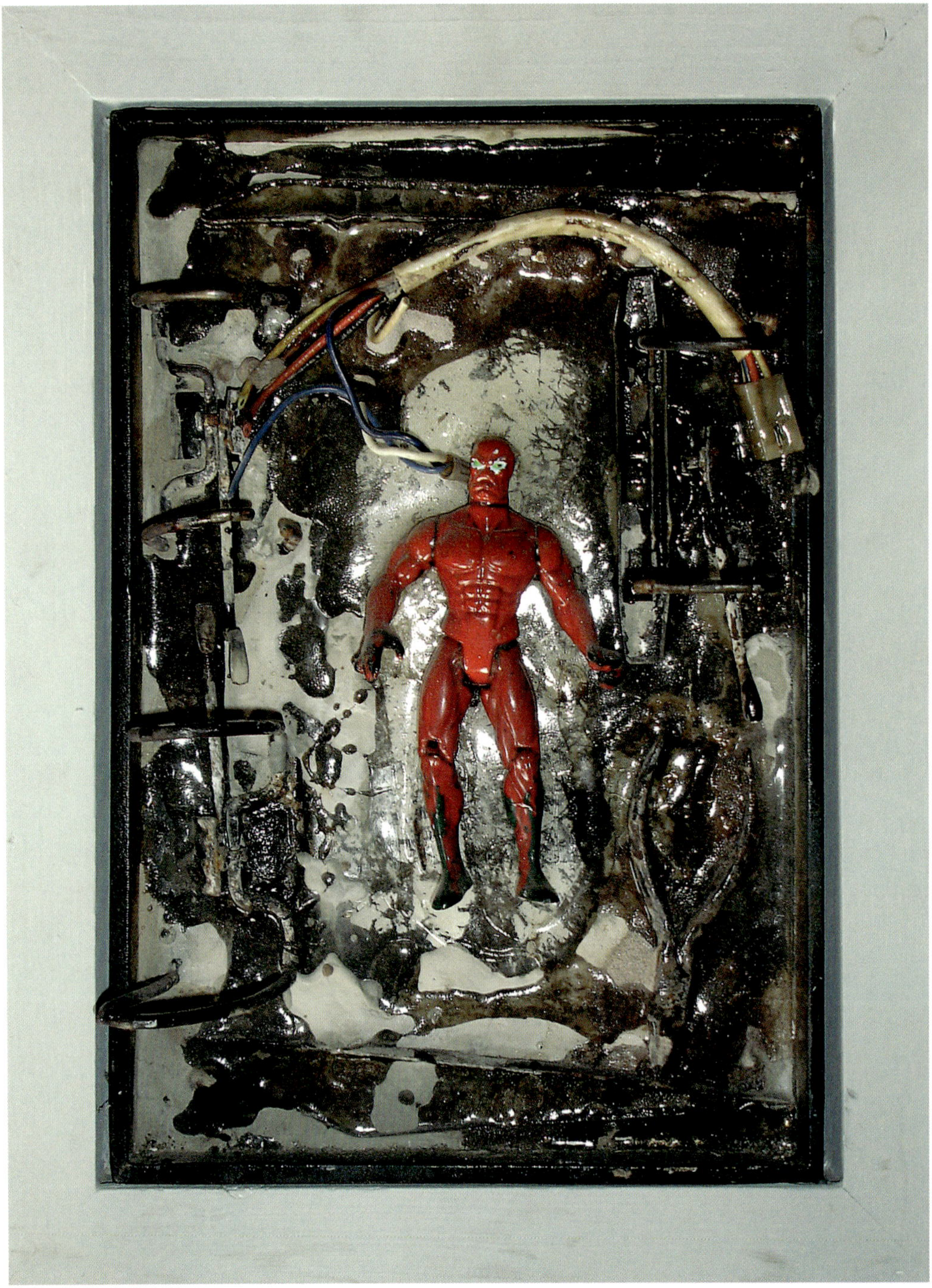

Time Machine, 2010

SARDINE CAN CONSTRUCTIONS

Falling between many art historical stools, Osborne's wall bound objects constructed from standardised sardine cans placed in rows à la Warhol break out of modular uniformity through the rich diversity of encased members. Toy soldiers, dinky cars, erotica or post-war paraphernalia impart the iconic singularity of the ready-made within a moving narrative of enigmatic and changing boxed objects. The serial compartments become solidified perspex 'bathtubs' full of dramatic innuendo and open-ended narrative. The uniformity of assembly line industrial manufacture is constantly undermined by perplexingly varied contents, forming a Pandora's Box of shocks and surprises.

With the sardine can constructions, moreover, Osborne creates a hybrid species of humorous, satirical post-dada objects. They fall again between the sculptural and pictorial as small plastic figures or segments from Airfix model planes, tin soldiers and random toy parts - themselves low forms of sculpture- are presented in separate pictographic compartments within the overall assemblage. There is interplay here between free association and abandonment on the one hand, and a clinical and rational collected order on the other.

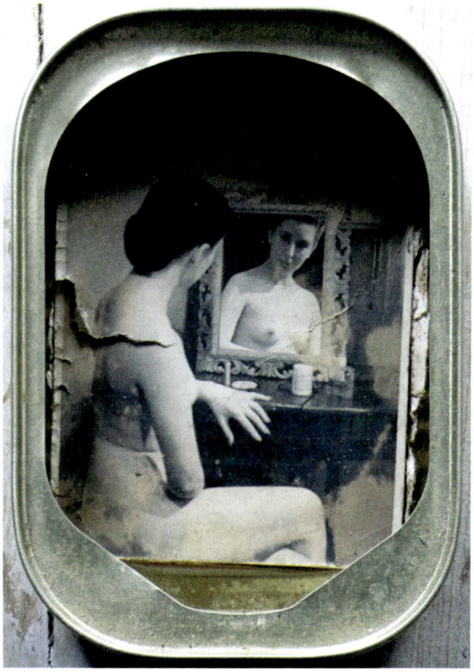

Goodbye to All That, 2010

The shining metal cans have a clean, pristine newness that emulate Pop sculptor Clive Barker's replication of 'real objects' in chrome-plated cast metal. The multi-faceted nature of these works, takes in the Duchampian tradition of the *objets trouvés* and utilises the process popularised by the French *Nouveau Realist* sculptor Arman of encasing the objects in a solidified but transparent perspex lacquer, a witty paraphrase of the rich preservative oil into which the sardines were originally 'embalmed'. Here Osborne bridges the gap between art and life through simulation and subterfuge.

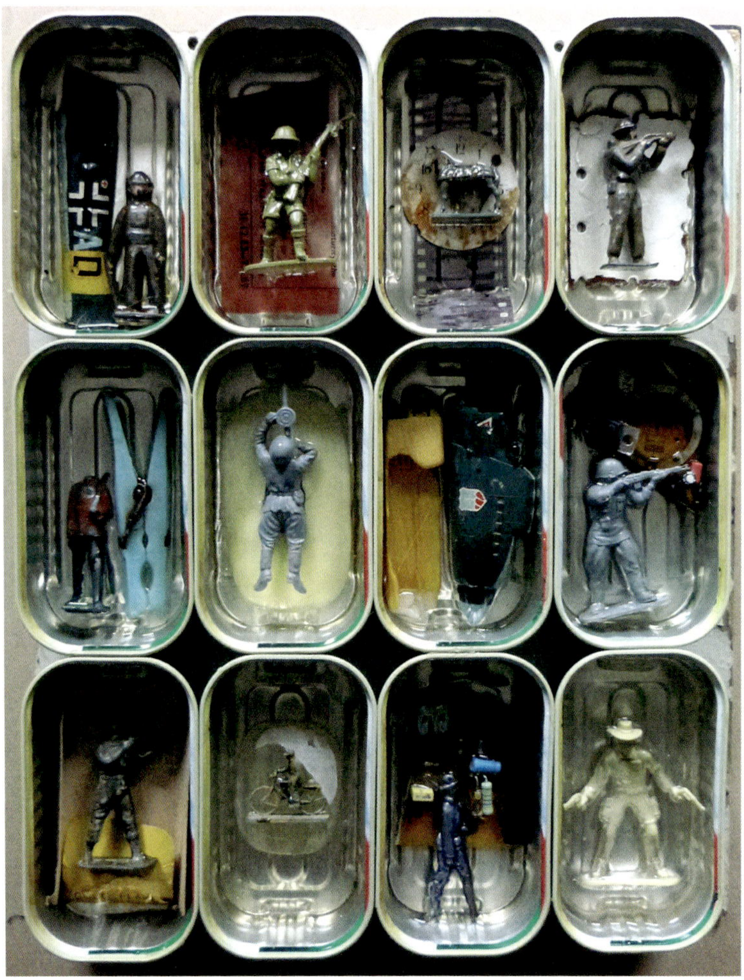

Things Fall Apart, 2010

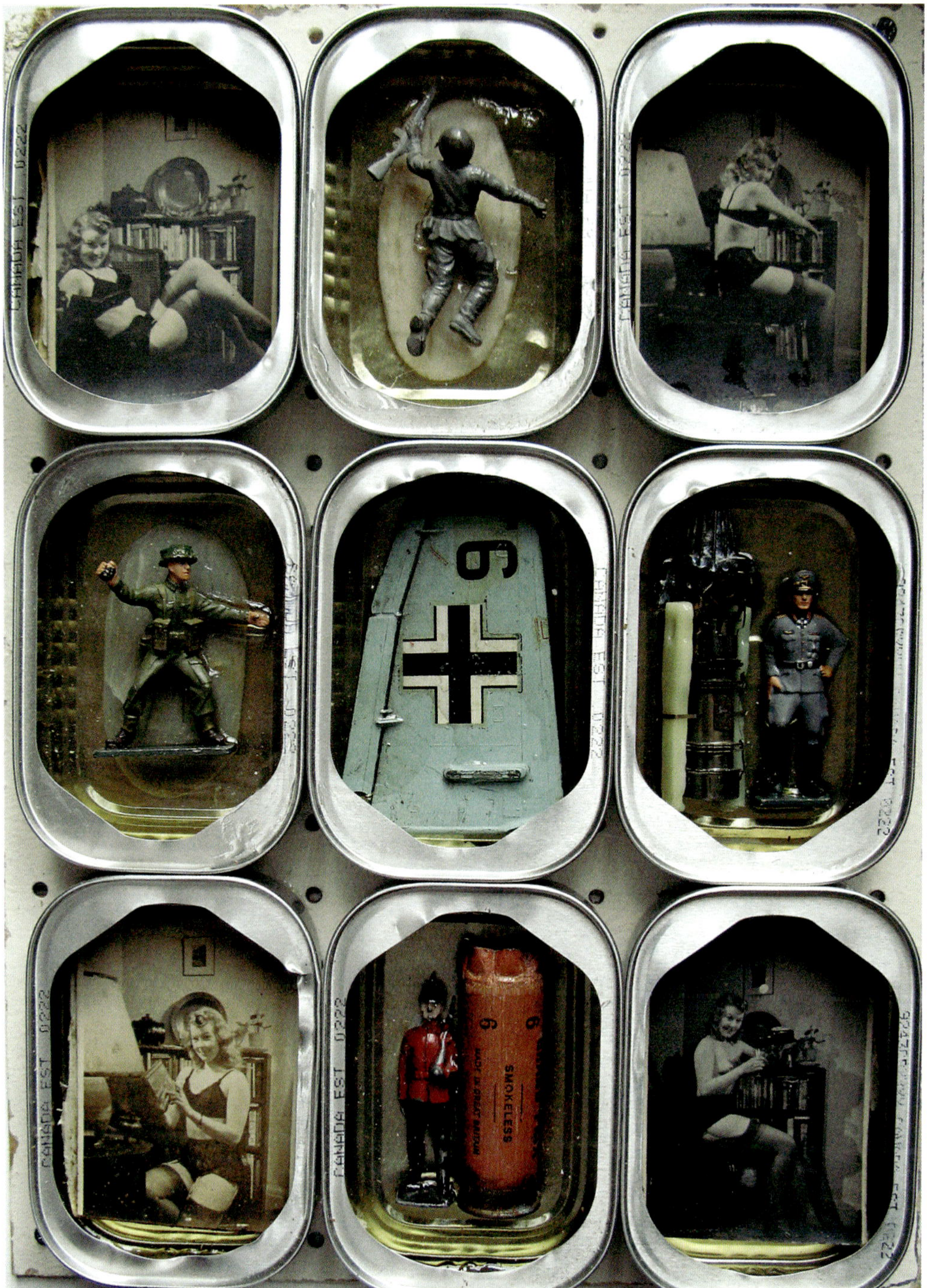

Keep the Home Fires Burning, 2010

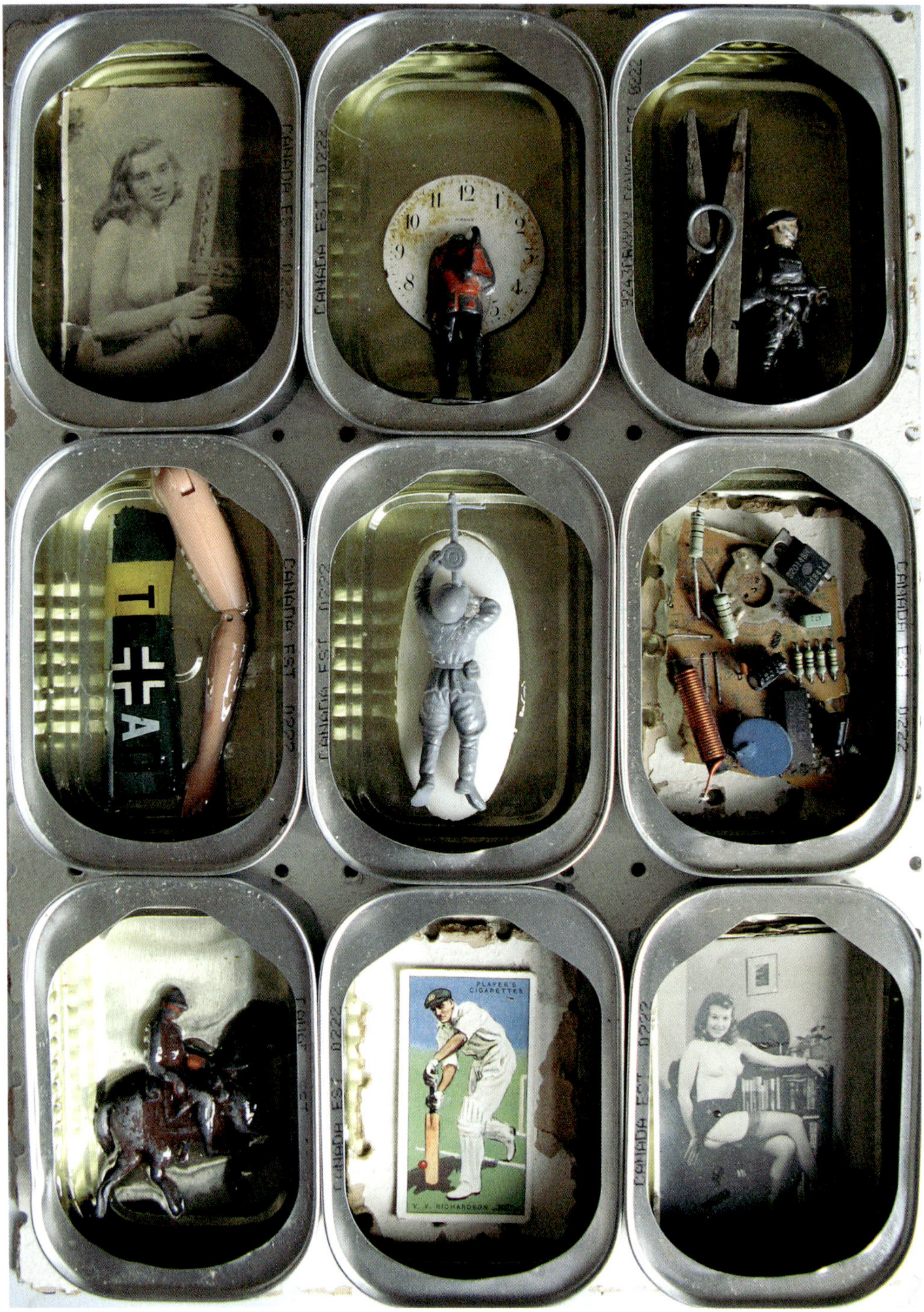

England Made Me, 2010

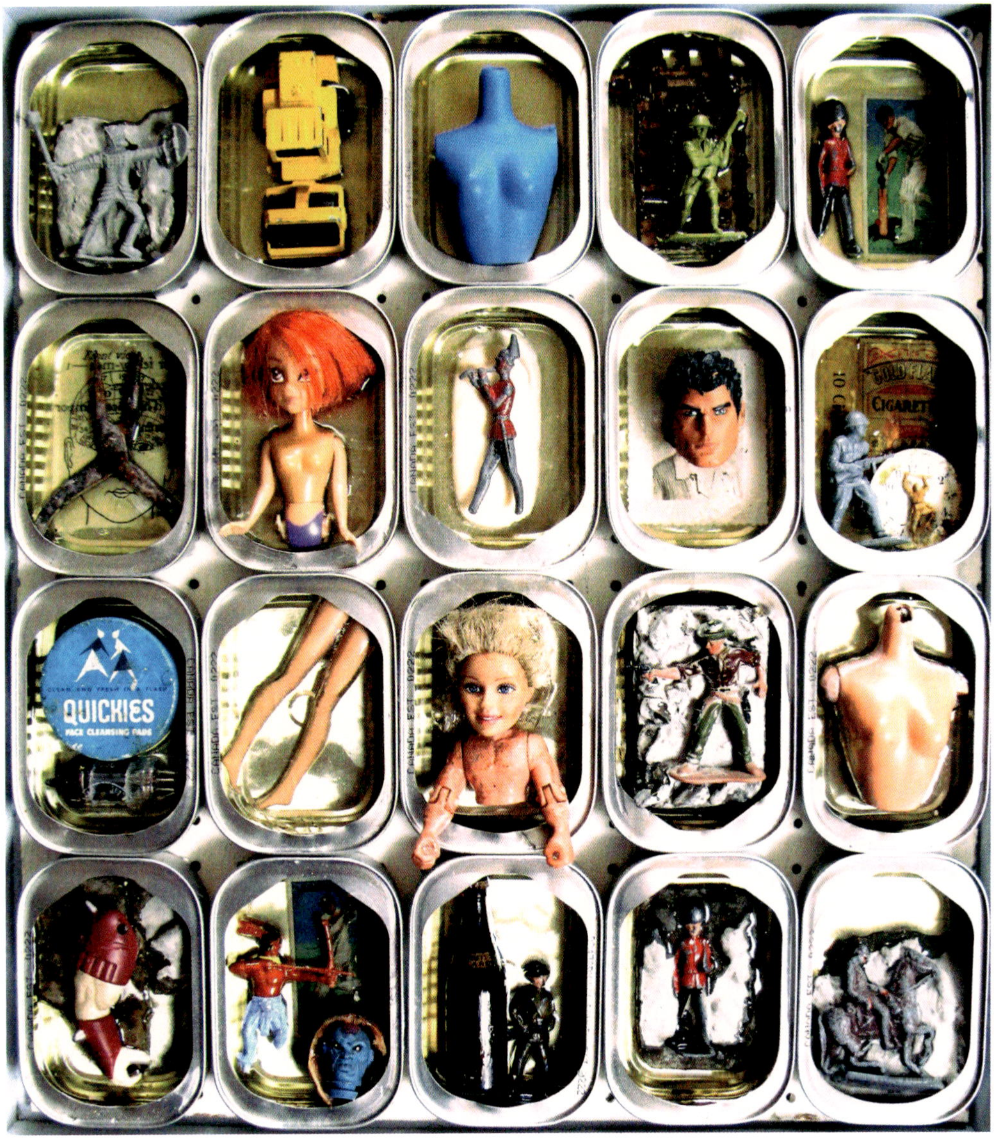

Uncanny, 2010

'He was like a man who has narrowly escaped a great danger.
Relief made him hilarious, and hilarity made him the best of company.'
– Graham Greene, *England Made Me*

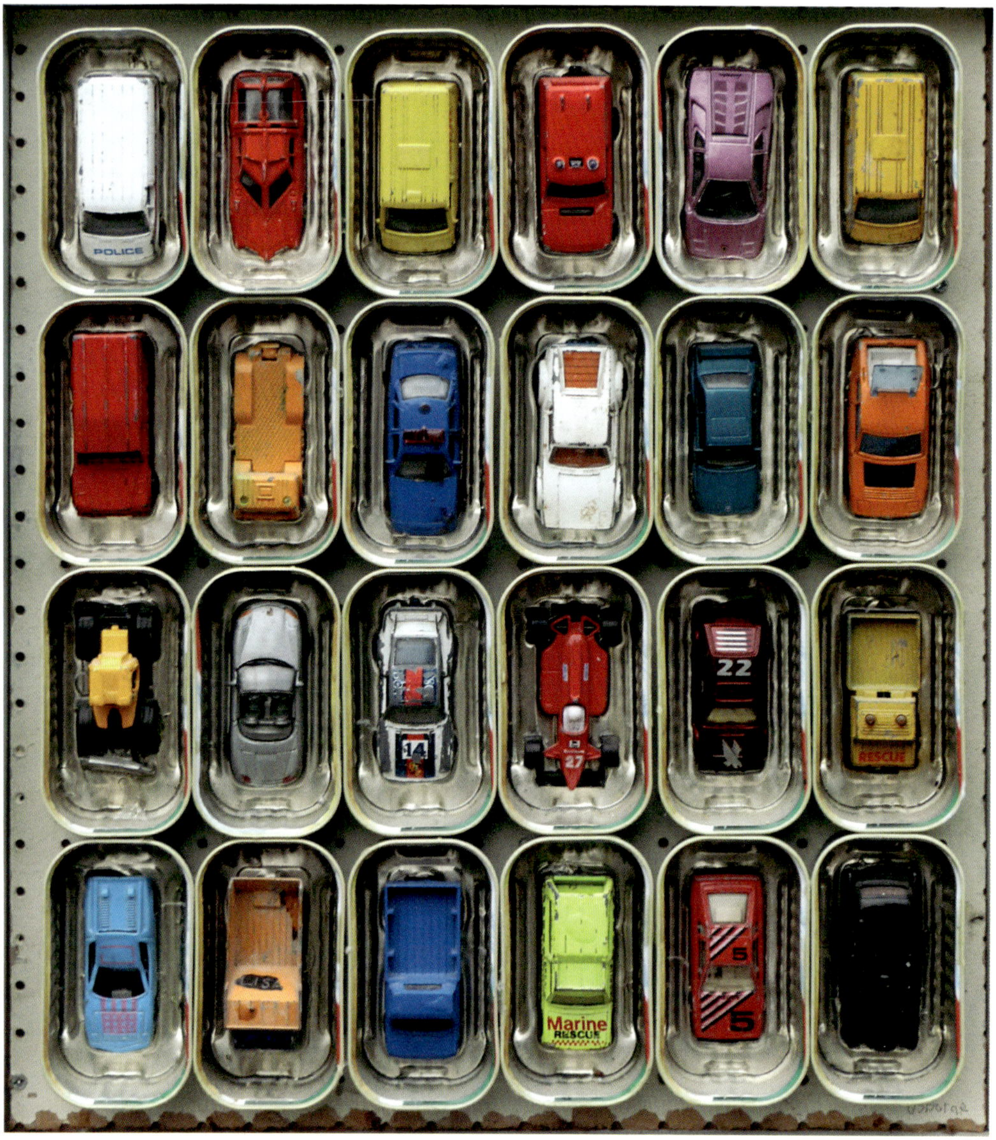

Cars, 2010

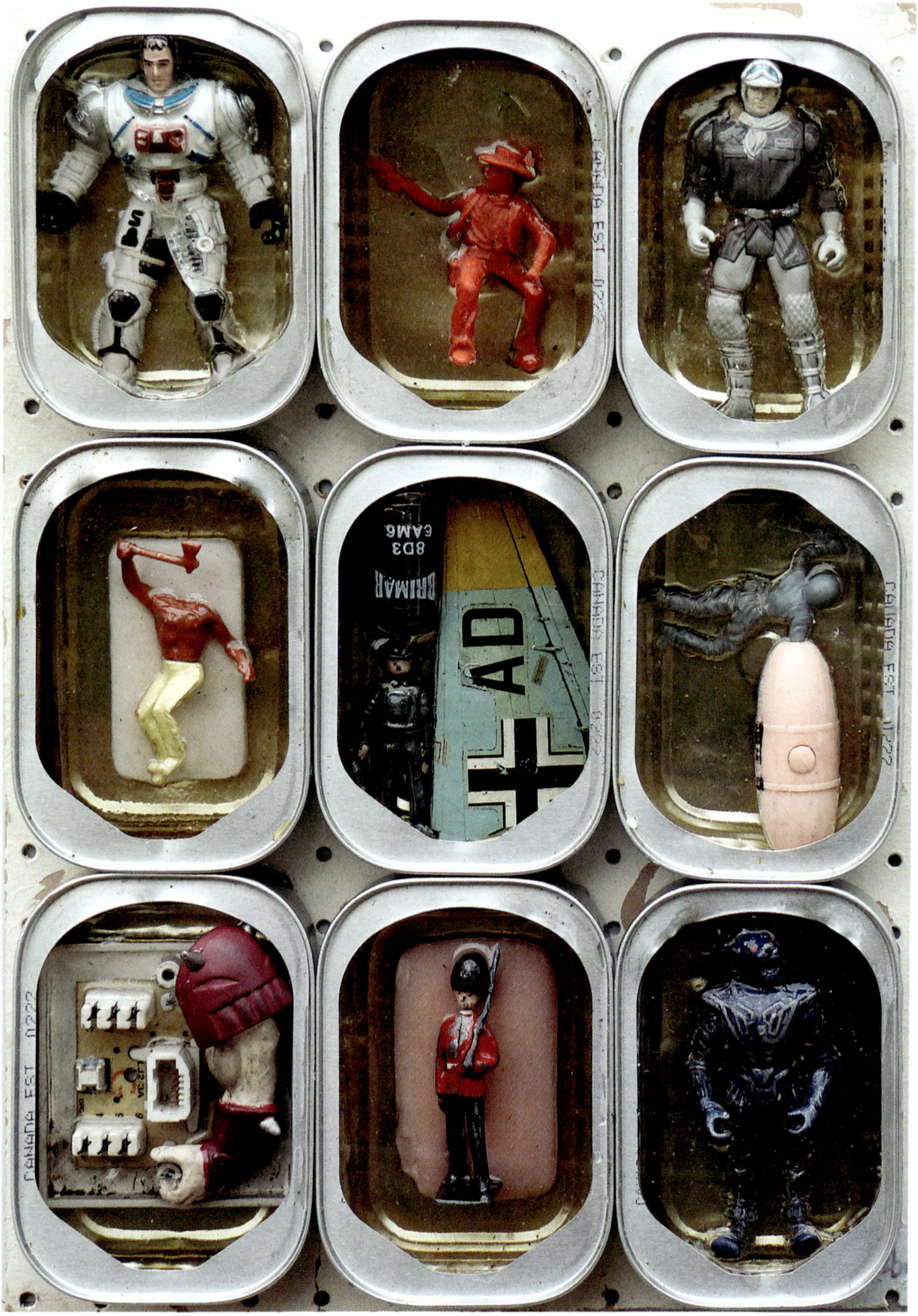

Mad in England, 2010

FOOTNOTES and CREDITS

Rebel Not Taken references:

Merriott Families Genealogy
The Monmouth Rebellion and the Bloody Assizes,
Geoff Sawers 2007 - Two Rivers Press
Plague Spot and Beauty Spot: Some History of the Dale,
Notting Dale Urban Studies Centre

Photographs:

Photographs of artworks by Rosie Osborne, Malcolm Ashton and loulou
Photo editing by Dave Jervis

Artworks:

Stencils: In collaboration with Rosa Osborne
Mousehole Window: courtesy of Katharine House Gallery
Sacking and Acrylic: courtesy of Sandra Blow Estate and DACS
52 pages of Glamour and *England Made Me:* courtesy of John Boden
Other works: courtesy of Jane Anderson, Melanie Buchan, Sally Osman

www.robertosborne.org.uk